Elections in Britain

Also by Dick Leonard

THE BACKBENCHER AND PARLIAMENT (*co-editor with Valentine Herman*)
CROSLAND AND NEW LABOUR (*editor*)
THE ECONOMIST GUIDE TO THE EUROPEAN UNION
GUIDE TO THE GENERAL ELECTION
PAYING FOR PARTY POLITICS
POCKET GUIDE TO THE EUROPEAN COMMUNITY
THE SOCIALIST AGENDA: CROSLAND'S LEGACY (*co-editor with David Lipsey*)
WORLD ATLAS OF ELECTIONS (*with Richard Natkiel*)
A CENTURY OF PREMIERS: FROM SALISBURY TO BLAIR

Also by Roger Mortimore

EXPLAINING LABOUR'S LANDSLIDE (*with Robert Worcester*)
EXPLAINING LABOUR'S SECOND LANDSLIDE (*with Robert Worcester*)
POLITICAL COMMUNICATIONS: THE GENERAL ELECTION
    CAMPAIGN OF 2001 (*editor, with John Bartle and Simon Atkinson*)

Elections in Britain

A Voter's Guide

Dick Leonard
Journalist and Author

and

Roger Mortimore
Senior Political Analyst, MORI

Fifth Edition

© Dick Leonard 1968, 1991, 1996
© Dick Leonard
Foreword ©

All rights reserved. No reproduction, copy or transmission of this
publication may be made without written permission.

No paragraph of this publication may be reproduced, copied or
transmitted save with written permission or in accordance with the
provisions of the Copyright, Designs and Patents Act 1988,
or under the terms of any licence permitting limited copying issued
by the Copyright Licensing Agency,
90 Tottenham Court Road, London W1T 4LP.

Any person who does any unauthorised act in relation to this
publication may be liable to criminal prosecution and civil
claims for damages.

The authors have asserted their rights to be identified as the authors
of this work in accordance with the Copyright, Designs and Patents
Act 1988.

First edition, *Elections in Britain*, by R. L. Leonard, published 1968 by
D. van Norstrand.
Second edition published 1991 by Macmillan Press Ltd.
Third edition, *Elections in Britain Today: A Guide for Voters and Students*,
published 1996 by Macmillan Press Ltd.
Fourth edition, *Elections in Britain: A Voter's Guide*, published 2001 by
PALGRAVE

Fifth edition, *Elections in Britain: A Voter's Guide*, published 2005 by
PALGRAVE MACMILLAN
Houndmills, Basingstoke, Hampshire RG21 6XS and
175 Fifth Avenue, New York, N.Y. 10010
Companies and representatives throughout the world

PALGRAVE MACMILLAN is the global academic imprint of the
Palgrave Macmillan division of St Martin's Press LLC and of
Palgrave Macmillan Ltd.
Macmillan® is a registered trademark in the United States,
United Kingdom and other countries. Palgrave is a registered
trademark in the European Union and other countries.

ISBN 1–4039–4255–2 hardback
ISBN 1–4039–4256–0 paperback

This book is printed on paper suitable for recycling and
made from fully managed and sustained forest sources.

A catalogue record for this book is available from the British Library.

A catalogue record for this book is available from the Library of
Congress.

10   9   8   7   6   5   4   3   2   1
14   13   12   11   10   09   08   07   06   05

Printed and bound in Great Britain by
Antony Rowe Ltd, Chippenham, Wiltshire

Contents

List of Tables and Figures   vi
Acknowledgements   viii
Foreword by David Butler   ix

1. Introduction   1
2. When Elections are Held   4
3. The Voters   12
4. Constituencies and the Electoral System   22
5. Political Parties: National   39
6. Political Parties: Local   73
7. Candidates   83
8. The Campaign in the Constituencies   104
9. The National Campaign   121
10. Polling Day   134
11. By-Elections, Local Elections, Euro-Elections and
    Referendums   144
12. Opinion Polls   164
13. How People Vote, and Why Some Don't   178
14. How Much Does it Cost – and Who Pays For it?   197
15. An Evolving System   208
Appendix 1:   British General Election Results, 1945–2001   212
Appendix 2:   Other British Election and Referendum Results   215
Appendix 3:   Proxy and Postal Voters   224
Appendix 4:   Election Timetable   226
Appendix 5:   Summary of Election Offences   228
Appendix 6:   Occupations of Candidates and MPs 2001   234
Appendix 7:   Opinion Poll Surveys Published during the 2001
              Election   236
Appendix 8:   Other Electoral Systems   238
Appendix 9:   The Single Transferable Vote   246
Appendix 10: Miscellaneous Statistics, 2001 General Election   248

Notes and References   249
Bibliography   264
Index   268

List of Tables

2.1   Duration of Parliament, 1918–2001   5
2.2   Dates of general elections, 1924–2001   9
3.1   Growth of the Parliamentary franchise, 1832–1985   14
3.2   Typical page from the electoral register   18
4.1   Large and small constituencies, 1992 and 1997 electorates   28
4.2   Conservative gains from redistributions, 1948–94   30
4.3   Percentage of seats and votes won by the parties, 1945–2001   33
4.4   Seats and candidates, 1945–2001   35
4.5   Voting figures in Feltham and Heston, 1987 and 1992: conventional swing   37
4.6   Voting figures in Feltham and Heston, 1987 and 1992: two-party swing   38
5.1   Conservative Party leadership election, 1997   53
5.2   Conservative Party leadership election, 2001   54
5.3   Labour Party leadership election, 1983   57
5.4   Labour Party leadership and deputy leadership elections, 1994   57
5.5   Co-operative Party candidates, 1945–2001   61
5.6   Scottish National Party and Plaid Cymru candidates, 1945–2001   65
5.7   Communist Party candidates, 1945–87   66
5.8   Far-right candidates since 1970   68
5.9   Ecology Party and Green Party candidates since 1979   69
6.1   Subjects most often raised with MPs, 1996–7   78
7.1   Women candidates and members, 1945–2001   97
7.2   Occupational backgrounds of candidates, 2001   99
8.1   Impact of campaigning, 1979–2001   114
9.1   Total readership of Conservative and Labour daily newspapers, 1964–2001   131
9.2   Daily newspaper partisanship and circulation in 2001   131
11.1   By-elections 1945–2001   146
12.1   Polls in the final week, 2001 election   167
12.2   Accuracy of final election polls   168
13.1   Party preference by parents' Conservative or Labour preferences, 1960s   180

13.2 Falling support for Labour principles, 1964–74 181
13.3 Labour voters on Tory aims, 1979 182
13.4 Class composition of the electorate 1964 and 1983 182
13.5 Head of household's class and vote, 1983 183
13.6 Social grade and vote, 2001 183
13.7 Support for Labour by social grade and class self-image, 2002 184
13.8 Support for Labour among union and non-union members by social grade, 2001 185
13.9 Housing, class and vote, 1997 186
13.10 Region and voting, 2001 186
13.11 Class, neighbourhood, region and vote, 1983 187
13.12 Class, education and vote, 1983 188
13.13 The 'gender gap' in voting, 1983–2001 188
13.14 Campaign's effect on vote choice, 2001 193
14.1 General election expenditure at national level 1979–2001 198
14.2 Breakdown of campaign spending, 2001 199
14.3 Expenditure by Parliamentary candidates, 1945–2001 202
14.4 Election expenses in Selby, 2001 203
A8.1 Largest remainder, four-member constituency 240
A8.2 Division by D'Hondt divisors, four-member constituency 240
A8.3 Quotas and divisors: the formulae 242
A8.4 Scottish Parliament seats and votes in the West of Scotland region, 1999 243
A8.5 Distribution of top-up seats, West of Scotland 243
A8.6 Estimated outcome of the 1997 election (GB only) under different electoral systems 245
A9.1 Galway West result, general election February 1982 246
A9.2 First preference votes and seats won 247

Acknowledgements

Table 13.1 is reprinted, by kind permission, from David Butler and Donald Stokes, *Political Change in Britain*, 2nd edition (London: Macmillan, 1974). Tables 13.4, 13.5, 13.11 and 13.12 are reprinted, by kind permission, from Anthony Heath, Roger Jowell and John Curtice, *How Britain Votes* (Oxford: Pergamon Press, 1985). Tables A9.1 and A9.2 are adapted by kind permission from Paul McKee, 'The Republic of Ireland', in Vernon Bogdanor and David Butler (eds), *Democracy and Elections: Electoral Systems and their Political Consequences* (Cambridge: Cambridge University Press, 1983).

Appendix 6 reproduces by kind permission a table from Byron Criddle, 'MPs and Candidates', in David Butler and Dennis Kavanagh, *The British General Election of 2001* (Basingstoke: Palgrave, 2002). Table 7.2 summarises the same data.

Appendix 8 is largely an updating of the introduction by Dick Leonard in Dick Leonard and Richard Natkiel, *World Atlas of Elections* (London: Economist Publishing Co., 1986), by kind permission of Economist Publishing Co.

Foreword

David Butler

Elections lie at the heart of democracy. But their detailed nature is little understood. Few people know in any detail about the rules and administrative arrangements that govern the franchise, or the casting and counting of ballots, or the way votes are translated into seats or the conduct and financing of campaigns. Fewer still comprehend what goes on in the minds of ordinary people as they decide whether to vote as they did last time or to switch to another party.

What decides elections? What do elections decide? The answers to these questions vary greatly in different countries and even in the same country at different times. Since Dick Leonard produced the first edition of this book in 1968 much has changed and continues to change in the nature of campaigning.

The contests of the 1990s saw a new professionalism in party headquarters in the use of direct mail and e-mail and focus groups, as well as in a 24-hours-a-day spinning of news. And since Labour's victory in 1997, new and different electoral systems have been installed for the Scottish Parliament, for the Welsh Assembly and for the Northern Ireland Assembly, as well as for the Mayor and Assembly in London. Moreover, the 1999 elections to the European Parliament saw the first nationwide use of proportional representation.

Furthermore, before the 2001 election the government set up the independent Electoral Commission, the first full-time professional body charged with supervising the administration of British elections, and also of investigating and recommending future reforms to the system, whether minor or major. Statutory spending limits now apply to parties nationally as well as in the constituencies, and parties must now submit comprehensive accounts of their income and expenditure.

The behaviour of the public is changing, too. Turnout has fallen across a whole range of British elections in recent years, and a smaller proportion of the electorate voted in the 2001 general election than on any previous occasion since the introduction of universal suffrage. Reversing this trend will pose a continuing challenge both to the Electoral Commission and the political parties.

Dick Leonard and Roger Mortimore are uniquely qualified to present a comprehensive, authoritative and down-to-earth guide for voters – and for others – to Elections in Britain.

1
Introduction

'The disadvantage of free elections', V. M. Molotov (the Soviet Foreign Minister in 1946) remarked to Ernest Bevin, 'is that you can never be sure who is going to win them.'

Perhaps, unconsciously, he had put his finger squarely on the feature which makes democratic systems of government so *interesting*. For it is the uncertainty which attends nearly every general election, at least in the United Kingdom, which adds spice to what might otherwise be regarded as a rather tiresome civic duty.

It is this, possibly, which explains a persistent paradox in British politics: that whereas only a tiny minority – probably less than 1 per cent – take an active part in politics between elections, around three-quarters generally turn out to vote, without any compulsion, whenever a general election is held. Yet the choice which is presented to the 30 million or so electors who record their votes at elections is largely determined by the few thousands who take a continuing part in the activities of the political parties. It is they alone who participate in the selection of Parliamentary candidates and it is they who have a *direct* influence on the policies adopted by the political parties.

At most general elections about 2 million young men and women are entitled to vote for the first time. It was in the hope that it would be of assistance to some of them, and also to those older voters who are perhaps puzzled or uncertain about particular aspects of the electoral system, that some years ago one of the present authors wrote a paperback entitled *Guide to the General Election* (later revised as *Elections in Britain*, subsequently as *Elections in Britain Today* and now – having acquired a co-author on the way – as *Elections in Britain: A Voter's Guide*). It was intended to fill a gap which at that time seemed to exist for a book which explained the complexities of the electoral system in a simple manner

1

and which also contained an account of how the political parties are organised, both locally and at national level, how their Parliamentary candidates are chosen and how the policies which they put before the electorate come to be adopted.

The years passed and major changes have occurred to the electoral system (votes for 18-year-olds, elections to the European Parliament, the coming of referendums, two fundamental reorganisations of local government and so forth), to electoral techniques (as television, computers and opinion polls have become more and more important) and to the party structure, with the creation of the Social Democratic Party and the subsequent merger to form the Liberal Democrats. With the election of the present government in 1997 the pace of change has quickened, with the establishment of an independent Electoral Commission, a plethora of changes in the administrative rules, and a swathe of elections to an entirely new tier of government, justifying another comprehensively revised edition only four years after the last.

This book is addressed to voters who support all political parties and to those who remain uncommitted. We have attempted throughout to describe *how* the system works rather than explain *why* we approve or disapprove of its different features. It should be emphasised that this work is an account of the British electoral system at the present time, together with some observations on how it has evolved and on how it may evolve in the future. It is not an historical work[1] or a general primer on the British constitution;[2] nor is it a work of comparative government.[3] Again, for the benefit of younger readers, however, it may be helpful to summarise in a few preliminary paragraphs the general characteristics of the British constitutional system in so far as it is relevant to elections.

1. The United Kingdom has a parliamentary form of government. The executive is not directly elected, but is formed from the membership of the legislature. Ministers are members of the legislature. The great majority, including those holding the leading offices, are members of the House of Commons. A minority are members of the House of Lords. This necessarily restricts the field of recruitment for ministers to a far greater extent than, for instance, in the USA.

2. It has evolved basically as a two-party system, though a third party – the Liberals – has invariably polled a substantial vote and has had a small representation in the House of Commons, and several smaller parties from Northern Ireland, Scotland and Wales are also represented in the House. The rise in support for the Liberals and the creation of the Liberal Democrats now places the whole concept in question.

But in the past an election campaign, like a debate in the Commons, was basically a confrontation between the Government and the Opposition. The party which won a majority of seats in the House of Commons formed a government, and its leader became Prime Minister. Most elections have produced a clear Parliamentary majority for one party or the other, though occasionally only a small one. When a single party has not gained a majority of the seats a minority government has been formed rather than a coalition, which is a form of government unknown in modern Britain except in wartime.

3. The electoral system requires a single ballot and the candidate with the largest number of votes wins, even if he or she has polled only a minority of the total votes cast. This is sometimes known as the 'first past the post' system. It is not a system of proportional representation, and it penalises minority parties and inhibits their growth.

4. General elections in Britain are not held at fixed intervals, unlike in a majority of democratic countries. Though the maximum length of life of a single Parliament is five years, it may be dissolved at virtually any time at the wish of the government. This gives the incumbent party a considerable advantage.

5. The United Kingdom has no written constitution: all laws, including electoral laws, may be changed by the passage of an Act of Parliament. It is technically easy, therefore, to change the electoral system at any time. But in practice only minor amendments are adopted with any frequency, and much of the present system is rooted in great antiquity. Nevertheless, the indications are that we may now be in the midst of a period of significant changes.

2
When Elections are Held

Apart from the result, the principal uncertainty about a British general election is its timing. Unlike in the USA and the great majority of democratic states outside the Commonwealth, there is no fixed date for British Parliamentary elections.

There is, however, a limit on the length of life of the House of Commons. In 1694 it was set at three years, which was increased to seven years in 1715. Under the Parliament Act of 1911 it was reduced to five years, which is the present limit. During both world wars annual Prolongation of Parliament Acts were passed after the expiry of this limit to avoid the inconvenience of a wartime election, but though such a measure would theoretically be possible in peacetime it is inconceivable that it would be attempted.

No peacetime Parliament has in fact run its full five years, though those of 1959 and 1992 came so close to it that the general elections at either end were more than five years apart. Table 2.1 shows the length of each Parliament which has sat since 1918, the first to be elected under the 1911 Act.

Except in the case of a minority government or one with a very small majority (as in 1950, 1964 and February 1974) it will be seen that most Parliaments have continued for a period of between three and four and a half years. Unless an election is precipitated by a government defeat on a vote of confidence in the House of Commons (which has not occurred, except to a minority government, since 1886), it is in effect the Prime Minister who decides the date of a general election.

In theory, the Sovereign may refuse the advice of the Prime Minister to dissolve Parliament. In practice, she could not refuse any but the most frivolous request. Especially after a Parliament has passed its half-way mark, the Prime Minister may safely recommend a dissolution at any time.

4

Table 2.1 Duration of Parliament, 1918–2001

General election	Duration of Parliament Years	Days	Original government majority
1918	3	265	263
1922	–	361	79
1923	–	266	None
1924	4	159	225
1929	2	105	None
1931	3	356	425
1935*	9	200	247
1945	4	189	186
1950	1	213	6
1951	3	183	16
1955	4	104	60
1959	4	342	100
1964	1	127	4
1966	4	41	97
1970	3	251	30
1974: Feb	–	195	None
1974: Oct	4	166	3
1979	4	4	43
1983	3	345	144
1987	4	274	102
1992	4	346	21
1997	4	7	177
2001	?	?	165

* Duration extended by annual Acts of Parliament during 1939–45 war.

The decision is the Prime Minister's alone. In earlier times the agreement of the Cabinet was always sought, but in 1918 Lloyd George successfully set the precedent, which has never since been challenged, of not consulting the Cabinet on this decision. The Prime Minister may seek the advice of senior colleagues, but is by no means bound by it. It is known that both in 1950 and in 1951, several senior Cabinet ministers disagreed with Clement Attlee's decision to go to the country.

Conversely, in September 1978 a large majority of Cabinet ministers were known to be in favour of an election in the following month, but James Callaghan abruptly informed the Cabinet that there would not be one until the following year. There was no discussion, despite the fact that Callaghan's decision had taken his colleagues, and virtually the whole country, by surprise.

In 2001, a May election had been expected but an outbreak of Foot and Mouth Disease in farming areas across the country led Tony Blair to decide to postpone it until June. The decision was leaked to the press, and Cabinet ministers travelling to a weekend summit at Chequers, at which they thought the election date was to be discussed, were presented with a *fait accompli* in their morning papers.

Numerous factors influence Prime Ministers in their choice of general election dates. The economic situation, the state of the government's legislative programme in the House of Commons, the need for the country to be represented at important international negotiations by a government with a fresh mandate from the people or, if the government majority is precarious or non-existent, as in the February 1974 Parliament, the desire to increase its Parliamentary support. This list could be extended indefinitely, but there is little doubt that the principal factor was neatly summed up by Lord Poole, then joint chairman of the Conservative Party, in 1963: 'The Prime Minister is likely to have a general election at the time when he thinks he is most likely to win it.'

The timing of general elections has become of crucial importance in British politics, as it is also in Australia, Canada and New Zealand where the government also has an effective choice of date. The Prime Minister's prerogative of choice is a powerful weapon for the government and a serious handicap to the Opposition. It has, moreover, assumed greater significance during the past half century when public opinion polls have provided a far more accurate and sensitive, if occasionally fallible, barometer of the relative standing of the political parties than existed in earlier periods. Traditionally, by-elections had been the main measure of political support, but the results of these can often be misleading. Thus in 1880, on the strength of two Conservative victories in by-elections at Liverpool and Southwark, Lord Beaconsfield (Benjamin Disraeli) went to the country, and saw his party defeated.

Sir Anthony Eden was, in 1955, the first Prime Minister to capitalise on the new precision with which public opinion polls enable a Prime Minister to choose a favourable moment for a dissolution, and all subsequent Prime Ministers have sought to follow in his footsteps. Nevertheless, a cautious Prime Minister takes many other factors and indicators into account, and should always bear in mind that a narrow opinion poll lead might melt away during the election campaign. By-elections are still a useful confirmation of what the polls are showing, as are local government election results, including council by-elections which are held periodically throughout the year, as a supplementary indicator.

When a government is clearly and firmly ahead, the Prime Minister can pick his or her moment. Thus Harold Wilson in 1966 waited until a highly encouraging by-election result confirmed the opinion poll evidence that he could increase his Parliamentary majority, which he did indeed when the election was called. Similarly in 1987, Mrs Thatcher had the encouragement of a sustained opinion poll lead, but waited until Conservative success in the May local government elections before calling a general election the following month, at which she was duly returned with a comfortable majority for a third term.

The advantage which 'naming the day' gives to the Prime Minister is perhaps best illustrated by the 1979–83 Parliament. In the early years of the Parliament, Mrs Thatcher's newly elected government plumbed the depths of unpopularity, and had the election been held in 1981 the polls and by-elections alike suggested that the newly formed SDP-Liberal Alliance would have swept the country. But after the Falklands War and a sudden economic upturn in 1982 the government's popularity recovered and, despite high unemployment, it was clear that many voters distrusted Michael Foot's Labour Party. By calling an election in June 1983, just over four years into her term, Mrs Thatcher was able to exploit the favourable circumstances before anything changed, in (justified) confidence that the ensuing general election would greatly augment her majority.

The decision is more tricky when the message of the polls is less clear cut – or, of course, if the polls are consistently suggesting that the government will lose. Should the Prime Minister wait in the hope that the position will improve, or grasp the nettle and make the best of it rather than risk allowing the position to deteriorate still further? In 1978, James Callaghan avoided an autumn election in which it seemed the outcome would be finely balanced. However, instead of the hoped-for upturn his standing was further undermined by the industrial unrest which came to be nicknamed the 'Winter of Discontent', and the following March all the opposition parties combined to defeat the government in a vote of confidence in the Commons, forcing an immediate election at which Mrs Thatcher was returned with a comfortable majority. In 1992, though, John Major facing a narrow poll deficit hung on to the last moment, 'waiting for something to turn up', and when he finally went to the country secured a narrow (if unexpected) victory.

The same considerations may apply even if the government is nowhere near the end of its term. Following the inconclusive election of February 1974, Wilson was able to choose his moment to call another general election in the hope of gaining an overall majority. This he achieved in October 1974, but only just – his majority was three seats, and this majority was wiped out by by-election losses over the next two years. Much more painful setbacks were suffered by Wilson in 1970, and by the Conservative Prime Minister Edward Heath in February 1974. Both called early elections which the opinion polls suggested they would win, and both lost.

Though the Prime Minister's advantage appears immense, the area of choice is more limited than is immediately obvious, for in practice there are normally only a limited number of possible dates between which to choose. The winter months are usually excluded from consideration for climatic reasons, and the summer is the holiday season. A spring election is one possibility, but unless it is held on the same day as the local elections, the first Thursday in May (as it was in 1979 and 1997),[1] it needs to steer clear of that date by several weeks to avoid the campaigning periods overlapping; it is also best to avoid Easter and the spring bank holidays. Early autumn is the only other period which normally would be seriously considered for electioneering. Apart from 1945, when the election was held on the earliest practicable date after the German surrender, all modern general elections have been concentrated in two periods – late February to early June, and October to early November. It may safely be assumed that the great majority of future general elections will take place during these 'windows of opportunity'.

Over the last 50 years, general elections and the great majority of by-elections, local government and other elections have been held on a Thursday (see Table 2.2).[2] However, in recent years there has been much discussion of moving polling day to the weekend, as in most of continental Europe, which it is suggested would be more convenient for many voters and would encourage a higher turnout. The change was tried on an experimental basis in a few local elections in May 2000, with voting spread over two days, Saturday and Sunday, to avoid causing problems for those electors who for religious reasons would be unable to vote on one day or the other. (It must be said, however, that the initial experiments were not a conspicuous success, and turnout fell rather than rose; more success has been achieved by experiments involving postal voting, which tackle the inconvenience of voting on a weekday in a different way.)

It was only in the twentieth century that voting on a single day became the norm. Before 1918, polling had been spread over a fortnight or more, and results in the first constituencies to poll were already known when voters in other constituencies went to cast their votes. This was sometimes alleged to cause a 'bandwagon' in favour of the party which made early gains. The only occasion since when voting has been staggered was in 1945 when, because of local holiday arrangements, 23 seats in the north of England and Scotland polled one or two weeks later. But as none of the votes in this election were counted until three weeks after the original polling day, to allow for servicemen's votes to be sent from overseas, there was no risk of a 'bandwagon' being created on that occasion.

Table 2.2   Dates of general elections, 1924–2001

Year	Day	Date
1924	Wednesday	29 October
1929	Thursday	30 May
1931	Tuesday	27 October
1935	Thursday	14 November
1945	Thursday	5 July
1950	Thursday	23 February
1951	Thursday	25 October
1955	Thursday	26 May
1959	Thursday	8 October
1964	Thursday	15 October
1966	Thursday	31 March
1970	Thursday	18 June
1974: Feb	Thursday	28 February
1974: Oct	Thursday	10 October
1979	Thursday	3 May
1983	Thursday	9 June
1987	Thursday	11 June
1992	Thursday	9 April
1997	Thursday	1 May
2001	Thursday	6 June

Dissolution of Parliament is effected by Royal Proclamation, but it is customary for the Prime Minister personally to break the news with a statement giving notice of the dissolution. In 1983, for example, Mrs Margaret Thatcher issued a statement on Monday 9 May, announcing the dissolution of Parliament on 13 May, and polling day was set for 9 June. The last-minute moves preceding the announcement were cryptically reported the following day in *The Times*:

10 a.m.   Close Cabinet colleagues and Conservative Party advisers gathered at 10 Downing Street for final meeting before the election date is announced.

11 a.m.   Mr Cecil Parkinson, party chairman, leaves briefly to break the news to Conservative Central Office.

11.15 a.m. Mr Parkinson returns to Downing Street for a Cabinet meeting where June 9 date is revealed.

12.20 p.m. The Prime Minister leaves for Buckingham Palace and asks the Queen to dissolve Parliament. After an audience lasting little more than half an hour, Mrs Thatcher returns to Downing Street at 1.10 p.m.

2.15 p.m.   The Press Association releases the text of an official statement headed 'General Election, June 1983', and personal letters from the Prime Minister are sent to Mr Michael Foot, the Labour leader, and Mr David Steel, the Liberal leader, informing them of the decision.

In subsequent general elections up to 1997, a broadly similar pattern was observed. However, as already mentioned, in 2001 the news seems to have been 'leaked' to selected journalists before any official announcement was made.

Polling day is 17 days after the date of dissolution. But in reckoning the 17 days, Saturdays and Sundays are excluded from the calculation, as are public holidays. The 1983 election was the first in which Saturdays were excluded, and the period also happened to include the May bank holiday. This meant that there were actually 27 days between dissolution and polling day, whereas the average number in post-war elections had been 20. But in giving only four days' notice of dissolution, whereas most of her predecessors had given ten, Mrs Thatcher's announcement came exactly one calendar month before polling day. This conformed almost exactly to recent practice, though there is no legal requirement to give any notice at all of dissolution. In 1987 Mrs Thatcher followed a virtually identical timetable, announcing on 11 May an election to be held on 11 June; and John Major followed the same course in 1992, announcing on 10 March that the election would be on 9 April. In 1997, however, believing that a long election campaign might give his government a better chance of winning, Mr Major announced as early as 17 March that the election would be held on 1 May, a full six and a half weeks' notice, and Parliament was prorogued (i.e. stopped sitting, though it had not been formally dissolved) just three days later. In 2001 the effective announcement was earlier still, the government confirming on 2 April that the local government elections were to be postponed until 7 June because of the Foot and Mouth Disease outbreak (which made it obvious that the general election was to be held on the same date, although no official announcement about the general election was made until Tony Blair formally asked the Queen for a dissolution on 8 May). It led to the longest general election campaign of modern times, since all the main parties had already booked advertising space in anticipation of a May election. But such exceptional circumstances are presumably unlikely to recur.

In so far as the government has the advantage of foreknowledge in making its preparations, it may be presumed to gain by giving as short notice as possible. On the other hand, there is nowadays usually so much advanced press speculation that the Opposition is not likely to be caught napping.

As soon as Parliament is dissolved, the Lord Chancellor is ordered by Royal Proclamation to issue writs for the holding of fresh elections throughout the country. The writs are issued as soon as practicable following the Royal Proclamation and are sent to the Returning Officers in each Parliamentary constituency. The Returning Officer is the person appointed to organise the conduct of elections, and in England is normally the sheriff of the county, the chairman of the district council or the mayor of the London borough in which the constituency is situated. In Wales he or she is the chairman of the county council or county borough council, and in Scotland a local government officer appointed by the council concerned. In Northern Ireland the Chief Electoral Officer for Northern Ireland, an official appointed by the UK government, fills the role. The Returning Officer normally appoints an Acting Returning Officer, who will be a local government official and who in fact carries out most of the duties of the office.

Not later than 4 p.m. of the second day after the writ has been received the Returning Officer must publish, normally by means of posters outside public buildings and on commercial advertising sites, notices of election stating the place and times at which nomination papers must be delivered and the date of the poll. The election will only then be officially in train, though most people concerned in it will already have been extremely busy with their preparations for several weeks.

3
The Voters

Any British citizen, citizen of any other Commonwealth country or Irish citizen, over the age of 18 and resident in the United Kingdom, with a very few exceptions, is eligible to vote in all elections in Britain – Parliamentary, local[1] and European. Some other categories may vote in some, but not all, British elections: British citizens over the age of 18, but living outside the UK, may vote in Parliamentary and European, but not local, elections, so long as they have been resident in Britain at some time in the past 15 years; citizens of other EU countries (apart from Britain and Ireland) who are resident in the UK may vote in European elections and local elections, but not Parliamentary elections.

However, a few groups who would otherwise be eligible are explicitly excluded. *Members of the House of Lords* may not vote in Parliamentary elections (though they may vote in local and European elections). *Persons suffering from severe mental illness* may not vote, except during 'lucid intervals'. A *convicted prisoner* detained in any penal institution is disqualified while serving his or her sentence (or while unlawfully at large). *Persons convicted of corrupt or illegal practices* in connection with elections (see Appendix 5) are ineligible to vote for five years from the date of conviction.

But apart from these exceptional cases, and foreign nationals from outside the European Union and the Commonwealth, all adult residents are eligible. The only other requirement, in every case, is that his or her name should appear on the electoral register.

Thus British Parliamentary elections are based on the principle of universal franchise. It was not always so; indeed it was only the abolition of plural voting (by university graduates and occupiers of business premises), by the Representation of the People Act of 1948, which finally established the principle of 'one man, one vote'. In local government, indeed, plural voting survived until 1969: occupiers of any rateable land or premises of a yearly value of £10 or more (this would apply mostly to businessmen and tradesmen) were also entitled to vote.[2] Like most developments in the British constitution, progress towards universal suffrage had been slow and gradual. Prior to 1832, voting was a privilege reserved for a mere 5 per cent of the population and it required five Acts of Parliament spread out over a period of 116 years for the transition from oligarchy to democracy to be effected. Women were not entitled to vote at all before 1918. The growth of the British Parliamentary electorate since 1832 is shown in Table 3.1.

Although all adults not excluded above are qualified to vote, they may not do so unless their names appear on the Register of Electors. The register is now compiled on a 'rolling' basis – that is, anybody who is eligible can (and should) apply to be added to the register immediately if not already included; the list is updated monthly. This is a new development. Until 2001 the register was compiled annually, and recorded only those who were eligible on a 'qualifying date' in the autumn:[3] anybody who became eligible to vote during the year had to wait until the autumn before they could be included, and there was then a further delay until the following February before the new register came into force.[4] (The only exception was those reaching their 18th birthday during the year, who – as now – were listed in the register together with their date of birth so they could vote immediately once they came of age.) This meant that people who moved house, for example, could only vote at their old address and not at their new home for anything up to 16 months, though they could of course apply to do so by post.

Since the rolling register introduced in 2001, however, it is only necessary to be qualified on the date that the application is made – but it is still be too late to be added to the register for an election once nominations have closed. Indeed, since there is some delay involved in compiling even a rolling register, the real deadline is earlier still: at the 2001 election, held on 7 June, only those who had applied by 5 April (in time to appear in the May update) were eligible to vote.

The rolling register was suggested as long ago as 1965–6, when the Speaker's Conference on Electoral Law recommended that a study of its feasibility should be made, but nothing came of the proposal. In those pre-computer days the administrative work involved would have been prohibitively expensive, but with modern technology it presents far fewer difficulties.[5]

The register is now revised annually following a canvass in the autumn, but also updated monthly during the rest of the year on the basis of applications made by electors.[6] The Electoral Registration Officer (ERO) of

Table 3.1 Growth of the Parliamentary franchise, 1832–1985

Representation of the People Acts		Provisions relating to voters' qualifications	Total electorate	Percentage of population 21 years and over
Prior to 1832	Counties	40s. freeholders.	509,000	5
	Boroughs	Various and unequal franchises.		
1832	Counties	40s. freeholders, £10 copyholders, £10 leaseholders, £50 tenants at will.	720,000	7
1867	Boroughs	£10 householders.		
	Counties	40s. freeholders, £5 copyholders, £5 leaseholders, £12 tenants at will.	2,231,000	16
	Boroughs	All occupiers of rated dwelling houses, lodgers occupying £10 lodgings.		
1884	Counties and Boroughs	A uniform franchise for householders and lodgers, giving a vote to every man over 21 who had a home.	4,965,000	28
1918	Men	Abolition of property qualification in counties. Qualification by either six months' residence or the occupation of a £10 business premises.	19,984,000	74
	Women	Enfranchised at the age of 30. Plural voting by university graduates and the holders of the business premises qualification restricted to two votes including the one for residence.		
1928		Women enfranchised at 21: male and female adult suffrage.	29,175,000	96.9
1948		University constituencies and all plural voting abolished. 'One man, one vote.'	34,915,000	*
1969		Voting age reduced to 18.	39,153,000	*
1985		Vote extended to certain overseas voters.	43,181,321	*

* Since 1948 the adult franchise has been almost 100 per cent, subject to the deficiencies of the registration process.

Source: This table is adapted and updated from *The Student Guide to Parliament* by Alfred J. Junz (London: Hansard Society, 1960).

each local authority distributes forms to heads of households[7] to discover who is resident on 15 October each year, requiring them to fill in details of all members of the household (including lodgers) who are eligible to vote. Any person who refuses to comply or who gives false information is liable on summary conviction to a fine not exceeding £1000 (though prosecutions are rare). The ERO is a council officer, and is usually the same person who when the time comes will be the Acting Returning Officer, who is responsible, in practice, for the organisation of elections in the different constituencies.

To be included in the register one must be resident in the constituency.[8] (In Northern Ireland it is necessary to have been resident at the same address for three months; this is to prevent residents of the Irish Republic crossing the border for a short period only and registering as voters.) People can legitimately register at more than one address if they are legally 'resident' at both. This applies mainly to two categories, those with second homes or holiday homes, and students who may be registered both at their home and term-time address. People who are registered at more than one address may only vote once (though they can choose at which address they will vote).[9]

In addition to eligible voters already over the age of 18, anybody who will be 18 before 1 December in the following year should be included on the form, since they will become qualified to vote before next year's canvass is completed. They will be registered as 'attainers', and the date of their birthday will appear on the printed register. They will accordingly be eligible to vote at any election occurring after they turn 18.

A further special category are service voters. Members of the armed forces (whether stationed at home or abroad), persons employed in the service of the Crown outside the United Kingdom (such as diplomats and British Council employees) and husbands or wives of either may register in the normal way at their home address (if living in the UK), or complete an annual service declaration to register either at their past address or at the address where they would be living if they were not serving abroad or in the forces.

The current register is displayed in post offices, public libraries and other public offices and is open to inspection. Claims and objections may be made to the ERO in respect of inaccurate entries or omissions. It is especially important that newly qualified voters or those who have recently changed their address should check that they are included; but there is no guarantee that voters who had been included in previous registers will be included in the next. If the head of the household has inadvertently failed to make an accurate return the voter might be wrongly deleted. There is also a possibility, on rare occasions, of a clerical error by the staff of the ERO. The vast majority of voters who do not bother to check the register nevertheless find, when they come to vote, that they have been properly included. On the other hand, thousands of qualified voters at each general election find that they are not on the register and it is then too late to do anything about it.

The same register is used for Parliamentary elections, local government elections and for elections to the European Parliament (with those not eligible to vote in one or more elections specially marked – see below), and the register is also used to select citizens for jury service.[10] This provides a further reason why it is important that the register should be complete and accurate: the fair administration of justice depends upon the assurance that jury selection is representative of the whole of the population and community.

Free copies of the register are provided for the agents of political parties and to Parliamentary candidates. They may also buy additional copies. Registers, or parts thereof, may also be purchased from the ERO by members of the general public, and most EROs are in a position to supply copies in electronic form. However, electors now have a legal right to have their names excluded from the version of the register sold commercially; the registration form must include a box to tick for exercise of this option. This 'ex-directory' registration or 'opt out' is a new provision. One group of frequent purchasers were direct mail advertising agencies, which angered some electors who felt that this use of the register was an invasion of their privacy; they are no longer able to buy the unedited register. However, the full register may still be used for 'other purposes such as the prevention and detection of crime and for checking your identity when you have applied for credit'.[11]

The register is divided into polling districts (each of which is distinguished on the register by an initial letter or letters). Polling districts are devised by the Registration Officer to give each voter the minimum distance practicable to travel to cast a vote. They vary in number between a mere handful of voters (sometimes less than a dozen) in remote hamlets to over 5000 in densely populated areas in the centres of cities. The most usual number of electors in polling districts is, however, between 1000 and 2000. There are about 40,000 polling districts in the whole of the United Kingdom.

There are normally between one and a dozen polling districts in each ward (the local government electoral area), several of which normally comprise a borough constituency. In country areas each village would be a separate polling district and towns and larger villages would be subdivided. Within each polling district the electors are listed in street order, except in villages, where they are often listed alphabetically. Each entry consists of, reading from left to right, the voter's electoral number (counting from one in each polling district), surname, first forename, the initials of any other forenames and the number or name of the house. Within each household the names are given in alphabetical order. Certain special categories of voters are indicated by letters printed in bold type immediately preceding the voter's surname, as follows:

- **L** voters are members of the House of Lords, who are not entitled to participate in the choice of representatives to the lower house; they may vote in local government and European Parliament elections, but not in Parliamentary elections.
- **G** voters are nationals of other countries in the European Union who are registered to vote in their own country (or some other country outside the UK) at European elections. They may only vote in local government elections.
- **K** voters are other EU nationals, who may vote in local government and European Parliament elections, but not in Parliamentary elections.
- **F** voters are overseas voters, who have the right to vote in Parliamentary and European Parliament elections, but not local government elections.
- **E** voters (a very small category) are overseas peers who have the right to vote only in European Parliament elections.
- Citizens of 'accession states', the ten countries that joined the EU on 1 May 2004, were listed on the register as **Y** voters in the run-up to enlargement.
- Attainers, those young people who will reach their 18th birthday, and therefore attain the right to vote, in the near future, are marked with their date of birth.

Before February 1987 no overseas voters, other than service voters, were able to vote in any elections in Britain. Under the terms of the 1985 Representation of the People Act and subsequent amendments, a limited right was granted to British citizens resident outside the United Kingdom. For 15 years following their departure[12] they may qualify to be 'overseas electors' in respect of the address at which they were last registered (or at which they would have been registered if they were too young to vote when they last lived in Britain). In order to do so, they need to register themselves annually through British consular posts. This will entitle them to vote, by post or proxy, at any Parliamentary or European Parliament election. Estimates of the potential number who could register have ranged as high as 3 million, but in fact only 23,600 were on the register in 1997, and numbers dip still further in years when no general election is expected.

A portion of a typical (but fictitious) register is shown in Table 3.2.

Table 3.2   Typical page from the electoral register

MINEHEAD ROAD

TP11 1PG

202	Watson, Alice A	1
203	Watson, David J	1
204	Watson, John H	1
205	Perryman, Jennifer	3
206	Timms, Laura A	5
207	Timms, Michael H	5
208	Topham, Elizabeth C	7
209	Mitchell, Paul T H	9
210	Mitchell, Rachel	9
211	Ellis, Cynthia	11
212	**11/04/1986** Ellis, Edward G	11
213	Swales, Charlotte	13
214	Newton, Lynn E	13

TP11 1PH

215	Whyte, Nicholas S	2
216G	Schmidt, Hartmut	4
217	Peters, Louise	6
218	Thompson, Richard	6
219	Marks, Rebecca	8
220	Marks, Terence G	8
221	Hill, Graham E	10
222	Hill, Philip	10
223	Lewis, Joanna	10
224	Morrell, Paula	12
225	McLean, Jack	14
226	McLean, Timothy J	14
227	McLean, Suzanne E	14
228	Burton, Keith G T	16
229	Burton, Maureen	16
230	Jackson, Andrew M	18
231	Jackson, Eileen H	18

One reason for the introduction of a rolling register is that the annual register was, necessarily, always out of date. It was already four months old when it came into effect and 16 months old at the end of its life. Thus at all times large numbers of dead people were on the register while people who had moved were not registered in respect of their current address (and probably only a minority of these applied for a postal vote or travelled back to their previous neighbourhoods to register their votes on polling day).

Many years ago the Government Social Survey made a study of the accuracy of the electoral register. They found that when compiled it was 96 per cent accurate (that is, 96 per cent of eligible adults were registered in respect of the address in which they were actually living on the qualifying date). By the time the register was published it was only 94 per cent accurate. There was thereafter a cumulative loss of 0.5 per cent per month, due to removals, until at the last month that the register was in force its degree of accuracy was only 87 per cent. A subsequent study in 1982 by the Office of Population Censuses and Surveys (OPCS) suggested that the situation had deteriorated further, and that the October 1981 register was only 93 per cent accurate at the time that it was compiled. In 1993 a further survey estimated that between 7.4 and 9.0 per cent of eligible adults in England and Wales were missing from the 1991 register. This meant that between 2.8 and 3.4 million adults were disfranchised.[13]

In some areas, and for some categories of voter, the position was a great deal worse than the national average, with voters in metropolitan areas being particularly liable to be excluded. The 1991 survey suggested that as many as 20.4 per cent of potential voters in inner London, and 10.3 per cent in outer London, were excluded. One reason for the large number of non-registrations in 1991 may have been that young people in particular, who wished to avoid paying the 'poll tax', had contrived to exclude themselves from the register.[14] In the inner cities registration tends to be particularly low, and both young people and ethnic minorities are significantly less likely than average to be registered. These factors are cumulative. Across the whole country by 1991, whereas non-registration among whites was 6.5 per cent, as many as 15 per cent of Asian and 24 per cent of black adults and of other groups were unregistered; and registration was especially low among those born outside Britain who retained citizenship of New Commonwealth countries, of whom 37 per cent were not on the register.[15] These figures seem to reflect a greater feeling among both the young and ethnic minority groups that elections are unimportant and have little to offer them, and these groups are also less likely to vote even if registered. The rolling register is too recent an innovation for there to be any reliable estimates available of its accuracy today. There are certainly more people who fail to register than was the case half a century ago, and there is of course still some delay in removing the names of those who have died or otherwise ceased to be eligible. Nevertheless, it seems possible that at least some of the deficiencies of the old system have been alleviated.

The total number of registered voters is now over 44 million. There are some 37 million electors in England, 4 million in Scotland, 2.2 million in Wales and 1.2 million in Northern Ireland. Altogether 33,614,074 people cast valid votes in the 1992 election, the largest number of electors ever to have gone to the polls in the UK. The percentage turnout however, at 76.7 per cent, was near to the post-war average, and far lower than the record 84.0 per cent who voted in 1950. On a significantly lower turnout in 1997, just over 30 million voted, and in 2001, when turnout hit a record low of 59 per cent, only 26.4 million did so. While the vast majority of voters still vote in person by going to their polling station on election day (as explained in Chapter 10), everybody in England, Scotland and Wales[16] now has the option of voting by post instead, provided they contact their local council early enough to request a postal ballot paper. They may either arrange a postal vote for one specific election, or if they prefer can be permanently classified as a postal voter and will be sent a ballot paper without having to take any further action for all future elections until they revoke their request.

In either case, the application must be made before 5 p.m. on the sixth day before polling day, excluding weekends and public holidays. Some local authorities include the appropriate forms with the annual electoral registration documents, but in any case they can always be obtained from the Town Hall, and often also via a council website. It is important to remember, however, that once an elector has been issued with a postal ballot paper for any election, he or she *will not* then be able to obtain a ballot paper at a polling station in the normal way. Postal ballot papers must be returned in time to reach the Returning Officer by the close of poll. (If necessary the voter may hand them in at a polling station or deliver them in person to the Returning Officer on election day rather than posting them.)

The universal availability of postal voting on demand is a new departure. Before the 2001 general election, postal votes were available only to those electors who for various reasons could not be reasonably expected to vote in person. These restrictions remain for those electors who prefer not to vote by post but to appoint a proxy to vote on their behalf.

Voters may also vote by post or, if eligible, by proxy in European and local government elections in Great Britain, including parish and community council elections in England and Wales, and elections to the devolved assemblies. Full details of those that are eligible for proxy votes, and of how to apply for postal and proxy votes, are given in Appendix 3; the effect of postal voting on the course of the election campaign is discussed in Chapter 8.

An absent voters' list, including the addresses to which postal voting forms must be sent, is compiled by the Returning Officer and is available for inspection at his or her office, as is a separate list of overseas electors. Copies of the list are supplied free of charge, on request, to each candidate or election agent. In copies of the election register supplied to polling stations, postal voters are marked on the register with the letter 'A' and proxy voters have the names of their proxies marked on the list.

4
Constituencies and the Electoral System

The House of Commons has at present 659 members, each of whom is the representative of a single-member constituency.[1] The origin of the different constituencies is diverse. Some constituency names, particularly those comprising medium-sized provincial towns, go back several hundred years, though the precise boundaries of the constituencies are unlikely not to have been altered at some time. The vast majority of constituencies were in fact newly delineated prior to the 1983 general election, and three-quarters were redrawn again before 1997.

The basis of representation in the House of Commons from 1264 to 1832 was, with a few exceptions, two members for each county and two for each borough. No attempt, however, was made to ensure that members represented equal numbers of voters, and enormous discrepancies in the size of constituencies had developed long before the 1832 Reform Act. Medieval boroughs which had declined almost to nothing retained their right to elect two members, while large cities such as Manchester, Leeds, Sheffield and Birmingham, which had grown up during the seventeenth and eighteenth centuries, had no separate representation. By 1832 the largest Parliamentary constituency had several thousand times as many electors as the smallest.[2] In 1832 and again in 1867 the worst anomalies were removed, but no systematic attempt was made to redraw the electoral map on the basis of approximately equal constituencies.

In 1885 a much more thorough redistribution was undertaken and the ratio between the largest and smallest constituency was reduced to 8:1. The 1885 Act also replaced the great majority of two-member constituencies with single-member seats, though the last of the two-member constituencies did not disappear until 1950. The Representation of the People Act of 1918 went one stage further and reduced the disparity in electorates to a maximum of 5:1. It also abolished the difference between the franchise in borough and in county constituencies; nevertheless, constituencies are still classified as either borough[3] (urban) or county (containing more than a token rural element), and this affects the amount a candidate may legally spend on his or her campaign.

Although the principle of approximately equal constituencies had been accepted in 1918, no provision was made to correct anomalies caused by future movements of population. Thus by 1939 the rapid growth of suburban fringes to London and other major cities had produced a large number of constituencies with an excessive number of electors, while depopulation of city centres and of remote rural areas had left many other constituencies with tiny electorates.

The Speaker's Conference on Electoral Reform in 1944 recommended the establishment of permanent machinery for the redistribution of seats, so that major anomalies should not again arise. An Act of the same year established four Boundary Commissions, one each for England, Wales, Scotland and Northern Ireland, which should make a general review of constituency boundaries at intervals of not less than three and not more than seven years.[4] Each Commission was to consist of three members, chaired by the Speaker of the House of Commons, though his or her role was to be largely nominal, and with a judge as the Deputy (and effective) Chairman.

The first reports of the Commissions were, with one major amendment (mentioned below), approved by the House of Commons in 1948 and came into effect at the 1950 general election. They provided the first systematic delineation of constituencies which had ever been attempted, and of the 625 seats which made up the 1950 Parliament, only 80 had retained their boundaries untouched.

Only two general elections were fought on the new boundaries. In November 1954 the Commissions produced their second reports, which came into force in time for the 1955 general election. Although the recommendations which they made were much less far-reaching than in 1948, major alterations were suggested to 172 constituencies and minor alterations to 43, with the creation of five additional seats, and they were greeted with a storm of protest. There was general agreement, with which the Commissions themselves concurred, that if redistribution had previously been too infrequent it now erred very much on the other side.

Two groups of people were particularly incensed by the effects of this second redistribution within barely five years – Members of Parliament and active party workers in the constituencies. MPs of all parties were agreed that the normal hazards of political life were severe enough, without adding the further hurdle of a fresh bout of redistribution every five years or so. For a stiff hurdle it proved in a number of cases: safe seats were to become marginal or even hopeless, and marginal seats might become safe for the other side. In 1950, of the 70 members who lost their seats at least half could blame redistribution, partly or wholly, for their defeat. In 1955 at least eleven members were in the same position. Sir Frank Soskice (Labour) and Sir Ralph Assheton (Conservative) were double casualties, losing their seats through redistribution on both occasions.

The inconvenience which redistribution brings, both to members of local political organisations and to ordinary members of the public, was well described by Kenneth (later Sir Kenneth) Thompson, then Conservative MP for Liverpool, Walton, in a speech in the House of Commons on 15 December 1954, which also encapsulated some of the strengths and virtues of the constituency system as a basis of representation. He said:

We in this House are compelled to face the facts of political life. Political party organisation consists of the little constituency club, a polling district committee, a ward organisation, a constituency organisation, all pyramiding up from the modest humble, unobtrusive men and women who knock on doors, write names and addresses and do the slogging day-to-day work of a political party. That is the system under which political organisation has grown. Every time a unit is taken from the electorate of a constituency, every time a boundary line is altered by however much or however little, some Mrs Jones is chivvied out of this organisation and hived off to what is to her a foreign land, where there are a lot of people who do not speak her language. At the whim – if that is not an offensive word – of the Boundary Commission, she is expected to accept this as her lot and destiny and the pattern of her future political activity.

That is the immediate concern of Honourable Members ... but it goes further than that ... It concerns itself also with the ordinary people who live in the streets and villages of our constituencies. Time goes on, and they may not like us very much, they may tolerate us but they do get to know us as their Member or candidate. Something happens in their lives, big or little ... and they think in the first place of their Member of Parliament. If he has done his job reasonably well over the passage of years, it is not difficult for them to recall his name or his face ... Then the Boundary Commission draws a line, and out of their lives completely goes this man or woman ... and in comes an entirely different individual ...

It has always seemed to me of the utmost importance that the individual elector should feel at ease and confident in the company of his Member of Parliament ... Once we play about with this relationship between the individual elector and the Member, we do our democracy no good.[5]

The strong reaction to the 1955 redistribution led to amending legislation being passed by the House of Commons in 1958 which extended the period between general reviews of constituencies to a minimum of 10 and a maximum of 15 years. Subsequent boundary changes have been introduced at the elections of February 1974, 1983 and 1997. Those of 1983 were especially sweeping, leaving only 66 constituencies unchanged, as they reflected the changes to the local government structure introduced in 1974–5, but all have involved at least alterations to the vast majority of constituencies with the complete abolition of some seats and creation from scratch of others. As part of this process, the total number of constituencies has steadily increased, from 615 at the time the Speaker's Conference first recommended setting up the Boundary Commissions in 1944, to 659 today. The Parliamentary Constituencies Act 1986 consolidated the law on redistribution, while the Boundary Commissions Act 1992 reduced the intervals between which redistributions are carried out to every 8–12 years, instead of the 10–15 years provided for under the 1958 Act. The Political Parties, Elections and Referendums Act 2000 provided that the newly created Electoral Commission will absorb the Boundary Commissions once the next review (due to be completed by 2007) is finished, but left the rules otherwise unaltered.

Most of the boundary revisions have caused some political controversy and have led to attempts to block or alter the recommendations. In 1948 the English Commission recommended systematically smaller electorates for county (average 55,360) than for borough constituencies (average 61,442), in apparent defiance of Parliament's instructions. The Labour government amended the proposals before enacting them (as part of the 1948 Representation of the People Act), adding 17 extra borough seats, which reduced the average borough electorate to 57,883. The Tory opposition angrily accused the Labour Party of 'gerrymandering', but the results of the subsequent general election showed that Labour had gained virtually no net benefit from the amendment, and that the overall effect of the redistribution was a Conservative gain of between 20 and 30 seats.

In 1954–5 and 1982–3 members of the Labour Party, fearing that the net effect of the changes would be to their disadvantage, challenged the proposals in the courts on various grounds, but on each occasion were unsuccessful; and in 1954–5 there was also a separate unsuccessful legal challenge by Conservative Party members to some of the local proposals. In 1969 the Labour Home Secretary, James Callaghan, attempted to implement only the proposals referring to Greater London, leaving constituencies elsewhere unaltered. He justified his proposal on the grounds that major local government reorganisation – which would leave the new constituency boundaries totally out of line with local authority areas – was imminent (except in Greater London, where local government reorganisation had already taken place); but the opposition Conservatives, who rightly believed that their party would gain from a redistribution, cried foul. The House of Lords voted down Callaghan's bill, and the government was forced to introduce in the Commons orders to implement the Boundary Commissions' proposals, but used its majority to defeat them. Accordingly the 1970 general election was held on the old boundaries established in 1955, but the newly elected Conservative government lost no time in re-presenting the orders to the House of Commons, which approved them, and they took effect at the next (February 1974) general election.

The statutory rules under which the Commissions operate are few and their provisions simply worded, but in practice they give the Commissions little guidance on how to decide between the conflicting principles they lay down. On the one hand, there is a numerical requirement: the total electorate in each of the four countries is divided by the number of constituencies to secure an 'electoral quota', and the number of electors in each constituency should 'be as near to the quota as is practicable'. On the other hand, the Commissions must avoid, 'so far as is practicable', recommending constituencies which cross local authority boundaries, a requirement which tends to work against numerical equality, since local government areas often have inconveniently sized populations. Further, they may 'depart from the strict application' of these two principles if 'special geographical considerations' seem to make it desirable, and they must take account of 'the inconveniences attendant on alterations of constituencies ... and of any local ties which would be broken by such alterations'.

This means that the Commission's task is to strike the best balance between these competing requirements and leaves a lot to its discretion;

there is no 'right' answer. Because reaching a satisfactory solution must involve detailed local knowledge, all controversial details in the boundary proposals are normally subject to a public inquiry, where an Assistant Commissioner hears evidence on the merits of various possible arrangements of the local boundaries before the Commission makes a final recommendation. Although all members of the public can attend and submit evidence to these inquiries, which must be advertised in the local press, in practice it is usually only representatives of the local political parties who will attend, each arguing for the arrangement which is most to their partisan advantage. However, the Assistant Commissioner in his or her report and the Commission itself in its final decision will be swayed only by how well each alternative has been shown to satisfy the statutory rules, and not by any considerations of the political outcome.

The number of constituencies in Scotland and Wales must not be less than 71 and 35 respectively, and in Great Britain not substantially greater or less than 613, while Northern Ireland is to have between 16 and 18 seats. This allocation gives more than their proportionate share of seats to Scotland and Wales, presumably as a sop to their national susceptibilities. Of the 659 seats in the present Parliament, 529 are in England, 40 in Wales, 72 in Scotland and 18 in Northern Ireland. However, under the devolution arrangements by which the Scottish Parliament was set up, Scotland will have its number of seats at Westminster reduced to its true proportionate share – 59 seats – with effect from the next general election.

At the 1992 general election, as Table 4.1 shows, the largest constituency, the Isle of Wight, had an electorate of 99,838 – more than four times as large as the smallest, the Western Isles (in Scotland) with an electorate of 22,784. Both of these constituencies, in fact, are special cases – the inconvenience and geographical impracticability of combining the Western Isles or part of the Isle of Wight with any other area are agreed by all concerned to outweigh any arguments of numerical parity. But the second and third biggest seats in England were twice as big as the two smallest, and the three biggest seats in Scotland much more than twice as big as the smallest mainland Scottish seat. But by 1992, some of the boundaries were in effect 16 years old. (In England, the previous boundary revision had been based on the electorates in 1976.) Between 1992 and 1997 revised boundaries were drawn up, and the table illustrates how effectively the Boundary Commissions were able to reduce most of the discrepancies, though Isle of Wight and the Western Isles were both left unaltered.[6]

Table 4.1   Large and small constituencies, 1992 and 1997 electorates

	1992		*1997*
Largest			
England			
Isle of Wight	99,838	Isle of Wight	101,680
Eastleigh	91,736	Bristol West	84,870
Berkshire East	91,527	Ealing Southall	81,704
Scotland			
Gordon	80,103	Eastwood	66,679
Inverness, Nairn & Lochaber	69,468	Inverness East,	
Ayr	65,481	Nairn & Lochaber	65,701
		Carrick, Cumnock &	
		Doon Valley	65,593
Wales			
Pembroke	73,187	Vale of Glamorgan	67,213
Llanelli	65,058	Caerphilly	64,621
Smallest			
England			
Kensington	42,129	Camberwell & Peckham	50,214
Surbiton	42,421	Birmingham Yardley	53,058
Newham North West	46,471	Brent South	53,505
Scotland			
Western Isles	22,784	Western Isles	22,983
Caithness & Sutherland	30,905	Orkney & Shetland	32,291
Orkney & Shetland	31,472	Caithness, Sutherland &	
		Easter Ross	41,566
Wales			
Meironnydd Nant Conwy	32,413	Meironnydd Nant Conwy	32,345
Montgomery	41,386	Montgomeryshire	42,618

As a result of the boundary changes, the number of English seats with electorates more than 15 per cent above the quota was reduced from 71 to 5, and those 15 per cent below the quota from 93 to 20. Only 4 English seats deviated by more than 20 per cent from the quota. In Wales, the number of seats more than 15 per cent from the quota was cut from 8 to 3, in Scotland from 23 to 10, and in Northern Ireland from 6 to 4.

Despite this, some of the discrepancies that remained are obviously very substantial. The difference between England on the one hand and Scotland and Wales on the other is, as has already been indicated, because both the latter nations are statutorily guaranteed a minimum number of seats which is higher than their strictly proportionate share – therefore their electoral quotas, the benchmarks by which their constituency electorates are judged, are lower. Even so, within each country some constituencies are larger than others. Why should this be, even when a redistribution has just taken place?

In most cases it is because the Commissions try to assign whole numbers of seats to each county or London borough and are reluctant to cut across their boundaries. Therefore in counties and boroughs with electorates very close to the borderline for gaining an extra seat, the average electorate will inevitably be some way above or below the electoral quota. The Isle of Wight, England's smallest county at the time of the last redistribution, illustrates the point well: it had either to have a single seat with 101,000 electors or two with an average of 50,500 each. The problem affects small units more than larger ones, where the shortfall or excess of electors can be spread over several constituencies, so London boroughs such as Ealing and Brent are particularly likely to appear in the lists. But in other cases, such as Bristol West, although it would have been possible to improve numerical equality the Commission preferred to avoid unnecessary change to a generally satisfactory if rather overpopulated existing constituency. In Scotland and Wales the inaccessible geography of the more remote areas justifies smaller electorates than the national average, and all the smaller constituencies here are of this type.

With the passage of time, many of the larger seats tend to experience a disproportionate population growth, while the smaller seats tend to become progressively depopulated. The consequence is that the disparities grow year by year, providing ample demographic justification for the next redistribution some years before it is due. The Boundary Commissions have the right, rarely used, to make recommendations concerning individual constituencies at any time. This is meant to take account of electorates which become abnormally large or small. The only occasion when this provision has been used to make substantial change was in 1990, when the Milton Keynes constituency, whose electorate was then 109,839 and growing fast, was divided in two; however, very minor changes to realign constituency boundaries after small alterations to the local government boundaries are more frequent.

The political impartiality of the Boundary Commissions is unquestioned, but their work certainly has a considerable effect on the fortunes of the political parties and some of their decisions, particularly those of the English Commission, have been the cause of fierce controversy. It is obvious that individual decisions by the Commissioners can greatly affect the political complexion of any particular constituency. Providing that there is no consistent bias in their approach, it might be thought that the overall effect of their decisions would be to cancel out the advantage which different parties enjoy. In fact the overall outcome of each periodic redistribution has been to benefit the Conservative Party. Table 4.2 shows the range of estimates by leading experts of the size of this benefit.

Table 4.2   **Conservative gains from redistributions, 1948–94**

Redistribution	General election	Net Con. gains in seats
1948	1950	20–30
1954	1955	2–10
1969	Feb 1974	16–22
1983	1983	15
1994	1997	5–24

The reason for the consistent benefit which the Conservatives have gained is that redistributions cancel out the advantage that the Labour Party gains invisibly each year between one redistribution and the next. For the seats which are becoming smaller are disproportionately Labour seats (mostly in declining inner city areas and in the north), while those which are growing tend to be Conservative constituencies in the suburbs and in the south and east of England. If there were no redistributions the Labour Party would build up an enormous cumulative advantage. As it is, the redistributions which periodically eliminate the smallest seats and split up the largest tend to overcompensate the Labour advantage, and for much of the post-war period there was a slight bias in the electoral system towards the Conservatives. That is to say, that for any given distribution of votes they tended to win more seats than the Labour Party. In 1983 for example, it has been estimated that if the Conservative and Labour vote had been exactly equal the Conservatives would have won 19 more seats.[7] By 1992, however, this bias had been significantly reversed, and the same experts estimated that Labour would have been no less than 38 seats ahead in the event of an equality of votes.[8] Nor was this Labour advantage significantly reduced by the 1994 redistribution. This had been expected – not least by the Conservative government which took steps to speed up the process – to yield an advantage of 20 or more seats to the Tories. When the review was concluded, however, most experts[9] took the view that the net Tory gain was only about five seats, and this was more than cancelled out at the next elections by changes in geographic voting patterns. On the basis of the distribution of votes in 1997, if the Conservative and Labour vote had been exactly equal

Labour would have won 79 more seats and an overall majority of 19.[10] In 2001 Labour's vote held up better in the marginal constituencies than elsewhere, further increasing their advantage to a likely lead of 140 seats on an equal split of the vote. Viewed another way, Labour would win an overall majority even if 3.7 per cent behind in the popular vote; the Conservatives would need an 11.5 per cent lead for a majority of their own;[11] the abolition of 13, mostly Labour, seats in Scotland at the next election will only slightly offset this.

A bias of this size means that in theory the 'wrong' side could win an election, and indeed it has happened twice. In the 1951 general election the Labour Party actually polled 231,067 votes more than the Conservatives, but a Conservative government was elected with 26 seats more than Labour, and a majority of 17 overall. Conversely, in the February 1974 election, the Labour Party won five more seats than the Conservatives, even though it polled 225,789 fewer votes, and was able to form a minority government.

While detailed criticisms can be made of the recommendations and procedures of the Boundary Commissions, in general the difficult problem of delineating constituencies appears to have been solved more satisfactorily in Britain than in many other countries, and serious accusations of gerrymandering are almost unknown. If there are injustices in the arrangements for British elections, they are due much more to the electoral system than to the work of the Boundary Commissioners. Without a change in the system, it is doubtful whether the method of revising constituency boundaries could be improved to any significant extent.

All Parliamentary constituencies are now territorial ones, though from 1603 to 1950 representatives of the universities (elected by graduates) sat in the House of Commons. University representation was abolished, in accordance with the principle of 'one man, one vote', by the Labour government of 1945–51.

The method of election within each constituency is the simplest yet devised. Each voter has one vote which is recorded by marking an 'X' against the candidate of his or her choice on the ballot paper. The candidate who polls the largest number of votes in the constituency is elected, even if supported by only a minority of the voters. Where three or more candidates are in the field this is of course a common occurrence, and in the 2001 general election no fewer than 337 out of 659 members were elected with a minority vote.

Where support for three or more candidates is very evenly balanced it is possible for a member to be elected with much less than half the votes. The lowest winning share of the vote in modern general elections came in a five-party contest for the Inverness, Nairn and Lochaber seat in 1992, where the winning candidate obtained little more than a quarter of the votes. The result was:

Sir Russell Johnston	(Lib Dem)	13,258	(26.0%)
David Stewart	(Lab)	12,800	(25.1%)
Fergus Ewing	(SNP)	12,562	(24.7%)
John Scott	(Con)	11,517	(22.6%)
John Martin	(Green)	766	(1.5%)
Lib Dem majority		*458*	*(0.9%)*

It is of course theoretically possible in multi-sided contests for a candidate to be elected with considerably less than one-quarter of the votes.

The combination of single-member constituencies and a 'first past the post' (or 'plurality') method of voting leads to considerable discrepancies between the proportion of votes polled by parties and the number of seats which their candidates obtain in the House of Commons. Between the two larger parties this normally has the effect of exaggerating the majority obtained by the more successful and thus ensuring a larger majority for the government in the House of Commons than it would achieve under proportional representation.

Way back in 1909, the so-called 'cube law' was propounded by James Parker Smith, who stated that if the votes cast for the two leading parties are divided by the ratio A:B, the seats will be divided between them in the proportion $A^3:B^3$. This relationship was actually observed, with minor variations, in British election results over the next 65 years, as well as in some other countries, such as the USA and New Zealand, which have a similar electoral system. Yet there is nothing hard and fast about this relationship between seats and votes, and progressively from the February 1974 general election the advantage which the leading party enjoyed over its main rival shrank. By the time of the 1983 general election the winning party's advantage was in fact even less than it would have been if a 'square law' had existed. In 1983 the Conservatives would have won 80 more seats and Labour 80 less if the cube law was still in operation.[12] Since 1983, the trend has reversed slightly, but the exaggerative effect still falls well short of the cube law.

The reasons why the cube law disappeared are complex, but they are due to population movements round the country and, in particular, to the fact that predominantly Conservative areas (in the south and in the country) have become steadily more Conservative, while Labour areas

(Scotland, the north of England, inner cities) have become progressively more Labour. There are thus fewer marginal seats which are liable to change hands at general elections. Whereas in the mid-1950s some 17 seats changed hands, on average, for each 1 per cent swing between the two leading parties, by 1979–83 only 10 seats were changing hands for each 1 per cent swing.[13] (For definition of 'swing' see p. 36 below.)

The other well-known consequence of the 'first past the post' system is that smaller parties tend to be seriously under-represented, especially those like the Liberal Democrats whose support is evenly spread across the whole country rather than being concentrated in geographical clusters (like the Scottish and Welsh Nationalists and the Northern Ireland parties). Table 4.3, which shows the proportion of votes and seats won by the three main parties since 1945, indicates the extent to which the Liberal Democrats and their predecessors have suffered.

Table 4.3   Percentage of seats and votes won by the parties, 1945–2001

	1945		1950		1951		1955	
	votes	seats	votes	seats	votes	seats	votes	seats
Conservative	39.6	33.2	43.5	47.7	48.0	51.3	49.7	54.5
Labour	48.0	62.2	46.1	50.4	48.8	47.2	46.4	44.0
Liberal	9.0	1.9	9.1	1.4	2.6	1.0	2.7	1.0
	1959		1964		1966		1970	
	votes	seats	votes	seats	votes	seats	votes	seats
Conservative	49.4	57.9	43.4	48.1	41.9	40.2	46.4	52.4
Labour	43.8	40.9	44.1	50.3	47.9	57.6	43.0	45.7
Liberal	5.9	1.0	11.2	1.4	8.5	1.9	7.5	1.0
	Feb 1974		Oct 1974		1979		1983	
	votes	seats	votes	seats	votes	seats	votes	seats
Conservative	37.8	46.7	35.9	43.6	43.8	53.4	42.4	61.1
Labour	37.1	47.4	39.3	50.2	36.9	42.4	27.6	32.2
Liberal/Alliance	19.3	2.2	18.3	2.0	13.8	1.7	25.4	3.5
	1987		1992		1997		2001	
	votes	seats	votes	seats	votes	seats	votes	seats
Conservative	42.3	57.8	41.9	51.6	30.7	25.0	31.7	25.2
Labour	30.8	35.2	34.4	41.6	43.2	63.6	40.7	62.5
Alliance/Lib Dem	22.6	3.4	17.8	3.1	16.8	7.0	18.3	7.9

It is clear from a glance at the Liberal performance that third parties are very much under-represented under present conditions. The system can also be capricious in the extreme: between 1992 and 1997 the Liberal Democrats' share of the vote fell, yet because their votes were concentrated in Conservative marginal constituencies their share of seats more than doubled.

The apparent injustice of the system has led to demands for the introduction of a system of proportional representation (or PR) as practised in a number of other countries. Such calls go back almost to the start of the twentieth century, and have come close to success in the past. Single Transferable Vote (STV) was almost adopted in 1918. A less drastic (and not really proportional) reform of the voting system, the Alternative Vote, was actually approved by the House of Commons both in 1918 and 1931, but defeat of the measure in the Lords in 1931, followed by a change of government, prevented it coming into force. (Both systems are described in Appendix 8.) The temporary decline of the Liberal Party from this point made the question less urgent, but the Liberal resurgence from the 1970s onwards and the growth in votes for minor parties have brought 'electoral reform' to prominence once more. Not only was the injustice to the Liberals and their successors considered a concern, but the low proportions of electors actually supporting elected majority governments raised questions about their democratic legitimacy. The Labour government elected in October 1974, with a majority of three seats, polled only 39.2 per cent of the votes cast (and just 28.6 per cent of the total electorate). Mrs Thatcher won three comfortable majorities with only just over two in five voters supporting her, and Tony Blair won two landslide majorities with 43 per cent and then 41 per cent of the vote.

Without distinguishing between different methods of PR, opinion polls in recent years have often shown large majorities in favour of changing the system, although when the question is phrased differently strong support can also be found for aspects of the existing system.

There is no consensus on which system should be adopted if 'first past the post' were to be scrapped. STV (which is used in the Irish Republic, for elections in Northern Ireland except to the House of Commons, and which is soon to be introduced for local government elections in Scotland) remains the preferred proportional system of many British campaigners, including the Liberal Democrats and the Electoral Reform Society. However, when proportional representation was finally introduced for some elections in Great Britain in 1999, two other systems were adopted instead – 'closed' regional party lists in the European elections, and the Additional Member System (based on the West German model and also recently adopted in New Zealand) for the Scottish Parliament and Welsh Assembly, as well as for the London Assembly elected in 2000. Yet another system, 'AV-plus', was recommended for general elections by a Commission under Lord Jenkins of Hillhead (the former Labour

Cabinet minister and SDP leader Roy Jenkins), which reported in 1998. However, the Labour government's enthusiasm for any change seems to have cooled and, as the Conservatives remain opposed to proportional representation, the prospect of a change in the electoral system in the near future has perhaps receded. Details of all these systems are given in Appendix 8.

Historically, it was quite common for there to be no contest in some constituencies at general elections in seats regarded as being very secure for the defending member or his party. Since 1951, however, every single seat has been contested at every general election. But before the 1980s many constituencies had 'straight fights', between only two candidates, Labour and Conservative, as the Liberal Party was not able to field a full roster of candidates. From 1983, however, the SDP-Liberal Alliance and later Liberal Democrats began to fight every constituency in Great Britain, which meant that there were at least three candidates in every constituency. In fact in both 1979 and 1983 there was an average of four per constituency. Table 4.4 shows the number of candidates in each post-war election (see also Appendix 1). There had been a steady rise since the mid-1950s, though there was a fall in 1987, probably due to the rise in the candidate's deposit from £150 to £500 (see p. 105). In 1997 the total number of candidates was the largest in British history, averaging 5.7 per constituency; it fell in 2001 to an average of five per constituency, but this is still higher than hitherto.

Table 4.4 Seats and candidates, 1945–2001

General election	No. of seats	No. of candidates	Average per seat
1945	640	1,682	2.6
1950	625	1,868	3.0
1951	625	1,376	2.2
1955	630	1,409	2.2
1959	630	1,536	2.4
1964	630	1,757	2.8
1966	630	1,707	2.7
1970	630	1,837	2.9
1974: Feb	635	2,135	3.4
1974: Oct	635	2,252	3.5
1979	635	2,576	4.1
1983	650	2,579	4.0
1987	650	2,325	3.6
1992	651	2,946	4.5
1997	659	3,724	5.7
2001	659	3,319	5.0

Although every seat is contested, relatively few change hands, even in elections when one party achieves a sweeping victory. Some 52 did so in 1992, about 8 per cent of the total. Up to 1997, fewer than 100 seats had switched sides at each of the post-war elections since 1945 when, in a 'landslide' election, some 227 seats out of 640 changed hands, just over one-third of the total. The 1945 election was the first in ten years, and came after wartime conditions had changed the face of British politics. But the 1997 election showed that on rare occasions a dramatic turnaround is possible even after a single five-year Parliament, and around 180 seats changed hands; yet even in this 'landslide', almost three-quarters of the seats were won by the same party as five years before. In 2001, by stark contrast, just 28 seats changed hands, the lowest number since 1955.

In practice, constituencies are regarded as falling into three categories: safe, hopeless and marginal. A safe seat held by one party is of course a hopeless seat for the others. A marginal seat is one where the existing majority is small enough for there to be a realistic prospect for it to be captured by an opposing party. For most of the post-war period the great majority of marginal seats were at issue between Labour and the Conservatives. Only a small minority of seats (outside Northern Ireland) were regarded as being vulnerable to attack by another party, either the Liberals or the Scottish or Welsh Nationalists (Plaid Cymru). But the emergence of the SDP-Liberal Alliance and foundation of the Liberal Democrats has created a whole new category of marginal seats, most of which were previously regarded as being strongholds for the Conservatives.

It is impossible to give precise definitions of safe and marginal seats, but in practice those with a majority of more than 10 per cent of the votes cast (or roughly 5000 votes) have been unlikely to change hands at a general election, though the 'landslide' election of 1997 was an exception to this. (Much larger changes occur at by-elections, where many more seats should be regarded as marginal.) On this rough-and-ready definition, some 130 out of the 659 seats in the House of Commons elected in 2001 can be regarded as marginal. Of these, 42 are defended by Conservatives, 58 by Labour members, 19 by the Liberal Democrats, 3 by the SNP, 1 by Plaid Cymru and 7 by various parties in Northern Ireland.[14]

It has become common practice to convert the voting figures in constituency contests into percentages. This enables the 'swing' to be calculated. The term 'swing' was first applied to elections by David Butler. It is defined as the average of one party's gain and another's loss. Thus if at one election the Conservatives poll 50 per cent of the votes and Labour 45 per cent and at the next election the figures are reversed, there has been a swing to Labour of 5 per cent. If both parties lose to a third it is calculated by taking half the difference between the two parties' losses; for example, if at one election the Conservatives poll 60 per cent and Labour 40 per cent and at the next the Conservatives poll 50 per cent, Labour 38 per cent and the Liberal Democrats 12 per cent, the net swing from Conservative to Labour is 4 per cent.

The utility of the swing concept is that it enables the overall change in a constituency between two elections to be expressed in a single figure, and thus allows easy comparison between the results in different constituencies. Table 4.5 shows an example from the 1992 general election.

Table 4.5 Voting figures in Feltham and Heston, 1987 and 1992: conventional swing

		1987	*(%)*		*1992*	*(%)*
Conservative		27,755	(46.5)		25,665	(42.8)
Labour		22,325	(37.4)		27,660	(46.1)
Lib Dem		9,623	(16.1)		6,700	(11.2)
Majority	(Con)	5,430	(9.1)	(Lab)	1,195	(3.3)
Swing to Labour:					6.2%	

The Conservative percentage vote in Feltham and Heston fell by 3.7 per cent, and the Labour percentage rose by 8.7 per cent, making a swing to Labour of 6.2 per cent. With this figure one can tell at a glance that Labour did better in Feltham and Heston than in the country as a whole, where the average swing to Labour was 2.5 per cent.

For some comparative purposes it may be more useful to exclude the votes obtained by third parties and only reckon the votes obtained by the two largest parties in calculating swing. This is known as 'two-party swing' or 'Steed swing', after Michael Steed who first developed this concept. (By comparison, 'normal swing' is sometimes referred to as 'Butler swing' or 'all-party swing'.) To take the earlier example for Feltham and Heston, the calculation of two-party swing would be as in Table 4.6.

Note that in the case of two-party swing, one party's gain is always equal to the other party's loss, and that this is the net swing. Unless otherwise stated, all swing figures given subsequently in this book will be normal ('Butler') swing. The swing figure required for a seat to change hands is exactly half the percentage majority of the defending party, plus one vote. This is because one party's gain is another's loss. Thus in the above example of Feltham and Heston, where the Labour candidate won by 3.3 per cent, a Conservative swing of 1.65 per cent would have been needed for the Labour majority to disappear.

Table 4.6   Voting figures in Feltham and Heston, 1987 and 1992: two-party swing

	1987	(%)	1992	(%)
Conservative	27,755	(55.4)	25,665	(48.1)
Labour	22,325	(44.6)	27,660	(51.9)
Total two-party vote	50,080		53,325	
Two-party swing:				7.3%

Nothing is static in British politics and over the years safe seats have become marginal and marginal ones safe. This is due partly to the movement of population, partly to the effect of redistribution and partly to changes in political opinion. Each new Parliament elected alters the status of different constituencies.

5
Political Parties: National[1]

Political parties are the lifeblood of electoral politics in Britain, as in almost every other democracy in the world. The overwhelming majority of Parliamentary candidates are party adherents, and it is an exceptionally rare event for an independent candidate to secure election. The reader may, therefore, be surprised to learn that their existence has been almost totally ignored by law, and in British general elections up to and including 1997, parties were unrecognised, unregulated and the elections regarded officially as wholly a contest between individual candidates. This has now changed. Under reforms introduced before the 2001 election, political parties have been recognised by law for the first time ever in Britain, their names registered, their accounts opened to public scrutiny and some of their activities regulated. Yet in reality, this reform of the law will make little real difference to the way British elections work. Though unrecognised by law for so long, political parties have been the dominant factor for well over a century, and it is impossible to understand how an election works without understanding how the parties play their part in it and shape it.

In this chapter and the next the organisation of each of the three major parties is examined in some detail, together with a brief survey of the more significant minor parties. Before discussing the individual parties it should be noted that there is a common pattern in the organisation of all three parties. Each party is made up of three elements – the Parliamentary Party, comprising the MPs and peers who belong to the party concerned, the party bureaucracy and the mass membership throughout the country. The third element is discussed in Chapter 6, the first two are dealt with here.

Parliamentary Party

Of these three elements, it is the Parliamentary Party which is dominant in each case. This is explicitly recognised in the Conservative Party, in which a strong Parliamentary group existed long before either a bureaucracy or a mass membership organisation was formed. The latter were set up in the mid-nineteenth century specifically to provide support for the Parliamentary Party and to ensure the continued election of Conservative MPs. In the Labour Party, the mass organisation was set up first, and in the early days of the twentieth century when there were only a few Labour MPs, they were clearly subordinate to the extra-Parliamentary organisation of the party. But, at least from 1924 onwards when the first minority Labour government was formed, the Parliamentary Labour Party secured for itself in practice, if not formally, a dominance comparable to that of the Parliamentary Conservative Party, though this has been diminished in recent years due to changes in Labour's constitution (see below). The Liberal Democrats were formed (originally as the Social and Liberal Democrats) in 1988 by a merger of the Liberal Party, whose history was similar to that of the Conservatives, and the Social Democratic Party (SDP), which was founded in 1981, mainly by a group of defecting Labour MPs. Its constitution owes something to both traditions, protecting the autonomy of its MPs while reserving to the mass membership the final decision-making powers.

In all three parties, the leader of the party in the House of Commons and the leader of the whole party are one and the same. The members of the Parliamentary Party – full-time professional politicians in daily contact with each other for eight months of the year – normally have little difficulty in monopolising the most important party decisions.

This used to be least true of the Labour Party, particularly in opposition. Labour Party leaders, and Labour MPs generally, have periodically had great difficulty in resisting dictation from the party's annual conference and from the National Executive Committee. In the early 1960s the conference successfully resisted an attempt by the then party leader, Hugh Gaitskell, to amend the party constitution, and against his wishes carried a resolution in favour of unilateral nuclear disarmament. Gaitskell was able to secure a reversal of this defeat the following year, 1961, and the supremacy of the Parliamentary Labour Party was reasserted. Twenty years later however, following Labour's severe defeat in the 1979 election, the conference once more insisted on voting for policies which the party leader and a majority of Labour MPs did not support, on EEC membership, disarmament and the expulsion of American bases from Britain. The conference then proceeded to amend the party's constitution to take away from the Parliamentary Labour Party the exclusive right to elect the party leader and to submit Labour MPs to a mandatory process of reselection before each general election.

These decisions precipitated the breakaway of nearly 30 Labour MPs and the foundation of the Social Democratic Party. At one time it appeared that the Parliamentary Labour Party had suffered a permanent loss of power and influence to the conference, at least while the party was in opposition; in the late 1980s, however, Neil Kinnock demonstrated a steadily tightening grip on the conference which has re-established the Parliamentary Party's position. His successors as party leader, John Smith and Tony Blair, built further on his achievements. When a party is in government, of course, much of the authority of the Parliamentary Party is assumed by the Cabinet, whose influence far outweighs that of any organ of the party, and a Prime Minister's unelected personal advisers may be far more influential than party officials or even senior MPs.

Party bureaucracy and party conference

The party bureaucracy in the Conservative Party used to be under the direct control of the leader through an appointed party chairman, but is now controlled by a governing board whose members include elected representatives of the party nationally as well as officials appointed by the leader. In the Labour and Liberal Democrat parties it has always been responsible to the elected representatives of the mass membership. Because many of these elected representatives are also Members of Parliament, the Parliamentary Party exercises a considerable indirect influence over the bureaucracy, and clashes of interest are rare.

In each case, the party bureaucracy consists of a national headquarters and a series of regional offices throughout the country, including separate and theoretically fully autonomous parties in Scotland, and, except for the Conservatives, in Wales; all the party headquarters are based in London, though Labour has moved around 50 of its staff to North Shields in Tyneside. In the 1970s the Conservative and Labour headquarters faced each other from different sides of Smith Square in Westminster, with the Liberal headquarters also in the same square. Conservative Central Office remained there until 2004 (it is now a five-minute walk away, in Victoria Street), but the Labour Party has moved several times – first to Walworth Road (across the river in Southwark), then back across the river to Millbank (just round the corner from Smith Square), and now to Old Queen Street, a quarter-mile to the north. The Liberal Democrats are now based at 4 Cowley Street (very near to Smith Square), which had been the home of the Social Democrats before the merger in 1988. Though more scattered than they once were, all three headquarters are still quite near to the House of Commons, emphasising their close relationship to their respective Parliamentary Parties.

Although each party headquarters undertakes the same tasks, there has traditionally been considerable difference in the efficiency with which these have been performed. The Conservative Party has usually had much the largest staff, although it was reduced considerably in the early 1980s to save money; it has also paid higher salaries, and has therefore often been able to attract better-qualified people to its employ. Over recent years, though, the Tory organisational advantage over Labour has diminished somewhat; but the Liberal Democrats remain very much the poor relations. In 2003, the Conservatives employed 177 permanent staff (all but 36 of whom were in Central Office) at a cost of £6.7 million, whereas the Labour Party had on average 240 full-time and 28 part-time staff over the same period (costing £8.7 million). The Liberal Democrats spent only £1.4 million employing an average of 43 staff.

Each party's headquarters is divided into a number of departments or directorates. In the Conservative Party these are directly responsible to the board; in the Labour Party each reports to an appropriate committee of the National Executive Committee (NEC); in the Liberal Democrats, the entire Federal Party HQ organisation is responsible to the party's Finance and Administration Committee. The overall functions of the party HQs are the same, although the division of responsibilities between departments is somewhat different (and complicated in the case of the Liberal Democrats by the party's federal structure).

Some of these departments are more directly involved in election work than others, but all are equally vital. The department in charge of research has an essential job, briefing the party's speakers on the wide range of subjects on which they are called to speak, especially vital when the party is in opposition; much of the material contained in the party's publications will also originate here, although they will actually be prepared by the communications department. Policy development, too, may begin here.

A key department in a modern general election is the one in charge of the party's relations with the press and broadcasting media, containing the public relations experts often nicknamed 'spin doctors', who are responsible for the image the party projects to the public. Supervision of the party's own television and radio broadcasts is an important part of this function, as is planning the extensive press and poster advertising campaign which will be needed. In recent years, though, the parties have become increasingly aware that good 'news management' can be the most potent of all. They must ensure that the party's spokesmen and prospective candidates are properly briefed and make a good impression when they appear on the TV news or are reported in the papers, and that the journalists covering the election are persuaded to cover the issues and stories that best suit the party and not their opponents. They need to be able to react instantly to unexpected news stories and to their opponents' speeches and initiatives, finding material for the party's speakers – the Labour Party's 'rapid rebuttal unit', using a computerised information-retrieval system called Excalibur, was particularly noted for its efficiency at this in the run-up to the 1997 election. Finally, the almost unavoidable occasional bad news story, assuming it cannot be stifled altogether by distracting the media's attention with some other topic, must be explained away or otherwise put in some new light so as to limit any damage to the party. Furthermore, this is all a continuing task, as it is vital to protect the party's reputation not only during elections but between them as well. The bureaucracy is also responsible for supplying speakers on demand for speaking engagements throughout the country, both at election time and between elections, and for ensuring that these are given proper media coverage. The development of this skill of news management, and the increasing prominence put upon it, is perhaps the most significant development in the last few decades in the way the national parties go about fighting an election. However, increasingly, leading politicians and government departments have their own spin doctors, and friction can arise between them and the party officials. Such conflicts of interest are potentially distracting and damaging.

Another central function crucial to electoral success is vetting, training and generally overseeing the party's Parliamentary candidates. Although all the parties allow the constituencies a great deal of autonomy in selecting their own candidates, every party headquarters maintains a list of approved names and if a candidate is to be endorsed as the representative of the national party, he or she must either be on this list already when selected or must be added to it. (This is discussed in more detail in Chapter 7.) Since the registration of political parties was introduced in 1998, the function of endorsement has been formalised into a legal process: each party HQ must appoint and register a 'nominating officer', and only candidates with a certificate issued by or on behalf of the nominating officer may use the party's name or symbol on the ballot paper.

Before 1998, the use of party names by candidates was effectively unregulated, and it was possible for mischievous or malicious candidates to use a misleading description so that they might appear to be the official candidate of a party when in fact they were not. Although such incidents were thankfully rare, there was widespread outrage in the 1994 European elections when a candidate describing himself as a 'Literal Democrat' took more than 10,000 votes, while the real Liberal Democrat (whose name appeared lower down the ballot paper) was defeated by a margin of only a few hundred.[2] This is no longer possible: party names are now officially registered with the Electoral Commission, which has the power to prevent misleading or confusing names being registered;[3] no candidate can now use the name of a registered party on the ballot paper unless he or she has been endorsed by the nominating officer; candidates not attached to any registered party will be described simply as 'Independent'.

The organising staff, who are responsible for maintaining an efficient vote-winning machine throughout the country, have perhaps the least glamorous job at the party headquarters, but nevertheless an essential one. Through their regional offices they keep a tight rein on the full-time constituency agents (although most of these are actually employed by the constituency parties), and are also responsible for ensuring that local parties are in a constant state of readiness to fight elections and that the selection of Parliamentary candidates proceeds according to the party rules. If there is any irregularity it is their function to bring the constituency party into line.

Head Office must also deal with such matters as local government, contacts with the European Parliamentary Party, keeping in touch with the party's overseas voters, relations with like-minded political parties in other countries, and the administration of maintaining membership records, collecting subscriptions and generally overseeing relations with the paid-up members, a task whose scale has grown in recent years as the parties have become more centralised.

Finally there is the crucial problem of fundraising. The maintenance of a party bureaucracy is an expensive business, and the difference in organisational efficiency is a direct reflection of the rival parties' financial resources. Historically the Conservative Party has been much the wealthiest party, but in recent years the gap between it and the Labour Party has narrowed considerably. For the two largest parties, members' subscriptions have provided only a fraction of the necessary resources, and both have been heavily dependent on individual and corporate donations and, in Labour's case, donations from trade unions. The sources of each party's funds, the scale of their fundraising and how the money is spent are discussed in Chapter 14.

The party bureaucracy is entrusted with the task of organising the party conference which provides the sole opportunity for the members of the mass organisation to give collective expression of their views. Traditionally the conference has been annual, the three parties holding them in rapid succession – first Liberal Democrat, then Labour, then Conservative – in September and October each year. Recently, the Liberal Democrats and now the Conservatives have started holding two conferences each year, of theoretically equal status; but the autumn conference, held at one of the small number of resorts which have the facilities to house such a gathering, still draws more attention.

Only Blackpool, Bournemouth and Brighton have a large enough conference centre and sufficient hotel accommodation to cater for the Labour and Conservative conferences, which rotate between these resorts each year. The other parties' conferences are somewhat smaller and a number of other towns, including Scarborough, Llandudno, Eastbourne, Harrogate and Cheltenham, have been favoured by the Liberal Democrats and their predecessors in recent years.

Each conference receives a report on the work of the party bureaucracy during the year and a Parliamentary report, and then proceeds to debate a large number of policy resolutions which have been sent in by constituency parties or, at the Labour conference, by trade unions.

The Conservative conference is a cumbrous affair with several thousand members, and acts as little more than a party rally. It has no formal power to do more than proffer 'advice' to the leader, and for many years it appeared to have only a small influence on party policy. Recent leaders, from Edward Heath onwards, have taken its deliberations more seriously, however, attending throughout the conference and taking care not to offend its sensibilities. The open contempt once shown by Tory leaders such as Arthur Balfour, who said he would no sooner take political advice from the conference than from his valet, is decidedly a matter of the past.

The Labour Party conference has about 1200 delegates of whom about half come from constituency parties, and the remainder mostly from trade unions. As the constituency delegates represent less than half a million members while the trade unionists represent over 5 million, the latter had in the past a predominating influence on the voting, though spokesmen from the constituency parties enjoyed the lion's share of the speech making. The constituency party delegates have had their voting weight magnified by recent constitutional changes, and now wield 50 per cent of the votes at the conference, leaving the affiliated bodies, predominantly the trade unions, with the remaining 50 per cent. Furthermore, in 1993 the trade union block vote (by which each union's entire voting weight had to be cast one way or the other) was abolished, and each union delegate is now free to vote independently. In the past it was the Labour Party conference which decided the policy of the party and especially the election programme on which it was to fight. Theoretically, therefore, its influence was immense. In practice, however, the Parliamentary leadership usually enjoyed the support of several of the larger trade unions and this normally guaranteed it a majority at the conference. It was only when one or more of the normally 'loyalist' trade unions disagreed with the Parliamentary leadership, as happened on the issue of defence policy in 1960, that the leadership ran a serious risk of defeat. This occurred with increasing frequency in the early 1980s; but things seemed to have settled back into their normal pattern by the end of the decade, and Conference has not been a serious obstacle to the leadership during Tony Blair's tenure of office. Nevertheless, its power remains.

The great amount of time and trouble which both the Parliamentary leadership and many busy trade union leaders devote to the conference is strong evidence that its influence, though less than decisive, is far from negligible. In the 1990s, however, the conference's power was somewhat diluted due to the creation of a new institution, the National Policy Forum. This is a much smaller body of around 100 members, which meets twice a year or more frequently and subjects all policy proposals to detailed scrutiny; it was under the auspices of this forum that party and union leaders met in July 2004 to thrash out a policy deal acceptable to the union movement on which the 2005/6 election would be fought. With Labour in government, however, ministers and their (unelected) advisers inevitably exercise substantial autonomy on policy details in any case. The election manifesto, which in 1997 had been submitted to a postal ballot of the national membership, was in 2001 decided entirely by the Cabinet.

The federal conference of the Liberal Democrats meets twice yearly. In theory it has considerably less power than the Labour Party conference, although it is the final arbiter of party policy. In practice, however, its influence is fairly strong; the small number of Liberal Democrat MPs leaves the Parliamentary leadership in a weak position, as it did in the old Liberal assembly, and Conference carries great weight.

Since the early 1960s the party conferences have received extensive coverage on television, and this has to a great extent modified their function. Traditionally, the Conservative conference was derided by its opponents as being 'stage managed' in order to provide a public image of unity and enthusiasm. Now all party managers exert themselves to achieve the same effect, and if they are successful they may well be rewarded by a spurt in their party's opinion poll ratings in the period immediately after the conference. Conversely, a fractious or quarrelsome conference can lead to a sharp fall in a party's popularity.

Major parties

The *Conservative and Unionist Party* is the oldest and most resilient of British parties. Its origins go back at least 300 years to Stuart times. The earlier name, Tory Party (still widely used by friends and foes alike), dates from 1679. 'Tory' was an Irish word meaning brigand and it was applied to the King's supporters, who were supposedly willing to use Irish troops against Englishmen to enforce the succession of James II. Tories were supporters of the Crown and drew their support principally from the squirearchy and the clergy.

The name Conservative was adopted following the Reform Act of 1832. Some 30 years later, finding themselves in a permanent minority in the then politically-dominant urban middle class, they set out under the inspiration of Benjamin Disraeli to form the basis of a mass party. Local Conservative associations were formed in many constituencies to secure the election of Conservative MPs. The 1867 Reform Act, which extended the vote to most urban working-class men, gave added impetus to this development, and in the following three years the party took on substantially its present shape.

The Liberal Unionists, who broke away from the Liberal Party in 1886 because of their opposition to Irish Home Rule, finally amalgamated with the Conservative Party in 1912, hence its present unwieldy name. Conservatives in Scotland and in Northern Ireland traditionally called themselves Unionists and Ulster Unionists respectively, but the term is infrequently used in England and Wales. The Ulster Unionist Party in Northern Ireland used to be the Conservative Party in the province. In 1972 however, the Conservative government, under Edward Heath, imposed direct rule on Northern Ireland. The Unionists broke away, and their party is now completely independent of the Conservatives. After some years of refusing to countenance the possibility, the Conservative Party finally yielded to pressure in 1989, and has now permitted the foundation of constituency Conservative associations in Northern Ireland.

Until 1998, the Conservative Party had no formal constitution. Under changes introduced after William Hague became leader, which were overwhelmingly approved by a postal ballot of the membership, this is no longer the case, and the relationships between the various parts of the party are now formally laid down and enforceable. Three distinct elements make up the modern Conservative Party: the Parliamentary

Party, the constituency associations (which send representatives to the National Conservative Convention) and Central Office. They are linked at the apex by the leader, who enjoys very considerable formal power (much more than his Labour or Liberal Democrat counterparts). The most influential of the three elements is undoubtedly the Parliamentary Party, which is composed of all Members of Parliament who take the Conservative whip. The management of the Parliamentary Party is the responsibility of the Chief Whip, who is appointed by the leader.

The Conservative leader retains the ultimate power in determining the party's policies, though this is naturally exercised in consultation with senior colleagues and taking into account the views of the party at large, as expressed in informal consultation, at the party conference and especially through the Conservative Policy Forum. In 1998, unprecedentedly, William Hague called a referendum of all members on the party's policy on the single European currency, but as the choices offered were simply to endorse or reject the leader's policies it was in reality no more than a demand for a vote of confidence in Mr Hague himself. The wide margin by which his policy was approved strengthened his hand in dealing with his Parliamentary rivals, by demonstrating that both he and his policy were acceptable to the party activists; but more broadly, it emphasised that policy is still the prerogative of the leader and that forcing a change of leader is the only way to force a change in policy.

From the Parliamentary Party and the Conservative peers, the leader chooses the Cabinet when a Conservative government is in power; when in opposition he or she appoints a 'Shadow Cabinet' and a deputy leader. The Parliamentary Party has a number of specialist committees on defence, foreign affairs, trade and industry, agriculture and so on. When the party is in opposition the committees are attended by both front and backbench members, when in government they are comprised entirely of backbench members.

An unofficial body which wields considerable power is the '1922 Committee' (known as such because it was originally formed on the initiative of the backbench members elected to the Parliament of 1922). This committee, known formally as the Conservative Members' Committee, meets every week while Parliament is sitting and consists, when a Conservative government is in power, of all the Conservative backbench members. When Conservatives are in opposition the 1922 Committee comprises the entire Parliamentary Party, and the backbench influence is diluted by the presence of the leading frontbench members. Its chairman, who is elected by the committee, is a prominent backbencher, and is a most influential voice in party affairs; when there is a vacancy in the party leadership or a vote of no confidence in the leader is called, the chairman is responsible for administering the voting.

The National Union of Conservative and Unionist Associations, dating from 1867, used to be the body representing the mass following of the Conservative Party throughout the country. It was a federation of constituency associations, and its annual conference was, in effect, the annual conference of the Conservative Party. In the reforms of 1998, the National Union was abolished, and constituency associations are now affiliated directly to the party itself, with constituency officers sitting *ex officio* on the party's main administrative organs. The annual party conference is now organised by a committee of the party's governing board, and is chaired by the Chairman of the National Convention. Each constituency association can send members as representatives, including its chairman, two deputy chairmen, the agent or secretary, and three other representatives (one of whom must be a member of Conservative Future, the party's youth wing). MPs, prospective candidates and leaders of the Conservative groups on local councils can also attend.

The board is the governing body of the party organisation and bureaucracy, in charge of all operational matters but taking no part in political functions such as policy formulation. The National Convention has taken the National Union's place as the organ of the mass membership. It meets at least twice a year, and consists of all constituency association chairmen together with area and regional officials, and representatives of other affiliated or recognised organisations such as Conservative Future and the Conservative Women's National Committee. Its function is to act as a link between party members and the leadership. It elects from its number a National Convention Executive, which carries on its day-to-day work and also represents the national membership on the board. The Conservative Policy Forum (formerly the Conservative Political Centre) is a consultative body within the party, charging a separate (£25) subscription to give members input into the party's policy-making mechanism.

The Conservative Party now provides for all members nationally to vote in its leadership election (although if a candidate is unopposed, as Michael Howard was in 2003, the power is of course only theoretical). This is a radical departure for the Conservatives. Until 1965, indeed, the party leader was not elected at all as such. The leader in those days used to be nominally 'elected' by the Party Meeting (a body which never otherwise met and which consisted of all the Conservative Members of the House of Commons and of the House of Lords, all prospective Parliamentary candidates and the executive committee of the National Union), but there had never been a contested election. The leadership was actually decided by a process of informal consultation between the leading party figures in both Houses of Parliament and only one name was put before the meeting for formal endorsement. When a Conservative government was in power the Sovereign was normally advised to send for whoever was designated and appoint him Prime Minister, even before the meeting to formally elect the new leader had been convened.

Following the Conservative defeat in the 1964 general election, the leader Sir Alec Douglas-Home instituted a one-man inquiry by the party chairman, Lord Blakenham, on the basis of which he announced that in future the leader would be chosen by a ballot of Conservative MPs. The system was clearly devised to assist the evolution of a compromise choice should there be a sharp division between two controversial and mutually incompatible candidates. A candidate needed to secure on the first ballot not only an absolute majority, but a lead of 15 per cent over his or her nearest rival; if the first ballot failed to produce a winner, a second ballot was held for which new nominations could be made. To be successful on the second ballot, a candidate needed only an absolute majority. If the second ballot was inconclusive a third and final ballot was held between the three leading candidates: voters were required to indicate their second as well as their first preference, and if necessary the second preferences of the least popular of three would be distributed between the other two to determine the winner.

When Sir Alec resigned in July 1965 the new system was put into effect. Three candidates were nominated, and on the first ballot Edward Heath received 150 votes, Reginald Maudling 133 and Enoch Powell 15. Heath had received an absolute majority, but his lead over Maudling was less than 15 per cent and a second ballot was therefore necessary. However, both Maudling and Powell declined re-nomination, and Edward Heath was elected unopposed.

The system initially contained no provision for periodic re-election, but in the autumn of 1974, following two successive Conservative election defeats, there was an overwhelming demand among Tory MPs for a fresh election, although Heath made it clear that he had no intention of resigning. Lord Home (as Sir Alec had now become) was asked to consider changes in the rules, and his three main proposals were:

1. There should be an annual election of the leader.
2. A candidate, to be elected on the first ballot, required not only an overall majority but also a lead over the runner-up equal to 15 per cent of those eligible to vote (rather than 15 per cent of those who actually voted).

3. Though only MPs had votes, the views of the Conservative peers and of the party in the country should be conveyed to them.

An unforeseen consequence of the altered system, which later came to assume considerable political significance, was that it allowed for 'stalking horse' candidates. An unpopular leader could be challenged by a minor figure, not expected to win but to 'test the water'; if discontent with the leader was high enough, there would be enough votes for the stalking horse and abstentions to ensure a second ballot, at which the real challengers could stand, having avoided the risk of showing their hand too early and of being publicly disloyal while still uncertain of victory.

Heath submitted himself for re-election the following February, and was disconcerted to find himself led on the first ballot by Margaret Thatcher by 130 votes to 119, with 16 votes cast for a third candidate, Hugh Fraser, while eleven MPs did not vote. He immediately resigned and four more candidates (William Whitelaw, James Prior, Sir Geoffrey Howe and John Peyton) were nominated for the second ballot, from which Fraser withdrew. This ballot produced an absolute majority for Mrs Thatcher, who won 146 votes, to 79 for Mr Whitelaw and less than 20 for each of the other three.

Although the new system provided for a theoretically annual election, even if the party was in power, the first contested election after 1975 was in 1989, when Sir Anthony Meyer was persuaded to stand against Mrs Thatcher (who had by then been Prime Minister for ten years) to enable MPs to express discontent and possibly to open the way for a challenge from a more senior figure should she fail to win outright on the first ballot. However, Mrs Thatcher polled 314 votes while only 33 MPs voted for Meyer, with another 27 abstaining; nevertheless, the public embarrassment for the party was considerable. The following year Mrs Thatcher was challenged again, this time by Michael Heseltine, in the wake of the resignation of her Deputy Prime Minister, Sir Geoffrey Howe.

Although more than half of the MPs voted for Mrs Thatcher in the first ballot, she failed by four votes to clear the hurdle of a 15 per cent lead over her rival. The result of this ballot, declared on 20 November 1990, was:

Margaret Thatcher	204
Michael Heseltine	152
Abstentions	16

Mrs Thatcher's immediate reaction was that she would fight on into the second round, but after having been warned by the majority of her Cabinet and by other senior party figures that her support was crumbling she withdrew, freeing both the Chancellor of the Exchequer, John Major, and Foreign Secretary, Douglas Hurd, to accept nominations. The result of the second ballot, declared on 27 November 1990, was:

John Major	185
Michael Heseltine	131
Douglas Hurd	56

Major was two votes short of the overall majority required on this ballot, but his two rivals immediately withdrew, making a third ballot unnecessary. The following morning Mrs Thatcher resigned as Prime Minister and Mr Major was appointed in her place.

Many Tory MPs, as well as Conservative activists in the constituencies, were highly resentful that an electoral system designed when the party had been in opposition had been used to unseat a Prime Minister, and after the election the Chairman of the 1922 Committee, Cranley Onslow, was asked to carry out an inquiry as to whether different rules should apply when the Conservatives are in power. It was subsequently decided to make it much more difficult to mount a challenge to the Prime Minister by requiring at least 10 per cent of Conservative MPs to sign the nomination paper of any challenger. Nevertheless, in the summer of 1995, discontent with John Major's leadership had grown to such an extent on the right wing of the party that a challenge in the autumn seemed inevitable. John Major decided to take the bull by the horns and resigned as party leader in July, daring his opponents to put up a rival candidate. John Redwood, the Secretary of State for Wales, resigned his Cabinet post and took up the challenge. Two other Cabinet ministers, Michael Heseltine and Michael Portillo, who would have been stronger runners, declined to be nominated, and Major succeeded in obtaining a sufficient majority to win on the first ballot. The result was:

John Major	218
John Redwood	89
Abstentions/spoilt papers	20

The result was generally deemed to have strengthened Major's position, even though it revealed that one-third of Tory MPs were not prepared to support him.

After defeat in the 1997 election, John Major immediately announced his resignation as leader. Five of his former Cabinet ministers stood for the leadership, with William Hague emerging the winner (Table 5.1).

Table 5.1 Conservative Party leadership election, 1997

	First round	*Second round*	*Third round*
William Hague	41	62	92
Kenneth Clarke	49	64	70
John Redwood	27	38	
Michael Howard	24		
Peter Lilley	23		

After Mr Hague's election, a new system was introduced as part of a wider reform of the party's structure. In future elections for leader, all members of the Conservative Party will have a vote, though the Parliamentary Party retains the privilege of initiating a contest, and if there are more than two candidates, MPs are balloted first, with only their two leading choices offered to the membership at large. There are no longer, even theoretically, annual leadership elections. When a vacancy occurs through the resignation or death of the sitting leader, a contest must naturally occur; if the leader does not resign voluntarily, however, he or she can only be challenged if 15 per cent of the Parliamentary Party write to the chairman of the 1922 Committee asking for a vote of no confidence in the leader. If sufficient signatures are raised and the party leader loses the confidence vote, he or she is debarred from running in the leadership election that follows; on the other hand, if the Parliamentary Party gives a simple majority expressing confidence in the leader, no further challenge is allowed for a year.

The new system was used for the first time to elect Hague's successor when he resigned following defeat in the 2001 general election. An unforeseen flaw immediately emerged when two of the five candidates in the first round of voting tied for last place, and it was realised that the rules made no provision for breaking the tie. At the second attempt there was a clear outcome, and all proceeded smoothly until the MPs had to reduce three candidates to the final two. To the consternation of many, Michael Portillo – thought to be much the most popular of the three candidates with the paid-up members – was squeezed out by a single vote, quite possibly by supporters of Kenneth Clarke voting tactically for the less well-known Iain Duncan Smith, whom they thought to be a less dangerous opponent. In the event, though, 'IDS' scored a convincing win in the poll of the mass membership (Table 5.2).

Table 5.2   Conservative Party leadership election, 2001

	First round	*Second round*	*Third round*	*Members' ballot*
Kenneth Clarke	36	39	59	100,864
Iain Duncan Smith	39	42	54	155,933
Michael Portillo	49	50	53	Excluded
Michael Ancram	21	17	Excluded	
David Davis	21	18	Withdrew	

The Duncan Smith leadership proved an unhappy period, however, and after just over two years, a handful of discontented MPs revealed that they had already written to Sir Michael Spicer (chairman of the 1922 Committee) calling for a vote of confidence, and urging others to do likewise. Mr Duncan Smith, perhaps rashly, challenged his opponents to 'put up or shut up', and within a few days Sir Michael announced that he had now received the requisite number of signatures and that consequently a ballot would be held. Mr Duncan Smith was defeated (although comparatively narrowly, by 90 to 75), and thus debarred from the leadership contest which was thereby initiated.

The widely anticipated bitter battle for the succession never materialised, however, with only Michael Howard being nominated and neither MPs nor mass membership therefore having any opportunity to vote, an unexpectedly swift and dignified conclusion to the affair. But some party workers in the constituencies expressed anger that the leader they had elected, and who many still preferred to the alternatives, had been ousted by the MPs without their being consulted. If Michael Howard's leadership proves not to live up to the hopes of his supporters, this may come back to haunt the party as a source of friction between the MPs and the grass roots. Since Howard was certainly not the only senior MP with leadership ambitions, one can only assume that his potential opponents came to the conclusion by some sort of informal consultation – or had it intimated to them – that they could not win and in the interests of party unity (and their own careers) should therefore not stand. In a sense the party's electoral mechanism has come full circle in 40 years.

The Conservative Party did not publish membership figures for many years. In 1953 it claimed 2.8 million members, but this was believed to have fallen to around 1.5 million members in the mid-1980s, and since then there has been a further sharp decline. In 1999 the party was claiming only 350,000, and even this was disputed as an exaggeration by their opponents; by 2004 it was down to around 300,000, although this still left it larger than that of any of the other parties.[4] The party is organised in each of the 641 constituencies in Great Britain, and it invariably contests every British seat at general elections except, on occasion, that of the Speaker; since 1987 it has also contested a number in Northern Ireland. Unlike the other parties, no fixed proportion of membership subscriptions is passed on to central party funds; instead each constituency association is assigned a 'quota' which it is expected to pay, based upon its potential resources, and may raise it however it prefers. These quotas are not always met, and it is not unknown for associations to deliberately withhold part or all of their share to make a political point.

The *Labour Party* differs from all others in possessing a large affiliated membership (mostly trade unionists) in addition to its individual members. In fact, for the first 18 years of its existence it was impossible to become an individual member of the Labour Party.

The party was formed, under the title of the Labour Representation Committee, at a conference in London on 27 February 1900. The conference was convened by the Trades Union Congress, following a resolution passed at the TUC conference the previous year. It was attended by representatives of 67 trade unions and three small socialist organisations (the Independent Labour Party, the Social Democratic Federation and the Fabian Society). The purpose of the organisation established at this meeting was to secure the representation of 'working-class opinion' in the House of Commons 'by men sympathetic with the aims and demands of the Labour movement'. In the early years the Labour Representation Committee (which became the Labour Party in 1906) did no more than co-ordinate the political activities of its affiliated organisations and all Labour candidates at that time were financially sponsored by one or other of these affiliates.

Success at first came slowly to the new party. Only two Labour MPs were elected in the 1900 election (one being J. Keir Hardie who had been the driving force behind the creation of the party). But in the period from 1906 to 1923 the Labour Party progressively replaced the Liberals as one of the two principal parties, becoming the official Opposition in 1922 and forming its first (minority) government in 1924.

In 1918 the party adopted a new constitution. This at last made provision for individual membership of the party, and the creation of constituency Labour parties throughout the country followed immediately after. The

1918 constitution also specifically committed the party for the first time to socialist objectives. This provision, 'Clause Four', remained in force until 1995. The most significant amendments before this, agreed at a special party conference in January 1981, altered the basis for electing the leader and deputy leader of the party. Previously there had been, in theory at least, an annual ballot of MPs, who elected a leader and deputy leader of the Parliamentary Labour Party. In practice such ballots virtually never occurred except on the death or resignation of the incumbent. From Clement Attlee's assumption of the leadership in 1935 to Michael Foot's resignation in 1983, only twice was there a contested election other than to fill a vacancy; these two challenges, both to Hugh Gaitskell's leadership (in 1960 and 1961) were exceptional occasions arising from the dispute in the party over unilateral nuclear disarmament; Gaitskell won both comfortably.

In January 1981, two months after Foot's election, Labour MPs lost the right to choose their own leader. Henceforth the Labour leader (and deputy leader) would be chosen by an 'electoral college' made up of MPs (with 30 per cent of the vote), constituency parties (30 per cent) and trade unions (40 per cent). Although nobody was nominated to run against Foot under the new procedure, his deputy, Denis Healey (who had been elected unopposed by the Parliamentary Labour Party) was challenged in 1981 by Tony Benn. Healey defeated Benn by a mere 0.8 per cent of the electoral college vote.

The first leadership contest under the new electoral system came in October 1983, following the resignation of Foot. The result is shown in Table 5.3. Neil Kinnock, with over 71 per cent of the electoral college vote, was easily elected on the first ballot. In a parallel election for the deputy leadership held later the same day, Roy Hattersley was also elected on the first ballot, with over 67 per cent of the electoral college vote.

In theory, Labour continued to hold elections for leader and deputy leader every year while in opposition. (If Labour is in government they occur only if a majority of conference votes for a contest, unless there is a vacancy.) However, Kinnock and Hattersley were challenged only once: in 1988 Tony Benn was nominated for the leadership and John Prescott and Eric Heffer for the deputy leadership. Kinnock and Hattersley were both re-elected extremely comfortably, Kinnock securing 88.6 per cent of the vote and Hattersley 66.8 per cent, each winning in all three sections of the electoral college.

Labour's electoral system was put into motion again in 1992 when, following Labour's election defeat, Kinnock and Hattersley stood down. In the subsequent ballots John Smith was overwhelmingly elected leader, with 91 per cent of the votes against a single opponent, Brian Gould, who polled 9 per cent. For the deputy leadership there were three candidates: Margaret Beckett securing 57 per cent, John Prescott 28 per cent and Brian Gould 15 per cent.

Table 5.3 Labour Party leadership election, 1983

	Trade unions, etc.	*Constituency parties*	*MPs*	*Total*
Votes				
Neil Kinnock	4,389,000	571	100	–
Roy Hattersley	1,644,000	12	53	–
Eric Heffer	7,000	41	29	–
Peter Shore	5,000	0	21	–
Total	6,045,000	624	203	–
Per cent				
Neil Kinnock	29.042	27.452	14.778	71.272
Roy Hattersley	10.878	0.577	7.833	19.288
Eric Heffer	0.046	1.971	4.286	6.303
Peter Shore	0.033	0.000	3.103	3.137
Total	40	30	30	100

In 1993 the rules were changed slightly, giving each of the three sections of the electoral college an equal weight and insisting that union members should vote directly on a 'one member, one vote' basis, with each union's vote divided in proportion to its members' preferences, rather than its leadership casting a block vote. The unexpected death of John Smith in May 1994 led to a further contest, easily won by Tony Blair against the opposition of John Prescott and Margaret Beckett. In the deputy leadership contest Prescott defeated Beckett. The result, published only in percentage terms, is shown in Table 5.4. Neither Blair nor Prescott has subsequently been challenged.

Table 5.4 Labour Party leadership and deputy leadership elections, 1994

	Trade unions, etc.	*Constituency parties*	*MPs*	*Total*
Leader:				
Tony Blair	52.3	58.2	60.5	57.0
John Prescott	28.4	24.4	19.6	24.1
Margaret Beckett	19.3	17.4	19.9	18.9
Deputy Leader:				
John Prescott	56.6	59.4	53.7	56.5
Margaret Beckett	43.4	40.6	46.3	43.5

The Parliamentary Labour Party (PLP) is made up of Labour MPs and peers, though the latter are relatively few in number and wield little influence. Each year when Labour is in opposition it now elects, by ballot, a Chief Whip and a Parliamentary Committee (or Shadow Cabinet) of 15 members in the Commons and three in the Lords. Policy and Parliamentary tactics are discussed at weekly meetings of the PLP and are frequently put to the vote, which is binding on the leader and the Parliamentary Committee.

The PLP elects a backbench member as chairman and, when Labour is in government, it comes to resemble more closely the Conservative 1922 Committee, though ministers are entitled to attend and to vote, and frequently do so. A regular interchange of views between a Labour government and its backbench supporters takes place through the 'Liaison Committee'. This consists of the chairman of the Parliamentary Labour Party, two elected vice-chairmen – also backbenchers – and an elected representative of the Labour peers, with the Chief Whip and the Leader of the House of Commons representing the government.

The party bureaucracy is controlled by a National Executive Committee, mostly elected by the mass membership and affiliated bodies. This committee, usually known as the NEC, consists of 33 members, and acts on behalf of the membership in the periods between annual conferences. In addition to the leader and deputy leader of the party, the general secretary, and the leader of the European Parliament Labour Party group, six are elected by a postal ballot of all members of the party to represent the constituency parties, twelve by the members of affiliated trade unions, two by members of the Association of Labour Councillors, one by the socialist and co-operative organisations and one to represent Young Labour. The Parliamentary Party and European Parliamentary Party together elect three members (who will be MPs or MEPs), and the Cabinet nominates three ministers. The party treasurer, elected by the conference, is also a member. The influence of Labour MPs is therefore very much a minor one, though the leadership can hope to be influential in the results in all the sections. In the past, MPs were often elected as the representatives of the constituency parties and in the election of women members (which used to be separate), ensuring a bigger influence, but this has now been banned, and the constituency representatives are high-profile activists outside Parliament. (Women are now assured representation by rules that at least half the members elected in each of the trade union, constituency party and local government sections must be women.)

The NEC, which normally meets monthly, appoints the general secretary who is the chief official of the party and who is responsible to them for the running of the national headquarters at Old Queen Street and of the party machine in the country. The NEC and its various subcommittees are also responsible for making appointments to other senior posts in the party bureaucracy.

At the end of 2003, the Labour Party had just 215,000 individual members, the lowest figure since the 1920s and barely half the 407,000 it claimed at the time of its victory in the 1997 election. However, it still has several million affiliated members. The vast majority of these affiliated members belong to one of the 21 trade unions which are affiliated nationally to the party, but there are also 16 other affiliated bodies, which include the Co-operative Party (see below), the Labour Students and other bodies such as the National Union of Labour and Socialist Clubs, the Fabian Society, the Socialist Educational Association, the Socialist Health Association, the Christian Socialist Movement and the Society of Labour Lawyers.

As recently as 1988, before the rules were changed, the biggest six affiliated unions commanded a majority of votes at the party conference. The largest of the affiliated trade unions at present are UNISON, the public sector workers' union,[5] the GMB (formerly the General, Municipal, Boilermakers and Allied Trades' Union), Amicus, the Transport and General Workers' Union, and the Communications Workers' Union. The most important unions not affiliated to the Labour Party mostly represent white-collar or professional workers, for example the Civil Service unions and the National Union of Teachers; however, one major union not currently affiliated is the RMT transport union, a founding affiliate of the party (as the Amalgamated Society of Railway Servants) but expelled in 2004 for allowing its local branches freedom to affiliate to other parties.

The unions pay an affiliation fee for each member which comes not from the general funds of the union but must, by law, come out of a special political fund established by a vote of all union members and from which any individual union member may contract out if he or she does not wish to support the Labour Party financially. Individual members of the party pay their subscriptions to their own Constituency Labour Party, and these were set in 2004 at £24 per year (£12 for pensioners, students and the unemployed, who collectively make up just under half of the individual membership) of which a proportion is passed on to the national party as an affiliation fee. Members of trade unions who pay the political levy, and members of affiliated Socialist Societies, pay a reduced subscription for individual membership.

The Fabian Society, which has been affiliated to the party from the beginning, is an independent socialist research organisation, whose principal function is the publication of books and pamphlets studying current political, economic and social problems from a democratic socialist viewpoint. Although it is an affiliated body it expresses no collective viewpoint within the party and in practice its relationship to it is very similar to that of the Bow Group to the Conservative Party. Founded in 1884, it restricts its membership to those 'eligible for membership of the Labour Party'. This means, in effect, that non-members of the Labour Party may join, provided they are not members of other political parties.

For most of its life the Labour Party has been in opposition, and this factor was undoubtedly reflected in its constitution which, unlike that of the Conservatives, was more fitted to a party in opposition than in government. Under the successive leaderships of Neil Kinnock, John Smith and Tony Blair, determined efforts were made to make the Labour Party more electable by shedding old dogmas and adjusting to changes in society, culminating in a special party conference in April 1995, when a new clause entitled 'Labour's aims and values' was adopted, replacing the old Clause Four of the constitution, which had called for the 'public ownership of the means of production, distribution and exchange'. Blair and many of his supporters took to describing the party as New Labour, though no attempt was made formally to change the party's name. The Labour Party normally contests every seat at general elections, except in Northern Ireland.

The *Co-operative Party*, founded in 1917, has been formally allied to the Labour Party since 1926, and its local branches are affiliated to constituency Labour parties. It does not put up its own candidates, and the only Co-operative nominees who are put forward for Parliament are those selected by constituency Labour parties as Labour candidates; they are normally designated as Co-operative and Labour candidates, but otherwise are indistinguishable from other Labour candidates – 29 Labour candidates in 2001 were endorsed as also representing the Co-operative movement. The Co-operative Party used to sponsor its candidates financially in the same way as the trade unions (see Chapter 7), but this practice was abolished before the 1997 election.

The Social and Liberal Democratic Party (SLD, usually known by the shorter title of *Liberal Democrats*) was formed in 1988 by the merger of the Liberal Party and the Social Democratic Party (SDP). Of these, the

Liberal Party was larger and far older. It grew out of the old Whig Party, which dated from the debates in 1679 over the attempted exclusion of the Duke of York, later James II, from the succession. The Whigs probably derived their name, which was at first meant contemptuously, from the Whiggamores, a body of Scottish Presbyterian insurgents who had marched on Edinburgh in 1648. The Whigs became identified as the party of those wishing to assert the authority of Parliament over that of the Sovereign, and later as the advocates of Parliamentary reform through extension of the franchise. The Liberal Party is generally held to date from 1859, when the Whigs joined with the Radicals and Peelites (free-traders who had broken away from the Conservatives), though the name had been gaining currency as an alternative title for the Whigs even before that. Unlike 'Tory', the term 'Whig' passed completely out of common usage by the end of the nineteenth century.

Table 5.5   Co-operative Party candidates, 1945–2001

Year	Candidates	Elected
1945	33	23
1950	33	18
1951	37	16
1955	38	18
1959	30	16
1964	27	19
1966	24	18
1970	27	17
1974: Feb	25	16
1974: Oct	22	16
1979	25	17
1983	17	8
1987	20	10
1992	26	14
1997	26	26
2001	29	28

Under the leadership, successively, of Palmerston and Gladstone the Liberal Party dominated the Parliamentary scene during the greater part of the Victorian era. In 1886, however, it suffered a major setback through the defection of the Liberal Unionists over the issue of Irish Home Rule.

In 1906 a Liberal government was elected with an immense majority, and remained in office until 1915, led successively by Campbell-Bannerman and Asquith, but by the 1920s the Liberals had been replaced by the Labour Party as one of the two main parties, a process which was aided by a bitter division between the supporters of the last two Liberals to be Prime Minister, Asquith and Lloyd George. The 1910–15 government was the last Liberal government; subsequently Liberals took part in the Asquith and Lloyd George coalition governments from 1915 to 1922, briefly in the Ramsay MacDonald National government from 1931 to 1932, and in the Churchill coalition government from 1940 to 1945. In 1977–8, under 'the Lib-Lab pact', the Liberal Party supported the Labour government of James Callaghan, which had lost its majority through by-election reverses, in the House of Commons, and there were regular consultations on policy matters. There were no suggestions, however, that the Liberal Party should join the government.

The electoral decline of the Liberal Party continued unabated until the early 1950s when it was reduced to a mere six seats in the House of Commons. After that it staged periodic revivals, but still only held eleven seats after the 1979 election.

The Social Democratic Party (SDP), founded in 1981, had been established as a breakaway by Labour MPs dismayed by Labour conference decisions and constitutional changes, as well as the general leftward trend of the party over the previous few years. The initiative was taken by the former Labour Chancellor of the Exchequer and Deputy Leader, Roy Jenkins, who had just completed four years in Brussels as President of the European Commission, and three younger ex-Cabinet Ministers, David Owen, Shirley Williams and William Rodgers. It was joined altogether by 26 sitting Labour MPs and one Conservative, and its Parliamentary strength was subsequently increased to 29 by the election of Shirley Williams and Roy Jenkins in by-elections.

The formation of the new party had been actively encouraged by the Liberal leader, David Steel, and both parties quickly approved a formal alliance for fighting elections. Apart from policy issues, on which there were few serious differences between the two parties, both had a strong common interest in aiming to change the electoral system to one of proportional representation. They were forced, however, to fight under the existing system, which meant that they would only do themselves harm by putting up candidates against each other.

The appeal of the new party was immediate. It rapidly attracted some 70,000 members, two-thirds of whom had not previously belonged to any political party. The Alliance went on to achieve a string of by-election successes, and easily led the other two parties in the opinion polls. By the spring of 1982, however, the momentum began to slow down, and the Argentine invasion of the Falkland Islands and the subsequent military campaign resulted in a patriotic rallying of support for Margaret Thatcher and the Conservative government. This, and economic recovery, enabled the Tories to sweep back into the lead in the opinion polls, where they remained until the 1983 general election a year later. The Alliance never recovered from the impact of the Falklands War, and despite running a close third to Labour in the 1983 election and polling a quarter of the vote could take only 23 seats, 17 of them Liberal. Although this total was slightly increased by by-election gains, their total vote fell off in the 1987 general election and shortly afterwards the parties announced that they were considering merger, which was approved by ballots of both memberships and took effect early in 1988.

A minority in both parties declared themselves implacably opposed to merger, and subsequently formed independent breakaway parties under the old names. Of the two, the new SDP seemed the more significant, having the allegiance of three MPs including former leader Dr David Owen, but by the summer of 1990 it had become increasingly obvious that they had no future as a national party, and the Parliamentary Party was dissolved, all three MPs continuing to sit as independents but none being re-elected at the following general election. The breakaway Liberal Party (see below) had no sitting MPs but has continued to fight elections, though with no conspicuous success. Meanwhile the newly formed Liberal Democrat Party, after a shaky start when it polled only 6 per cent at the 1999 European elections, doubled its representation in the House of Commons at the 1997 general election and with further gains in 2001 now holds more than 50 seats. (See Appendix 1 for details in the growth of its number of candidates, share of the vote and MPs elected.)

The Liberal Democrats' leader is elected by a postal ballot of all members of the party, of whom there were about 70,000 in 2003. In the first election, shortly after the party's foundation in 1988, Paddy Ashdown won the leadership, gaining 41,401 votes to Alan Beith's 16,202. Elections take place in theory at least every two years, though the Parliamentary Party has the power to call for an election outside the normal two-year cycle by passing a motion of no confidence in the leader. In practice, as with the two largest parties, contested elections have been rare – in fact Paddy Ashdown was never challenged during his eleven years in office. On his retirement in 1999, five MPs stood for the leadership, and members voted using the Alternative Vote system (see Appendix 8). David Rendel, Jackie Ballard and Malcolm Bruce were eliminated in the first three rounds of counting, and in the final count Charles Kennedy defeated Simon Hughes by 28,425 votes to 21,833.

The Liberal Democrats are organised in three separate party structures, one each in England, Scotland and Wales (the party does not organise in Northern Ireland), with their own constitutions, bureaucracies and conferences, co-ordinated by a federal party headquarters in London and represented on the main organs of the national party, the Federal Executive Committee and Federal Policy Committee. For most purposes the supreme body is the twice-yearly federal conference, which consists of representatives of the constituency parties in proportion to the party's strength in each constituency; however, the constitution also provides for decisions by a direct postal ballot of all party members.

The number of candidates put in the field by the Liberal Party in elections in the quarter-century after the end of the Second World War fluctuated wildly, but during the 1970s they began to attempt to contest as many seats as the Conservative and Labour Parties. In 1983 and 1987, in conjunction with the SDP, they contested all seats in Great Britain, as did the Liberal Democrats in 1992 (with the exception of two seats defended by former SDP MPs). In both 1997 and 2001 the Liberal Democrats stood down in a single constituency in favour of an independent candidate,[6] and did not contest the Speaker's seat, but fought every other constituency.

The *Scottish National Party* (SNP) was founded in 1928 with the aim of securing self-government for Scotland. Its first Parliamentary seat, Motherwell, which was won at a wartime by-election in April 1945, was lost three months later at the 1945 general election, and it had to wait until the Hamilton by-election in 1967 for its second success. This, however, heralded the start of an upsurge in strength which led to its capturing one seat in the 1970 general election, seven in February 1974 and eleven in October 1974, when it polled 30.4 per cent of the Scottish vote. This prompted the then Labour government to propose a separate elected assembly for Scotland (and also for Wales), but the proposal was stalled when a referendum in Scotland failed to produce 40 per cent of the electors in favour, as the House of Commons had stipulated, despite winning a narrow majority of those who voted. The SNP has not subsequently been able to repeat its 1974 performance, though it reached 22 per cent of the vote and six seats in 1997. Since the inaugural elections to the Scottish Parliament it has been the second largest party in that legislature.

The SNP has contested all seats in Scotland in recent elections (except Orkney and Shetland in 1987, where it stood aside for the candidate of the separate Orkney and Shetland Movement).

Table 5.6   Scottish National Party and Plaid Cymru candidates, 1945–2001

| Year | Scottish National Party | | | Plaid Cymru | | |
	Candidates	Percentage of vote in Scotland	Elected	Candidates	Percentage of vote in Wales	Elected
1945	8	1.2	0	8	1.2	0
1950	4	0.4	0	7	1.2	0
1951	1	0.3	0	4	0.7	0
1955	2	0.5	0	11	3.1	0
1959	5	0.8	0	20	5.2	0
1964	15	2.4	0	23	4.8	0
1966	23	5.0	0	19	4.3	0
1970	65	11.4	1	36	11.5	0
1974: Feb	70	21.9	7	36	10.7	2
1974: Oct	71	30.4	11	36	10.8	3
1979	71	17.3	2	36	8.1	2
1983	72	11.8	2	38	7.8	2
1987	71	14.0	3	38	7.3	3
1992	72	21.5	3	35	8.9	4
1997	72	22.1	6	40	9.9	4
2001	72	20.1	5	40	14.3	4

Plaid Cymru (the Party of Wales, or more descriptively Welsh Nationalist Party) was established in 1925 and has contested all Welsh constituencies in all elections since 1970, though in 1992 it fielded joint candidates with the Green Party in three constituencies. It won its first Parliamentary contest in a by-election at Carmarthen in July 1966, but lost the seat in 1970. However, since February 1974 it has always been represented in Parliament, winning two to four seats at each general election. Its programme is self-government for Wales, and its greatest strength lies in the Welsh-speaking areas of north and west Wales. It is the second largest party in the Welsh Assembly.

Minor parties[7]

More than 260 smaller political parties are registered with the Electoral Commission in Great Britain, and a further 40 in Northern Ireland, but only a handful are, or were ever, liable to make a national impact.

The *Communist Party* of Great Britain (CPGB), founded in 1920, was once the most prominent of the minor parties with a national following and was the last to win a seat in the Commons. Communist MPs were elected to Parliament in 1922, 1924, 1935 and 1945, but the party has been without Parliamentary representation since 1950. From then it was in continuous decline, polling a smaller percentage vote than any other Communist party in the western world, reduced by 1987 to contesting a mere 19 constituencies, in which its average vote was only 0.8 per cent. In 1991 the CPGB disbanded itself as a political party; dissident members founded a new party under the same name which, however, contested only six seats in 2001.

Table 5.7   Communist Party candidates, 1945–87

Year	Candidates	Elected
1945	21	2
1950	100	0
1951	10	0
1955	17	0
1959	18	0
1964	36	0
1966	57	0
1970	58	0
1974: Feb	44	0
1974: Oct	29	0
1979	38	0
1983	35	0
1987	19	0

Other far-left socialist groups of Trotskyist persuasion have tended to overshadow the Communist Party in recent years, but have done no better at the polls. The most active was the *Workers' Revolutionary Party*, which put up 20 candidates in 1983 who polled an average of 0.4 per cent of the votes each, despite the active participation of the actress Vanessa Redgrave in their campaign. The *Socialist Workers' Party* (SWP) has also put up a sprinkling of candidates at recent general elections with even less success; in 2004 it joined *Respect*, a coalition of socialist parties and individuals led by the left-wing MP George Galloway, which attacked the government over British involvement in the invasion of Iraq, and looks set to contest the next general election under that banner.

The *Scottish Socialist Party*, formed in 1998, has had more concrete success. Its best-known member, Tommy Sheridan, fought both the 1992 and 1997 general elections under different labels as a left-wing opponent of Labour, gaining respectable shares of the vote on each occasion, and in 1999 he was elected to the Scottish Parliament as a regional member for Glasgow. In 2003 the party secured 6.7 per cent of the vote across Scotland, and increased its representation at Holyrood to six seats. It was less successful in the 2001 general election, averaging 3.3 per cent and saving ten deposits.

The *Socialist Labour Party* was founded by the miners' leader Arthur Scargill, disgusted at the changes in the Labour Party introduced by Tony Blair. He was immediately cold-shouldered by many of those to whom he appealed, but went ahead and nominated a candidate for the Hemsworth by-election in February 1996, who barely saved her deposit. The party was formally established in May 1996, and had 64 candidates in the 1997 election, three of whom saved their deposits including Scargill himself; but in 2001 it averaged only 1.4 per cent of the vote in the seats it fought, and all but one of its 114 deposits were lost. The *Socialist Alliance* also fought 98 seats, averaging 1.8 per cent but saving three deposits.

On the extreme right, various racialist parties have contested recent general elections, the best known of which was the *National Front* (NF), founded in 1966. Its candidates, who mostly contested working-class seats in areas with many Commonwealth immigrants, polled an average vote of over 3 per cent in its first three general election campaigns, which encouraged it to fight on a much broader front in 1979, contesting nearly half the British seats. Its vote declined substantially, and went down again in 1983, despite concentrating on its strongest areas; in 1987, blaming the increased deposit, it put up no candidates. It returned to the fray in 1992, but has made no impact.

Another far-right party, the *British National Party* (BNP), which split off from the National Front in 1983, has subsequently polled slightly better than its parent. The BNP created a short-lived sensation by winning a council by-election in the London Borough of Tower Hamlets in September 1993 in a low poll, but lost the seat in the local elections the following May. More recently it has exploited public disillusionment with the established parties to win a number of seats in local government. Its impact at national level, however, has been far smaller, winning on average only 3.9 per cent for its 33 candidates at the 2001 general election, and securing 4.9 per cent of the vote in the 2004 European elections, under a proportional representation system that is generally helpful to small parties.

The strongest established minor party in Britain is now probably the *Green Party*, which was founded as the Ecology Party in 1975 and changed to its present name in 1985. After securing little success in their first three general elections, the Greens were spectacularly successful in the Euro-elections in June 1989 when they won 14.9 per cent of the votes, more than twice as many as the Liberal Democrats, without however winning a single seat. It seems likely that at this election they benefited from a large anti-government protest vote which might otherwise have gone to the Liberal Democrats, who were in a state of turmoil following the amalgamation of the Liberal and Social Democratic Parties, which was something of a public relations disaster.

Table 5.8   Far-right candidates since 1970

Year	Candidates	National Front Average share (%)	National Front Highest share (%)	Candidates	British National Party Average share (%)	British National Party Highest share (%)
1970	10	3.6	5.6	–	–	–
1974: Feb	54	3.3	7.8	–	–	–
1974: Oct	90	3.1	9.5	–	–	–
1979	303	1.3	7.6	–	–	–
1983	60	1.1	2.4	54	0.5	1.2
1987	0	–	–	2	0.6	0.8
1992	14	0.8	1.2	13	1.2	3.6
1997	6	1.0	1.2	55	1.3	7.5
2001	5	1.5	2.2	33	2.1	7.8

The Green Party returned to earth at the 1992 general election, when having nominated 253 candidates it saw them average only 1.3 per cent, slightly lower than in 1987. Following the 1992 election, there were severe splits in the party leading to the departure of many of its best-known members. In the 1997 election it was able only to field 96 candidates, all of whom lost their deposits; in 2001 ten of its candidates saved their deposits and its total vote topped 165,000 (averaging a 2.8 per cent share, but 9.3 per cent being the highest).

Nevertheless, despite never having come close to winning a Parliamentary seat, the Greens have had limited success at local level, with a number of county and district councillors being elected. The introduction of proportional representation systems for some elections in 1999 has revolutionised prospects for the Greens. In May 1999 they secured a seat in the Scottish Parliament and the following month elected their first two Members of the European Parliament (MEPs) with a national share of 6.3 per cent of the vote; in 2000, they took 11.1 per cent of the vote and three seats on the London Assembly. In 2003 they increased their representation in the Scottish Parliament from one to seven members, and in 2004 held their two seats in the European Parliament, though losing one of their three in the London Assembly.

In 1992 the *Liberal Party*, made up of the minority who had resisted the amalgamation with the SDP and who stayed out of the Liberal Democrats, put up 73 candidates. Their aim was partly to spoil the chances of well-placed Liberal Democrats, an objective which yielded no tangible result; their presence was reduced to 55 candidates in 1997 and only 9 in 2001, when they saved one deposit (with a second-placed 14.9 per cent in Liverpool West Derby).

Table 5.9 **Ecology Party and Green Party candidates since 1979**

Year	Candidates	Average share (%)	Highest share (%)
1979	53	1.5	2.8
1983	108	1.0	2.9
1987	133	1.4	3.6
1992	253	1.3	3.8
1997	96	1.4	4.3
2001	145	2.8	9.3

The *Official Monster Raving Loony Party* was created by the pop singer Screaming Lord Sutch, who fought numerous by-elections under this and similar labels over a 30-year period, yielding himself much publicity but few votes. His party contested 30 seats in 1992 (in three of which he himself stood as the candidate) and 24 in 1997 (though Sutch personally was unable to compete). Sutch died in 1999, a colourful presence in elections who will be missed by many, but his party continues, putting up 15 candidates in 2001; on average, they polled 1.0 per cent.

The most successful minor party in the 1997 election was the *Referendum Party*, launched in 1995 by Sir James Goldsmith, campaigning for a vote on Britain's continued membership of the European Union. The party briefly had an MP when the Conservative member for Reigate, Sir George Gardiner, defected after being deselected as Conservative candidate. Fighting unquestionably the most lavishly financed minor party campaign in British electoral history, it was reported to have spent £7.7 million on advertising, but its candidates averaged 3.0 per cent of the votes in the constituencies where they stood, and following Goldsmith's death shortly after the election the party was wound up.

Its place as the principal anti-EU grouping has been taken by the *UK Independence Party* (UKIP), first formed to fight the 1994 Euro-elections. It has had no success in Parliamentary elections, losing its deposit in 192 of the 193 constituencies it contested in the 1997 general election, and in 422 of the 428 it fought in 2001, when it averaged 2.1 per cent of the votes. It has been a different story in European Parliament elections, however. Although UKIP's 24 candidates averaged only 3.3 per cent of the vote in 1994, the introduction of proportional representation in

1999 enabled its sympathisers to vote for it with a reasonable prospect that their vote would not be wasted. Its vote rose to 7.0 per cent in 1999, giving it three MEPs, then in 2004 to 16.1 per cent and twelve MEPs, pushing the Liberal Democrats back into fourth place.

The *Pro-Life Alliance*, an anti-abortion pressure group, put up 56 candidates in 1997 (enough to qualify for a party election broadcast, which caused considerable controversy), and 37 in 2001. Its candidates averaged only 0.7 per cent of the vote.

All the minor parties are severely handicapped by the 'first past the post' system, and there is little prospect of any of them gaining Parliamentary representation in the foreseeable future, unless electoral reform is introduced. Nevertheless, their presence is by no means an irrelevance, since the votes they capture from the bigger parties can easily swing the result in a close contest.

Northern Ireland parties

The party system in Northern Ireland is radically different from that in Great Britain, the major political divide being religious. The Protestant majority mostly divides its support between two parties, both calling themselves Unionist.

The *Ulster Unionist Party* (UUP, but known for a period as the Official Unionist Party or OUP), which until 1972 was affiliated to the Conservative Party, is the largest; its leader, David Trimble, is regarded as the spokesman of moderate Unionist opinion in the Province. The *Democratic Unionist Party* (DUP), led by Ian Paisley, split off in 1971, and has adopted a more stridently sectarian stance. In the 1997 general election the UUP won ten seats and the DUP two, with another seat being won by an independent Unionist, Robert McCartney, running under the label of United Kingdom Unionist;[8] but in 2001 the eleven Unionist seats were split almost equally, five to the DUP and six to the UUP.

On the Roman Catholic side, the majority of votes have usually gone to the moderately nationalist *Social Democratic and Labour Party* (SDLP), which won a single seat in 1983, but gained a further one in a by-election in 1986, a third at the 1987 general election and a fourth in 1992. In 1997 it slipped back to three seats. Its then-leader, John Hume, won a share of the 1998 Nobel Peace Prize together with David Trimble, for their contribution to the peace process. The party has also won one of Northern Ireland's three seats in the European Parliament at each election before 2004.

Sinn Féin, which is the political wing of the Provisional IRA, also won a seat in 1983 and 1987, two seats in 1997 and four in 2001; it has refused to take up its seats as a protest against British rule. In the last couple of years its support has moved ahead of the SDLP's, and in 2004 it won a seat in the European Parliament for the first time.

The non-sectarian *Alliance Party of Northern Ireland*, founded in 1970, tries to straddle the gap between Protestants and Catholics. It puts up candidates in most Northern Irish seats, and won 8.0 per cent of the votes in the province in 1997, without coming near to winning any seats.

In the election for the Northern Ireland Assembly in June 1998, a large number of parties took part, including Sinn Féin and two groups representing Protestant paramilitaries. Altogether eleven parties gained seats in an election under the Single Transferable Vote system of proportional representation. The Assembly's power-sharing Executive took office in 1999, with members of the four largest parties (UUP, DUP, SDLP and Sinn Féin) all holding portfolios; however, tensions between the parties led to a breakdown in political dialogue, and devolved government was suspended on 14 October 2002. New elections were held in November 2003, at which both the DUP and Sinn Féin made substantial gains, but the Assembly remains in abeyance. (See Appendix 2 for the Assembly election results in detail.)

Independents

A wide variety of *Independent* candidates, often wearing bizarre labels, offer themselves at each general election and at almost every by-election. Few independent candidates poll more than a few hundred votes, except when one of the major parties does not contest the constituency (a rare event). Independents play a much more significant role in local council elections, however, frequently securing seats and in some cases even controlling the council. In Northern Ireland occasional independents have been elected, but this has normally been with the tacit or open support of one of the main Northern Irish parties. The only independents elected to Parliament in Britain between 1945 and 1997 were former MPs who had fallen out with their political parties and stood again as independents in their own constituencies. There have been a handful of such candidacies at most recent elections. It is most unusual for the rebel to win in Parliamentary elections (though three Labour MPs did so in the 1970s[9]). In 1992, five Labour MPs and one Conservative stood against their former parties, and in 1997 the Conservative MP Sir George Gardiner, after being deselected at Reigate, joined the Referendum Party and stood as their candidate for the seat; all saved their deposits but none came close to winning. Away from Westminster, recent rebels have found more success: Ken Livingstone (as Mayor of London in 2000), Dennis Canavan (for the Scottish Parliament in 1999 and 2003) and John Marek (for the Welsh Assembly in 2003) were all established Labour figures who were elected as independents defeating official Labour candidates after being denied the party's nomination.

The last two general elections, however, have each produced an independent MP in rather different circumstances. In 1997, the sitting MP at Tatton in Cheshire, normally an ultra-safe Conservative seat, had been re-nominated by his party despite accusations of 'sleaze' against him which led many Conservative supporters to feel they could not vote for him. The Labour and Liberal Democrat candidates both stood down to give a free run to the respected BBC reporter Martin Bell, who had no affiliations to any party and who they hoped could unite their own supporters and dissident Tories. Bell duly won the seat but was committed to serving only a single term, and was defeated when he tried to win a different constituency in 2001.

Bell's 1997 achievement was matched in 2001, however, at Wyre Forest in Worcestershire. A retired doctor, Richard Taylor, stood against the Labour MP, a junior minister who had failed to prevent the closure of the hospital in Kidderminster, the constituency's main town. The Liberal Democrats stood down, although the Conservatives (who had regarded the constituency as a safe seat for themselves as recently as 1992) refused to do so, and Dr Taylor took 58 per cent of the vote. His supporters, organised as the *Kidderminster Hospital and Health Concern Party*, have subsequently won control of Wyre Forest council in local government elections – even though it is a local authority with no health service powers or responsibilities.

The only other members to be elected since 1945 without being official party nominees were the Speakers of the House of Commons (who on a number of occasions have been elected without opposition from the main political parties in the seats which they had formerly represented as Conservative or Labour MPs).

6
Political Parties: Local

The national organisations of the political parties monopolise publicity in the press and on radio and television, but it is the local branches with which the voter is likely to come into contact. The main parties have branches in each of the 641 constituencies in Great Britain. The Conservative Party also established branches in Northern Ireland in the early 1990s; Labour and the Liberal Democrats now also accept members from Northern Ireland, but do not contest elections there.

A constituency party (or association as it is called by Conservatives) is not normally the nearest the parties get to the grass roots. Local branches are organised at ward level in towns and cities, and in villages and small towns in country areas. Here, however, the main parties' coverage is less complete. In hopeless constituencies in industrial towns, there are some constituencies where the Conservative ward organisation is rudimentary or non-existent. In the counties, similarly, there are many villages and small towns without any Labour organisation. Liberal Democrat organisation below constituency level is even more patchy.

It is the ward or local party, at least in the Conservative and Labour Parties, which is the basic level of party organisation. The ward party is the actual unit to which party members belong: it is responsible for recruiting new members and collecting subscriptions and for the great majority of party members it is the only organ of the party with which they have any contact. The typical ward or village party meets every month, usually in the house of one of its members, sometimes in a hired school room or village hall, occasionally on party premises. The number of members varies enormously, both according to the size of the electorate in the area covered (which will range from a tiny village to a large ward in a city with anything up to 20,000 electors) and the strength of the party in that area. In practice the membership is unlikely to be less than half a dozen nor more than 1500. The great majority of members do no more than pay their subscriptions to the party. The attendance at most ward or local party meetings is likely to range between 6 and 40, averaging between 5 and 20 per cent of the members in most towns, though in country areas the percentage attendance may well be higher.

The minimum subscription to each of the parties is small – very small when compared to the subscriptions paid to political parties in most other countries. The Labour Party's standard rate subscription is £24 (£12 reduced rate for groups such as the unemployed or retired, and also for levy-paying members of affiliated trade unions). The Conservative Party minimum subscription is £15 (though only £3 for members aged under 23). The Liberal Democrats have no formal subscription, but solicit donations and state that any donation of £5 or more entitles an eligible donor to party membership.

Members of all parties are encouraged to pay their subscriptions annually by post, direct debit or credit card, but they are otherwise collected by an annual visit to the member's home. In most areas the Labour Party made arrangements, in the past, for the monthly or even weekly collection of smaller amounts. With the fall in the value of money, however, such arrangements are now an exception. Most Labour members now subscribe quarterly or half-yearly, while an increasing proportion make a single annual payment. There is a great deal of inefficiency in the machinery for collecting subscriptions and it is apparent that each party loses a substantial amount each year because of this. Many branches with a potentially larger membership refrain from attempting to recruit new members because of a lack of volunteers to act as collectors.

The minority of members who attend the monthly meeting of the party often find only a small part of its agenda is devoted to political matters. Many ward meetings have a speaker to address them on a subject of national importance, and there may be a resolution to discuss on the social services or a foreign policy issue. It is equally likely, however, that the agenda will consist almost exclusively of administrative matters, particularly those concerned with fundraising. It is not unusual for a local party to spend more time discussing who is to look after the sweet stall at the party's jumble sale than it devotes to considering possible resolutions for the annual conference of the party. It follows from this that local party branches are as much social as political affairs and the sense of comradeship at this, the lowest level of party politics, is strong.

In areas in which parties are weak, local and ward parties often have an ephemeral existence depending for their existence primarily on the enthusiasm of one or two members who provide the impetus for the others. A loss of interest on the part of one or two individuals, or their leaving the neighbourhood, may cause the branch to collapse altogether and go out of existence. Then, after an interval of perhaps several years, an enthusiastic newcomer will start things up again and, with the aid of old and unreliable records, will call on long-dormant members and try to rekindle their interest. Even in areas in which a party is strong, its local branches will not necessarily be flourishing. The absence of challenge from the other side may breed apathy and the party organisation, however strong on paper, may be sickly and lethargic. It is in marginal constituencies or council areas, where there is a constant electoral challenge, that the local parties on both sides are most likely to be large and active organisations.

There is a wide variation in the nature and circumstances of local branches. Differences within each of the three main parties are often greater than those between them, and exceptions to most of what follows can be found in all parties. At this, the lowest level of organisation, the procedures and functions of branches of all political parties are very similar, so much so that there is no need here to distinguish between them.

Depending on its strength and its circumstances, a local branch will have a number of officials. The minimum is normally a chairman, honorary secretary and honorary treasurer, though in very small branches even these offices might be doubled up. There are normally also one or more vice-chairmen and a number of other functional offices, of which canvassing officer, social secretary, membership officer, literature secretary, and raffle officer or tote organiser are most common. There may also be an assistant secretary and, in the case of the larger and more active branches, an executive committee whose membership would include most or all of the officers listed above.

The most active members of the branch will also be delegates to the managing body of the constituency party, usually known as the Executive Council in the Conservative Party and the General Committee (GC) in the Labour Party. (In the Liberal Democrats all party members are entitled to attend the area party concerned.) It is this body which contains the hard core of militants, usually of between 20 and 100 attending members (though the nominal membership may be higher), who keep the wheels of the party organisation turning throughout the country. At this level there is a notable difference between the parties. The managing body of a Conservative or Liberal Democrat constituency association will contain, in addition to representatives of ward and local branches, representatives from women's organisations and of Conservative Future and the Young Liberal Democrats respectively. A Labour GC similarly contains representatives from wards, Young Labour and women's sections but will also include delegates from affiliated organisations – trade unions, co-operative organisations and, perhaps, a local Fabian Society. For every individual member of the Labour Party there are many affiliated members, and the nominal membership of a great many GCs is made up predominantly of the delegates from affiliated bodies. Many of these are inactive, and it is very rare for there to be a majority of delegates of affiliated organisations among those actually attending. On special occasions, however, it sometimes happens that a meeting of a GC is crowded out by an influx of unfamiliar delegates who may never appear again.

The governing bodies of constituency parties are important and influential organisations. They are responsible for fighting elections, both Parliamentary and local government, and for all practical purposes are the voice of the national party within their own areas. Most of them meet monthly and, as in the case of local branches, much of their time is devoted to discussing financial and administrative matters. Constituency Labour parties, particularly those which are strongly left-wing, frequently pass resolutions of a political nature, which are sent to Old Queen Street for consideration by the National Executive Committee. Protests at the actions or omissions of the party leadership or of Old Queen Street officials are also frequently registered, with little apparent effect. Conservative associations make their views known to their respective head offices with far less frequency. Liberal Democrat local parties behave more like those of the Labour Party.

Constituency parties elect delegates or representatives to the annual party conference, who may or may not be instructed on how to cast their votes on the most controversial issues to be debated at the conference. It is usual for each constituency party to send one resolution to the annual conference, though here again the right is more often asserted by Labour and Liberal Democrat parties than by Conservative associations. The most important *political* act of constituency parties is undoubtedly, however, the selection of Parliamentary candidates. This is discussed in detail in Chapter 7.

The ward and local parties are, in most respects, definitely subordinate to the constituency parties. Each constituency party has a full panoply of officers – chairman, vice-chairman, honorary treasurer, secretary, assistant secretary, and numerous other people designated to do specific tasks. In the Conservative and Labour Parties, subcommittees of the constituency party's governing body, known respectively as the Finance and General Purposes Committee (Conservative) and the Executive Committee (Labour) are responsible for the day-to-day running of the constituency party. Conservative constituency organisations normally have several other standing subcommittees and make provision for both Conservative Future and women members to be represented on all organs of the party.

The principal function of constituency parties is to maintain an electoral organisation in a constant state of readiness. Constituency parties able to maintain a full-time agent find this a much more manageable task, but there are far fewer of these than there used to be. The Conservatives are usually much better placed in this respect. At the time of the 1997 general election they employed 287 full-time agents (including all 100 of their targeted key seats), although many of these were employed by Central Office rather than the constituencies. At the same time the Labour Party had just 20 full-time constituency agents and around another 40 operating from regional headquarters.[1] In 1966 there had been 499 Tory agents, 202 Labour and about 60 Liberal.

The decline in the number of agents in recent years has been caused principally by the difficulties of the constituency parties in meeting their salaries. The headquarters of the Conservative and Labour Parties have a limited amount of money at their disposal to help constituency parties to employ agents. Their money is channelled into the marginal constituencies: other constituency parties wishing to employ an agent are expected to pay their own way. Full-time agents normally act as secretaries to the constituency parties which employ them.

The activities of constituency parties between elections are varied. Among the most important is to keep the name and activities of its Member of Parliament or prospective Parliamentary candidate (PPC) continually in the public eye. (Candidates are invariably known as *prospective* candidates[2] in the period until the general election campaign begins. Otherwise, money spent on the candidate's activities between elections might be legally chargeable to his or her election expenses, which are restricted by law. See Chapter 14 below.) The traditional method of doing this is the public meeting, addressed by the MP or prospective candidate and two or three other speakers. With the spread of television and other mass media, interest in public meetings has declined in the post-war period. Few constituency parties in borough constituencies now organise more than four public meetings a year, and most these days do far less. Such meetings can still sometimes draw a respectable audience, especially those where the party leaders or other nationally known figures are speaking. It may be that, more so than in the past, those who attend are only the party faithful; but even a friendly reception from a partisan audience should justify some coverage in the local media.

Most Members of Parliament and some prospective candidates hold regular 'surgeries' to which their constituents may come with their personal problems. An extremely wide range of problems are referred to MPs for their help and advice. Often it is a question of referring the constituent to the proper authority – the Department for Work and Pensions, the housing department of the local council or the public health authority, for example. Sometimes, however, a member can be of direct assistance by taking up a case personally with a minister or agency, or asking a question in Parliament. This 'welfare work' of MPs is one of their most important activities and it consumes an increasing proportion of their time and energies. In so far as MPs have a personal vote, it is more likely to be built up laboriously over the years through diligent application to the personal problems of constituents than by any more flamboyant action or gesture. Of course, as well as the personal contact with their constituents at 'surgeries', MPs expect a huge postbag of local problems to deal with; and an increasing number are also setting up websites and e-mail addresses on the Internet, so that their constituents can also contact them in this way. However the contact is made, MPs who are attentive to their constituents can hope to gain a reputation as 'good constituency members' which will stand them in good stead at future elections. Table 6.1 shows the topics which MPs said were most frequently raised with them, in a survey just before the 1997 election. It will be seen that there is some difference between the issues raised with members of different parties; for the most part this simply reflects the different nature of the constituencies that they are likely to represent.

Table 6.1   Subjects most often raised with MPs, 1996–7

Q. *Which of the subjects on this list do you receive most letters about in your postbag, or receive most approaches about from individuals in clinics or other ways?*	All MPs %	Conservatives %	Opposition %
Child Support/Child Support Agency	78	87	69
Housing	72	60	85
Law and order	65	79	50
Social security	65	52	80
Health service	59	61	57
Education/schools	52	63	46
Animal welfare/hunting	48	43	54
Pensions	38	31	45
Dangerous weapons/guns and knives	35	46	25

Source: MORI survey of 102 Members of Parliament, November 1996–January 1997.
Adapted from a table in *British Public Opinion* newsletter, January–February 1997.

The agent or secretary will always be on the look out for other ways of pushing the MP or prospective candidate into the limelight. If a local organisation – a church, school or youth club, a dramatic society, a rotary club or any one of a hundred others – wants somebody to open a bazaar, distribute prizes or make a speech (quite often on a non-political subject) he or she has just the person for the job. The value of such assignments for prospective candidates lies at least as much in the report which will follow in the local newspaper as in the activity itself.

Most constituency parties organise membership drives from time to time in which their members call from house to house, usually in what are regarded as favourable areas, trying to persuade people to join. Little time is normally wasted on attempting to convert 'hostile' elements, but anyone who shows interest will be carefully fostered. In such cases a further visit by the Parliamentary candidate or party secretary may well be arranged.

A different sort of canvassing is designed to provide a reliable record of voting intentions of the electorate. The purpose is to obtain a 'marked register', so that the party has a good idea of where its support lies when the election is due. Copies of the election register are cut up and stuck on hard boards – and party members are asked to mark 'F', 'A' or 'D' against the name of each voter after calling at their houses. These abbreviations stand for 'for', 'against' and 'doubtful'. Nowadays, many local party organisations have computerised records, and canvassers are issued with computer printouts. The proceedings at each house are crisp and seldom prolonged. Most canvassers adopt an apologetic stance and mumble something along these lines: 'Good evening, Mrs Jones? I'm calling on behalf of the —— Party. We wonder whether we can rely on your support at the next election.' The response to this enquiry is varied, but rudeness is extremely rare. 'Yes, you can depend on us' or 'We always vote on the day' are likely rejoinders from party supporters. 'I'm afraid we're on the other side' or 'You've called at the wrong house, old chap' are the limits to the hostility which the average canvasser can expect to encounter. There are voters who will say: 'If I had a hundred votes I wouldn't give one to your lot' or even 'If you come this way again I'll set my dog on you', but they are few and far between.

A subsidiary object of house-to-house canvassing is to discover invalids and other people who might use postal votes, so that they may be helped to claim them. Relatively few voters take this initiative themselves, without prompting from their party. As postal votes are now available to any voter that wants them, rather than being restricted to the minority who could not reasonably be expected to vote in person, this is now more important than ever before. The party which organises the largest number of postal votes in a marginal constituency may find that this has made all the difference between victory and defeat. There is no doubt that the Conservatives used to be more alive than the other parties to the need to build up a large postal vote and that they used to enjoy much greater success in this sphere. Labour, and in some areas the Liberal Democrats, may well have closed the gap in recent elections.

Elections to local authorities absorb a great deal of the time and money of many constituency parties. In some districts elections are held three years in every four, on the first Thursday in May, a third of the council being elected each time. In counties with a county council this is also elected once every four years, in the year in which there are no district elections. Other areas, including London, elect the borough or district council as a whole once every four years. Some towns and cities now also have a directly elected mayor, again serving a four-year term. So some local parties are fighting elections annually, while others do so only once every four years. Local elections help parties to keep their electoral organisation in a state of readiness for the general election and the canvassing results help the party to maintain an up-to-date 'marked register'.

It can happen, however, that excessive preoccupation with local government matters can hinder a constituency party's ability to fight an effective general election campaign. The more able members may have become councillors and may devote so much time to council affairs that they have little to spare for the party. If the party controls the district council, unpopular decisions by the council, such as raising council house rents or approving a controversial planning application, may adversely affect the party's electoral appeal at a Parliamentary election.

The ownership or tenancy of premises can have a similarly two-edged effect on a constituency party. Parties employing a full-time agent obviously need premises to provide an office in which to work and to store the party records. It is a great advantage, too, to have a hall in which to hold meetings and to use as committee rooms at election time, and a permanent headquarters acts as a focus for a wide variety of party activities. There is danger, however, that if the premises are used extensively for social activities the political work of the party will suffer. In such circumstances the premises may be a heavy drain on the party's funds without producing any equivalent benefit to its electoral prospects.

Money raising is a perennial problem for constituency parties. Few of them derive sufficient income from subscriptions and donations to meet even their most essential commitments. There is no regular analysis of information about the funds of constituency parties, but the Committee on Standards in Public Life commissioned research from the academic Justin Fisher for its 1998 report on the funding of political parties.[3] He found that in 1997, the average Conservative constituency association had an income of £33,000 (down from £43,000 in 1992), whereas for constituency Labour parties the average was £8900 and for the Liberal Democrats £6200, and substantially less in non-election years. For Labour, the principal sources of local funds were individual donations (£2000 a year), donations from trade unions (£2000 in election years, though little at other times) and membership subscriptions (£1500); fundraising events might contribute another £1200. The Conservatives were heavily reliant on individual donations (£16,500), but company donations (£2500), though much smaller than they once were, still provided more than the unions could do for Labour; fundraising contributed on average £7200, and other income (of which rent on party-owned properties was often a significant component) the remainder. The nature of fundraising events in all parties is varied, but appeals to the gambling instinct – the raffle or whist drive, the bingo session, the football pool or tote scheme – are still popular, although in recent years this income has, of course, been hit by the introduction of the National Lottery.

Each of the parties has youth organisations, which are made up of branches formed on a constituency basis or to cover a smaller area within a constituency. The branches are represented on the governing bodies of constituency parties.

The Young Conservatives, though there are no published membership figures, were undoubtedly for many years much the largest and most powerful of the three organisations. Many of their branches have been primarily social organisations, but Young Conservatives, particularly in suburban areas, provided much of the manpower for canvassing teams and other electoral activities. There is no doubt that they represented a valuable asset to the Conservative Party. In more recent years, though, their size has shrunk. In 1998 the Young Conservatives were combined with the Conservative student organisations into a single new body, Conservative Future, which claimed 10,000 members across Britain in 2004.

The Labour Party Young Socialists had around 17,000 members in 550 branches at the time of the 1987 general election. More political than their Conservative counterparts, they often embarrassed the Labour Party by embracing policies well to the left of the leadership. Many branches played an important part in the party organisation, particularly at election times, but overall the Young Socialists undoubtedly proved less of an asset to their party than the Young Conservatives did to theirs. Since 1992 the organisation has been re-formed as Young Labour, and by 1995 had 23,000 members, substantially more than the Young Conservatives or the Young Liberal Democrats. A further reorganisation saw another name change, to Labour Youth, but the name Young Labour has now been re-adopted.

All three parties have flourishing student organisations with membership in universities and colleges throughout the country. In recent years Labour Students has been substantially the largest of the three bodies, and as many of the university towns contain marginal seats their members are an important factor in the party's general election efforts. In 1992, when the general election was held in the university vacation, the sharp rise in the postal vote in most constituencies with a student presence was testimony to the vigorous organising and campaigning role of all the student branches. Many of the active student members will also be members of their ward parties.

7
Candidates[1]

Who is eligible?

No special qualifications whatever are legally required of Parliamentary candidates; the only positive requirements are virtually those which also apply to voters – that is, to be a British or Commonwealth subject or a citizen of the Republic of Ireland, and to have reached the age of 21. (This has remained the minimum age for candidates, even though the voting age was reduced to 18 in 1969. An Electoral Commission report in 2004[2] recommended that the age for candidature be reduced to 18, but the government had made no indication of its intentions at the time of writing.) Much the same rules apply for candidacy in European, local and devolved assembly elections. It is not even necessary to be on the election register. There are, however, a number of disqualifications which together exclude a considerable number of people from being elected. People in the following categories are disqualified:

Aliens cannot sit in Parliament, although those who have acquired British citizenship through naturalisation are eligible, as are citizens of Commonwealth countries and the Republic of Ireland. Nationals of other EU countries are eligible to stand for local authorities and for the Scottish Parliament and Welsh and Northern Irish Assemblies, and also for the European Parliament provided they are not simultaneously a candidate in some other member state of the EU.

Peers. Members of the House of Lords have always been disqualified from sitting in the House of Commons. In the past, the prohibition included Scottish peers (not all of whom sat in the Lords but who used to elect some of their number to sit as Representative Peers), though Irish peers were not excluded unless they also had British peerages. However, with the reform of the House of Lords and exclusion of most – eventually, all – of the hereditary peers, only those who are actually members of the upper house are excluded from candidacy for the Commons.[3] Peers have always been able to stand for the European Parliament and local authorities, and are eligible for the Scottish Parliament, Welsh Assembly and Northern Irish Assembly.

Certified lunatics.

Bankrupts. Since the Enterprise Act 2002, bankruptcy is no longer a disqualification in itself, but nobody may be elected or remain an MP, MEP, councillor or member of any of the devolved assemblies while the subject of a bankruptcy restrictions order (BRO), or, in the case of local authorities in England and Wales, an interim BRO.

Another recently abolished prohibition was that on the *clergy*. Ordained clergy of the Church of England or the Church of Ireland, ministers of the Church of Scotland, Roman Catholic priests and former Roman Catholic priests were all ineligible to sit in Parliament. Clergy of the Church of Wales and non-conformist ministers, however, were not disqualified. These archaic restrictions were lifted by the House of Commons (Removal of Clergy Disqualification) Act of 2001.[4]

Convicted criminals. Convicted persons serving a sentence of more than one year, or an indefinite sentence, while they are either detained or unlawfully at large; the election or nomination of such a person is void. (This provision was enacted in 1981, following the Bobby Sands case. Sands, an IRA hunger striker in the Maze Prison in Belfast, was elected MP for Fermanagh and South Tyrone in April 1981. He died shortly afterwards as a consequence of his fast.)

Corrupt and illegal practices at elections. Persons convicted of such offences may be disqualified for varying periods (see Appendix 5). In elections to the European Parliament, citizens of foreign EU states who have been disqualified for similar offences by the courts in their own country are also disqualified from standing in the United Kingdom.

Residency. Unlike many countries such as the USA, there is no residency requirement for candidates in Parliamentary elections: a candidate need not live in the constituency which he or she hopes to represent. However, such a requirement does exist in local elections, including those for the devolved assemblies: a candidate must be a local government elector for the area of the local authority concerned, or have resided there or worked there for twelve months preceding the date of the election. Candidates for Mayor of London or the London Assembly must either live or work in London.

Disqualification by office or service. Much the largest number of people disqualified from membership of the House of Commons, however, are those who hold offices listed in the House of Commons Disqualification

Act of 1975. Most of these are what are known as *offices of profit under the Crown.* This includes sheriffs, judges, policemen, civil servants and a very wide and varied list of office-holders, many of whom receive only nominal remuneration for their services.

Before 1957, when a consolidated list was embodied in legislation for the first time, there was an immense degree of confusion as to what offices were actually disqualified. Members elected to the House of Commons who performed public service, such as membership of Rent Tribunals, found to their dismay and astonishment that they were disqualified from membership of the House and liable to pay extremely high monetary penalties (£500 per day) for sitting and voting in the House. The confusion was due to the fact that the different disqualifying offices had resulted from over a hundred Acts of Parliament enacted over a period of 250 years. The position was clarified, however, by the 1957 House of Commons Disqualification Act which contained two schedules, one listing specific offices which do disqualify, the other listing those which do not; this has now been supplanted by the 1975 Act. It is highly advisable for all would-be candidates to study these lists before accepting nomination, as there is now little excuse for candidates who transgress through ignorance. It should perhaps be added that, though civil servants are disqualified from membership of the House of Commons, schoolteachers, employees of nationalised industries and local government employees are all eligible.

For local government there are a number of additional disqualifications, the most important being that employees of a local authority may not seek election to it. This excludes quite a number of people, for example teachers, who would otherwise be eligible. However, a teacher employed by a county council is not excluded from seeking election to a district council, even if his or her school is situated in its area. Former councillors who have been adjudged guilty of incurring or authorising unlawful expenditure may also have been disqualified from being a candidate in the future.

Also ineligible to sit in the Commons are *members of Legislatures outside the Commonwealth and Ireland.* These would normally be excluded as aliens, but the effect of this provision is to disqualify the exceptional case of people with dual nationality. Members of the Seanad and Dáil of the Republic of Ireland were formerly also disqualified, but have been eligible to sit since 2000.[5]

Armed forces. The final category of people disqualified from membership of Parliament are members of the regular armed forces. However, it used to be normal for a serviceman seeking nomination to be discharged. Then in 1962 an ingenious soldier, Malcolm Thompson, who had been refused a discharge in order to enrol as a university student, offered himself as an independent candidate at a by-election at Middlesbrough West and consequently secured his demobilisation. Other servicemen followed his example, discovering that they did not even have to be nominated (and thus have to pay a deposit of £150) to secure their discharge; it was sufficient just to apply for nomination papers. No less than 174 requests were received for nomination papers at the by-election at Colne Valley, and 493 at Rotherham. However, the introduction the following year of an advisory committee appointed by the Home Secretary to vet such applications, recommending that no discharge should be granted unless they were satisfied that the potential candidate's parliamentary ambitions were genuine, stemmed the flow, and the vogue for servicemen applying for nomination papers faded as quickly as it had arisen.

Although all the above categories disqualify from membership of the House of Commons, there is no means of preventing a disqualified person presenting himself or herself as a candidate, which indeed is not strictly speaking illegal. (An exception to this is the case of convicted criminals, who are specifically barred from candidacy as well as from membership of the Commons.) The responsibility of a Returning Officer in vetting a nomination is confined to ascertaining that the nomination form has been properly filled in and signed by the requisite number of electors. Returning Officers are not required to satisfy themselves that candidates are not disqualified persons.

In practice no political party, at least outside Northern Ireland where Sinn Féin has frequently done so, would normally agree to support a candidate known to be disqualified. Occasionally, however, such a candidate is nominated as a gesture. In 1961 Tony Benn (at that time officially Viscount Stansgate) successfully contested, as the Labour candidate, the by-election in his constituency of Bristol South-East caused by his succeeding to his father's peerage. This triggered a change in the law, under the 1963 Peerage Act, which enabled hereditary peers to disclaim their titles.

In the event of a disqualified person being elected, it is open to his or her defeated opponent to apply to the High Court to have the election declared void. When this has occurred, the committee has held that if the facts leading to the disqualification had been generally known to the electors, those who have voted for the disqualified candidate should be deemed to have thrown their votes away, and the runner-up has been declared elected in his place. This indeed happened in the case of Tony Benn.[6]

Where a disqualified person has been elected without the facts leading to the disqualification being generally known to the electorate, the runner-up is not declared elected, but a by-election is held to find a successor. This occurred in Belfast West in 1950, when the Rev. J. G. MacManaway, a clergyman of the Church of Ireland, was elected, and it was not established until later that he was disqualified. Similarly, a successful candidate who subsequently becomes disqualified after being elected forfeits the seat, ceasing to be an MP, and a by-election must be held (see chapter 11.)

How candidates are chosen

The procedures of the three main political parties for selecting Parliamentary candidates differ in a number of important details, but are basically similar. In each case the selection is the responsibility of the local constituency party.

In the Conservative Party, procedures are not entirely uniform. The party constitution states that 'associations ... have autonomy to select candidates subject to the condition that all selected candidates must be included on the Party's Approved List of Candidates'. There are well-established procedures within the party which limit, however, the degree of local variation in methods of selection. Party members may put themselves forward for consideration. The constituency chairman is expected to obtain from the Central Office a list of names of suitable people, together with biographical details. A subcommittee of the national party board is responsible for maintaining an official list of approved potential candidates from among whom a number of names would be sent. Any member of the Conservative Party may apply to be included on the official list. Since 1980, weekend residential selection boards (based on army, civil service and business executive recruitment practice) have been arranged for batches of candidates before they are interviewed; and all approved candidates now join a centrally run Candidates' Association which arranges further training. In recent years only about 40 per cent of the applicants have been approved.

Together with the names obtained from Central Office, the selection committee considers any members of the constituency association who have expressed an interest in the candidature and also the names of Conservatives who may have written asking to be considered.

The Labour Party's selection procedure is laid down in more detail in the party rules, and it is complicated by the existence of two classes of membership, individual and affiliated (principally trade unions). When a constituency party decides to select a candidate, its executive committee first consults with the regional organiser of the party to agree a timetable for the selection. The regional organiser is the representative of Old Queen Street and has the responsibility of ensuring that the selection takes place according to the party rules. When the timetable has been approved by the general committee of the constituency party, the secretary writes to each local or ward party or affiliated organisation inviting them to make a nomination before a certain date, normally a minimum period of one month being allowed for this.

No person may be considered for selection unless he or she has been nominated by a local party, an affiliated organisation or by the executive committee, which may also make one nomination. There is no provision in the Labour Party for members to nominate themselves, though if a member has good personal contact with organisations with the right to nominate, it is often not difficult to obtain a nomination. Trade union branches are also able to nominate candidates, whose standing is the same as that of nominees of ward or local Labour parties.

Like the Conservative Central Office, Old Queen Street maintains a list of possible Parliamentary candidates. The executive committee of a constituency party may ask for copies for its own reference or to circulate to affiliated organisations, but there is no compulsion on them to do so, and frequently, particularly in the case of safe Labour seats, they make no effort to obtain the list; they can be quite sure in any case that if the seat is winnable any good aspiring candidate will be well aware of the vacancy.

The Liberal Democrats' procedures differ in several respects from those of the two larger parties. The party maintains a national panel of approved candidates, and whenever a local party proceeds to select a candidate it must advertise the vacancy to people on the panel who are invited to apply to be considered. Biographical details and a statement in support of candidacy are demanded from all would-be candidates, and the local party is required to follow a precise procedure set out in the party's constitution.

Shortlisting

The next stage, for all parties, is the reduction of the nominations to a manageable shortlist. The number of nominations made varies enormously. In a 'hopeless' constituency there may be as few as two or three. In a safe Conservative seat it is not uncommon for a selection committee to have over a hundred names from which to choose. In

Labour's case the maximum number is limited by the number of bodies eligible to nominate candidates, but in a safe seat, with many affiliated organisations, there is likely to be anything from 10 to 25 nominations, and even the latter figure is often exceeded.

The executive council of a Conservative association wishing to select a new candidate appoints a selection committee, usually of about six members, who would be amongst the most influential and senior members of the association. The chairman of the association is invariably included unless, which is not infrequently the case, the chairman has ambitions to be selected him- or herself. The purpose of the selection committee is to consider all the possible aspirants for the candidature and reduce them to a small number from which the final choice may be made.

The selection committee quickly whittle the number down to about seven or eight, and in the case of a safe seat few of the applicants would have much chance of surviving to this stage unless they were nationally known figures, were obviously extremely well qualified or were personally known to a member of the selection committee. The seven or eight people chosen are invited to attend to be interviewed by the selection committee which then chooses normally two or three names from whom the selection conference may make its final choice. Occasionally however, when the selection committee decides, in the words of the Central Office pamphlet, that 'a candidate is available whose record is so distinguished and whose qualifications are so outstanding that his adoption is practically a foregone conclusion' only one name is put forward to the executive council.

Before this stage is reached the names of any of the surviving nominees who are not included on the national list of approved candidates are submitted to the national party board's relevant subcommittee for endorsement. If endorsement is refused and the constituency proceeds to select a nominee in spite of this, he or she is not regarded as an official party candidate at the ensuing election (and would not, for example, be entitled to use the party's emblem on the ballot papers). Cases of an association selecting a candidate who has not been previously approved are, however, extremely rare.

In Labour's case, once the period of nomination has passed it is the responsibility of the executive committee to consider all the nominations received and to draw up a shortlist. If there are fewer than half a dozen nominations this is normally unnecessary, but this is a rare event, except in unwinnable seats. The executive committee may decide to interview all the nominees before drawing up a shortlist, or it may send them questionnaires to fill in. Often, however, it does neither.

The executive committee usually recommends a shortlist with from four to six names and this is reported to the general committee for its approval; at least one woman must be included in the shortlist if there are any female nominees. It is open to any member of the GC to move the addition, substitution, or deletion of names and this occurs with considerable frequency, though more often than not amendments are voted down.

There have been occasional cases in recent years where executive committees have been accused of bowing to pressure from the national party, either by shortlisting outsiders for whom Old Queen Street wishes to find a seat or by excluding popular local candidates not favoured by the national party. Ultimately, though, the CLP remains the sovereign body and Old Queen Street has few direct powers to impose or exclude a candidate at the shortlist stage without local co-operation. Even when someone recommended from headquarters is included it is by no means always an advantage for this fact to be known. Once an officially recommended nominee is on the shortlist he or she takes a chance with everyone else.

In the Liberal Democrats, the executive committee of the local party draws up a shortlist, perhaps after interviewing the applicants, and it is required to include at least three and no more than seven names. The shortlist must include both men and women nominees and 'shall be drawn up with regard to the desirability of securing proper representation for members of ethnic minorities'.

The selection conference

The shortlisted candidates next attend a selection conference. In the Conservative Party, this may consist of the executive council but nowadays is more likely to be open to all paid-up members of the association, as is the case in the Labour Party. Normally each makes a short speech (usually limited to a period varying between 10 and 30 minutes) and answers questions put from the floor. A secret ballot is then held to choose who will be the candidate.

There is no provision in Conservative Party rules as to the conduct of this ballot. It is possible for the nominee leading on the first ballot to be chosen forthwith, even though only a minority may have voted for him. It is far more usual, however, for an exhaustive ballot to be held, with the bottom candidate falling out if no overall majority is obtained on the first ballot. The Labour Party prescribes an exhaustive ballot, and absent members are allowed to vote by post.

The actual selection conference is the most dramatic stage in the selection process. It has been described by a former Tory MP, Nigel Nicolson, as 'a gala occasion for the selectors; slow torture for the candidate',[7] and it imposes considerable strain on the would-be candidates, as the senior author knows only too well from personal experience:

> The nominees are asked to attend a conference lasting anything up to three or four hours, though most of the time they are cooped up in an ante-room with the other contenders while procedural matters are being discussed or one of their number is making his speech. There is a certain tactical advantage in being the last to speak (the order is normally decided by lot), but this is often offset by the tension of waiting until all your rivals have spoken. All one can hear of the proceedings are occasional muffled sounds of applause from which one imagines that one's rivals are making an extremely good impression. In fact the audience normally goes out of its way to encourage the nominees, whose ordeal they can imagine, and they are very free with their applause.
>
> At last it is your turn. You are ushered into the conference, which as often as not is housed in a bleak Nonconformist church hall or school, but may occasionally be in the more regal surroundings of the council chamber of the town hall. Before you are perhaps 80 people, predominantly middle-aged, and you search eagerly for the encouragement of a familiar face, probably in vain.
>
> You reach your seat on the platform, shake hands with the chairman, who announces that you are Mr X, whose biographical details have been circulated to all the delegates. You have fifteen minutes to speak and another fifteen minutes for questions. After fourteen minutes the chairman will sound a warning bell and after fifteen you will be stopped – if necessary in mid-sentence.
>
> You stand up, try to show a confidence which you do not feel and launch into a well-prepared speech, which has been carefully timed in front of your bedroom mirror to last fourteen and a half minutes. In the event, you have either sat down after nine and a half minutes or are rudely cut short after fifteen minutes – less than a third of the way through your oration. You then deal rather better than you had expected with three or four questions and are surprised to hear that another fifteen minutes have gone by.
>
> Back to the ante-room and the interminable wait while a succession of ballots is taken. At last after two or three false alarms the regional organiser of the party will come into the room, look you straight in

the eye and announce that Mr Y has been selected. You shake hands with Mr Y and utter a few modest words of congratulation. Meanwhile that blithering idiot Mr Z is slapping Mr Y on the back and saying he had always known that Y would be chosen.

Back to the conference chamber with the other nominees. Deafening applause. The chairman says that all the nominees were absolutely first class (even if this was patently not the case). They would have liked to have chosen all of them, nevertheless they had to make a choice, however difficult, and the mantle had fallen on Mr Y. He was quite sure that such excellent people as Messrs W, X and Z would have no difficulty in being chosen soon by another constituency, and the members of his constituency would follow their future careers with interest. Then votes of thanks all round, a few words from the selected candidate and a final rousing call from the chairman to rally round and ensure that Mr Y becomes the next member for the constituency.[8]

This description, written some years ago, still remains generally true, though today some of the candidates would certainly be 'Mrs', 'Miss' or 'Ms' rather than 'Mr'. In some cases the proceedings may be more elaborate. In 2004 the Kensington and Chelsea Conservatives secured the services of the journalist Andrew Neil, who 'grilled' each of the candidates for selection in front of the meeting, so the members could judge their ability to cope with a hostile TV interviewer.

It is not easy for nominees to decide what to talk about in their set speeches. Should they talk about party policy or their personal records of work for the party? There is no set formula for success. The speech which would be an utter failure in constituency A may turn out an unqualified success in constituency B. All the nominee has to go on is experience and the degree of his or her knowledge of local feeling. The main consolation is that all his or her rivals are confronted by the same dilemma.

The Liberal Democrat procedure is a little different. Details of the shortlisted applicants are circulated to the entire membership of the area party, and a meeting or series of meetings are held to which all the shortlisted applicants are invited to speak and answer questions. This somewhat resembles the selection conference procedure of the other parties, but there is no voting at the conclusion of the meeting(s). Instead, a postal ballot is held, in which all members of the local party may take part, irrespective of whether they have attended any meetings.

In all cases, the candidate selected must subsequently be endorsed by the national party. This is normally a formality, but on very rare occasions this endorsement is withheld. This can be either because of alleged personal shortcomings by the candidate or because of the unorthodoxy of his or her political views. In the Labour Party it has in practice been used only to exclude those with strong Communist or Trotskyist connections. Even then such intervention rarely occurs. For example, eight supporters of the Trotskyist Militant Tendency were selected before the 1983 general election and none was refused endorsement. Two were elected as Labour MPs. Even in 1986, after Neil Kinnock had spent two years fighting the Militant Tendency, and had succeeded in getting a number of its adherents expelled from the party, a leading Militant supporter, Pat Wall, was endorsed as prospective candidate for Bradford North. He was subsequently elected in the 1987 general election. More recently, in 1995, a candidate selected from an all-women shortlist in the Leeds North-East constituency was rejected because of her left-wing activities. In the Conservative and Liberal Democrat Parties, it is even rarer for selected candidates to be black-balled for political heterodoxy, though four Tory candidates were dropped or withdrew before the 1992 election because of Central Office pressure. However, the Conservative experience in the 1997 election (when Central Office was unable to block the re-nomination of a sitting MP, Neil Hamilton, even though the allegations of corruption against him were believed to be damaging the national party's reputation) led to the setting-up of an Ethics and Integrity Committee with the power to veto candidacies in certain cases. Even more rarely, Labour's NEC has the power, by a rule change approved by the party conference in 1988, 'to require a CLP to select its nominee in the interests of the party' – though the power is not normally used except in by-elections.

The methods of selection of minor parties differ considerably from those of the major parties, principally because they have so few members. Decisions normally taken in the larger parties by constituency associations are more likely to be taken by the national committees of the smaller parties. Selection conferences of the type described above are the exception rather than the rule.

One general point which may be made about selection procedures of all parties is the small number of people involved in making the choice. The drawing up of the shortlist – a vital stage – is the responsibility in the Conservative Party of less than a dozen people and in the Labour Party of less than 20. The final selection is seldom made by more than 200 people in the two largest parties and most often by between 50 and 150. In the Liberal Democrats even smaller numbers are normally involved, though they sometimes achieve a substantially higher figure through the use of their postal ballots.

That said, candidate selection procedures are in a state of change at present, and it may be that in a few years' time the structure will be almost unrecognisable. Before 1997, the biggest political unit for which candidates had to be selected was the European Parliament constituency, consisting of perhaps half a dozen Westminster constituencies, which were of a practicable size to lump all the party activists together and proceed in much the traditional way; selection of local government candidates is also by a similar process, in some cases with local branches in charge of their own selections and in others with the constituency association selecting all its candidates collectively. But new elections and the adoption of proportional representation for the European Parliament have put candidate selection on an entirely new scale – parties need to be able to select at regional level a candidate for Mayor of London, list candidates for the London Assembly and European Parliament and, on a slightly smaller scale, list candidates for the sub-regions used in Scottish Parliament and Welsh Assembly elections. New procedures have been invented for these tasks and, coupled with an increasing enthusiasm among grass-roots members for participatory democracy within the parties, may well have knock-on effects in causing changes to Westminster selection procedures.

The involvement of a fairly small number in drawing up shortlists is perhaps inevitable, unless Britain were to move to an American-type system of full-scale primary elections (where the immense cost of campaigning tends eventually to reduce the names on the ballot paper to a manageable number). But greater involvement at later stages will probably become the norm. For example, in the system devised by the Conservatives to select their candidate for Mayor of London in 2000, a committee appointed by Central Office reduced the hopefuls to a long shortlist of eight; this was reduced to four by an electoral college consisting of representatives of every constituency association; these four were cut to two at a selection meeting of party members from throughout London – the meeting filled Westminster Central Hall – and the decision between the final two was left to a postal ballot of all members. To the embarrassment of the party, this process had to be run twice after the originally selected candidate, the novelist Jeffrey Archer, resigned following revelations in a Sunday newspaper which subsequently led to his being jailed. In the initial selection, the Central Office committee had allowed all the best-known candidates onto the shortlist without interference. However, after Archer's resignation the party leadership was much criticised for having allowed his candidacy to proceed in the first place, and in the re-run selection they veered to the opposite extreme, excluding a sitting MP and also initially barring the former MP Steven Norris, who had been runner-up in the original process. The furore over this decision was arguably quite as embarrassing as anything that might have been anticipated from selecting a controversial candidate.

Labour reduced its mayoral candidates to a shortlist of three after interviews by a committee appointed by party headquarters (which was specifically empowered to exclude candidates it thought might be opposed to the party's manifesto, though in fact it did not do so). These names were then submitted to an electoral college, similar to that used to elect the party's leader: a third of the votes for paid-up members, a third for London's affiliated organisations (trade unions and co-operative societies) and a third for its Labour MPs, MEPs and (already selected) Greater London Authority (GLA) assembly candidates. These rules were not announced until well after the identities of the likely candidates were known, and were widely seen as an attempt to 'rig' the process against the left-wing MP and former Greater London Council (GLC) leader Ken Livingstone. It had previously been understood that the selection would be on a 'one member, one vote' basis, which Mr Livingstone might have expected to win; but with a third of votes going to MPs, MEPs and assembly candidates, who could be controlled by the leadership (and who did not have the benefit of a secret ballot), the odds were much more heavily stacked against him. He did not win the nomination. There can be little doubt that the proceedings were damaging to Labour's image in the capital, and contributed to the ease of Mr Livingstone's victory in the election, standing as an independent.

Who is chosen?

Looking at it from the other side, what are the members of the selection conference looking for in their candidate? This varies with the nature of the constituency, and especially according to the prospect of electoral success. If it is a marginal constituency the delegates are most likely to be impressed by the vote-winning prospects of their candidate and a pleasing personality would be the number one qualification. In a safe seat delegates are conscious of choosing the future member rather than a candidate and are more concerned to choose a man or woman with the requisite knowledge and experience to perform what they conceive to be the functions of an MP. In a hopeless constituency energy and enthusiasm count a great deal, and younger candidates are much more likely to be chosen.

Policy differences are not all-important. It is commonly anticipated that left-wing constituency Labour parties are certain to select left-wing candidates and that right-wing Conservative associations, similarly, will pick extremist candidates. In fact this happens much less frequently than is imagined. Selection conferences of all parties will often pick the man or woman who 'looks the part' rather than to insist on the nominee whose political views most exactly coincide with their own.

Local interests undoubtedly often play a part. If one is nominated for a farming constituency it is prudent to show some knowledge of and interest in agriculture, similarly with industrial areas where one industry is predominant. But in mixed industrial areas and especially in suburban constituencies there is likely to be more interest in national than in purely local issues.

Age may play an important part in deciding between nominees, though this again will vary very much. There are a few parties which would regard a man of 50 as a 'young stripling', while others would regard a 40-year-old as a has-been. In general, the optimum age range is from 35 to 45, with a certain preference for younger candidates in hopeless and marginal seats and for older ones in safe constituencies.

Unlike in the USA and certain other countries, it is not customary for a candidate to be resident in the area where he or she is standing for election. In fact, a large number of candidates in British Parliamentary elections are 'carpet baggers' with no personal stake in the community they seek to represent. At some selection conferences it is a major advantage to be a local man, but equally often it can be a handicap. To come in from outside, with no previous connections with local factions, can in many cases be a strong recommendation.

Two striking biases in the profile of those selected to stand for Parliament have received considerable attention in recent years, the considerable imbalance between men and women and the small number of candidates from ethnic minorities.[9] The number of female candidates has been rising steeply with each election since 1966 (see Table 7.1), but there are still proportionately fewer women MPs than in most other European democracies. Many fewer women than men are selected and they tend to be chosen for the less hopeful seats. However, all the parties have taken steps to increase the number of women selected, though the Conservatives have been less successful than the others, partly through greater reluctance of the national party to interfere with the autonomy of local associations. The Labour Party conference decided in 1993 to try to increase the party's female representation by a measure of positive discrimination, intending that half of all winnable marginal seats and half of existing Labour seats where the MP was retiring should select women as candidates. The choice of constituencies to have all-women shortlists was to be made through consultation with the constituency parties concerned, but in the event of disagreement the NEC reserved the power to impose such a list. By mid-1995, 35 constituencies had agreed to select from all-women shortlists, and in one – highly publicised – case, in Slough, the NEC had imposed a list against the wishes of the local party. However in January 1996, after a challenge by two party members, all-women short-lists were ruled illegal under equal opportunities legislation by an industrial tribunal; more recently, though, the law was changed by the Sex Discrimination (Election Candidates) Act of 2002, legitimising the practice, and Labour has resumed the imposition of all-women shortlists in some seats. Even before the change, the number of women fighting winnable seats was considerably increased, and with Labour's sweeping victory in 1997 the number of women in the Commons was doubled to 120.

Table 7.1   Women candidates and members, 1945–2001

General election	Con		Lab		Lib/SDP/LD		Other		Total	
	Cands	MPs	Cands	MPs	Cands	MPs	Cands	MPs	Cands	MPs
1945	14	1	45	21	20	1	8	1	87	24
1950	28	6	42	14	45	1	11	0	126	21
1951	29	6	39	11	11	0	0	0	74	17
1955	32	10	43	14	12	0	2	0	89	24
1959	28	12	36	13	16	0	1	0	81	25
1964	24	11	33	18	25	0	8	0	90	29
1966	21	7	30	19	20	0	9	0	80	26
1970	26	15	29	10	23	0	21	1	99	26
1974: Feb	33	9	40	13	40	0	30	1	143	23
1974: Oct	30	7	50	18	49	0	32	2	161	27
1979	31	8	52	11	51	0	76	0	210	19
1983	40	13	78	10	115	0	87	0	280	23
1987	46	17	92	21	106	2	85	1	329	41
1992	59	20	138	37	144	2	227	1	568	60
1997	66	13	155	101	139	3	312	3	672	120
2001	92	14	149	95	139	5	256	4	636	118

Sources: David Butler and Gareth Butler, *Twentieth Century British Political Facts 1900–2000* (Basingstoke: Macmillan, 2000), p. 261; Byron Criddle, 'MPs and Candidates', in David Butler and Dennis Kavanagh, *The British General Election of 1997* (Basingstoke: Macmillan, 1997), p. 199; Electoral Commission, *Election 2001: The Official Results* (London: Politico's Publishing, 2001), Tables 20 and 21, p. 310.

In elections to the Scottish Parliament and Welsh Assembly, most of the parties apart from the Conservatives have been able to go further because of the list system of proportional representation used for those elections (see Appendix 8). Labour, the Liberal Democrats and both the nationalist parties all used the practice of 'zipping', that is ensuring that candidates on each list were alternately male and female (fitting together like the teeth in each side of a zip fastener). This greatly increased the number of women who won seats (though because only a minority of the seats were allocated by the list element of the electoral system it did not achieve full equality), and at the 2003 Welsh Assembly election exactly half the successful candidates were women, making it the only legislature in the world with equal membership of women and men.

No doubt the proportion at Westminster will also continue to increase. One major stumbling block has always been the unsocial hours worked by the House of Commons (which used to sit from 2.30 p.m. until 10 p.m., and often late into the night). This militated against family life and was undoubtedly more of a barrier to women MPs than to men. The adoption of more conventional working hours for the Commons under the present government may help encourage more high-quality female candidates to apply.

One other category which has been seriously under-represented among candidates and MPs is members of minority ethnic groups. Although three Asians had been Members of Parliament at an earlier time, no black or Asian MPs sat between 1931 and 1987, and only a sprinkling of ethnic minority candidates had been nominated. In 1987, when the number of black and Asian candidates increased to 28 (14 Labour, 8 Alliance and 6 Conservative), four were at last elected – all for Labour seats. In December 1990 the Conservative Party in Cheltenham, a Tory-held seat, selected a black barrister as its prospective candidate, a decision which was later challenged by a section of its members. He was defeated by the Liberal Democrat candidate in the 1992 election, but a Sri Lankan-born candidate held the Brentford and Chiswick seat from 1992 to 1997, becoming the first Asian Conservative MP in nearly 90 years. Altogether, six non-white candidates were elected in 1992, five of them Labour, and nine in 1997, all Labour.

It is not only women and minority ethnic candidates who have been rare in the Conservative Party. Despite frequent appeals from Central Office, it has proved almost impossible to persuade Conservative constituency associations to select working-class candidates. A rare exception is Patrick McLoughlin, a former miner, who has been the Conservative MP for West Derbyshire since winning a by-election in 1986. The occupational backgrounds of candidates and elected members in the 2001 election are shown in Table 7.2; a more comprehensive analysis is contained in Appendix 6.

In the professions category the law, particularly the bar, is dominant in the Conservative Party, and is very well represented in the Labour Party and the Liberal Democrats. There are a number of reasons for this. Traditionally, the bar and politics have been associated professions. By virtue of their training and professional practice barristers are skilled at arguing a case and it may be expected that they would face a selection conference with more confidence than most. Barristers and solicitors also undoubtedly find it easier than most to organise their time in such a way that they can combine their profession with their Parliamentary work.

Table 7.2   Occupational backgrounds of candidates, 2001

	Conservative		Labour		Liberal Democrat	
	Elected (%)	Defeated (%)	Elected (%)	Defeated (%)	Elected (%)	Defeated (%)
Professions	39	36	43	50	52	41
Business	36	43	8	12	27	25
Miscellaneous	25	20	36	32	19	29
Workers	1	1	12	6	2	5

Source: The information in this table has been drawn from a more comprehensive table in David Butler and Dennis Kavanagh, *The British General Election of 2001* (Basingstoke: Palgrave, 2002), p. 204. The full table is reproduced below, as Appendix 6.

There is a fair sprinkling from the other professions among the candidates of all parties, but it is only teaching – at both school and university level – which comes near to challenging the predominance of the law. In fact teachers form by far the largest occupational group among Labour candidates, almost a quarter of whom in the 2001 election were teachers, either at university, adult education or school level. In the Liberal Democrat Party, too, large numbers of candidates came from the teaching profession. Far fewer Conservative candidates have been teachers, though the number is growing.

It will come as a surprise to nobody to discover that business is largely represented in the Conservative Party. It made a good showing, too, in the Liberal Democrat Party. The smaller number of Labour candidates with a business background are not really comparable, as a majority of these are small businessmen or employees of larger companies, whereas a majority of the Conservatives in this category are company directors or senior executives.

Prominent in the miscellaneous category are journalists (in all parties) and farmers (nearly all on the Conservative side). Public relations and advertising men are well represented too, particularly in the Conservative Party. A growing category in all parties is political organisers; an increasing number of MPs have never held any job outside politics before first being elected. Amongst the workers, the largest single category is still the ex-miners, though there are barely a third as many of these as a generation ago. Eleven miners stood for Labour in 2001, all being successful. In the 1966 general election there had been 35 miners standing as Labour candidates, 32 of whom had been elected. A good proportion of the 'workers' who stood in 1992 and 1997 were full-time trade union officials, but many were working at their trades when first elected, and each general election brings to the Labour benches of the House of Commons reinforcements of members straight from the workbench (though the proportion is dropping steadily – in 1992, 22 per cent of Labour MPs were workers, in 2001 only 12 per cent).

Only a derisory number of workers have at any time been selected as Conservative or Liberal candidates, and fewer still have been elected. In the Labour Party a majority of candidates would have been classified as workers in the period up to 1945. But since that date the proportion of professional men (especially teachers) has greatly increased, and this has been largely at the expense of 'workers'. In very many cases the new aspirants have come from working-class families; but unlike their parents have enjoyed the benefits of a grammar school and/or university education. Ironically, workers have stood a much better chance of being chosen to fight safe Labour seats rather than hopeless or marginal ones. This was because of the system of trade union sponsorship. Until 1995, a great many Labour candidates were financially sponsored by trade unions. Under the so-called Hastings Agreement, dating from the Labour Party conference at Hastings in 1933, a trade union was permitted to contribute up to 80 per cent of the election expenses incurred on behalf of its nominee and a maximum of £750 a year, or 70 per cent of the agent's salary, to the constituency party.

There was thus a strong temptation for hard-up constituency parties to choose a sponsored candidate, and this applied especially in safe Labour seats in industrial areas. Many constituency parties took a pride in choosing the best nominee available irrespective of financial considerations and many sponsored nominees were able and public-spirited men. There were, however, certainly cases where more competent nominees were passed over in favour of a mediocrity whose principal recommendation was the income which his selection would ensure. It also means that when Labour is in government, especially with a big majority as in 1997, the Parliamentary Party tends to be far less working class than when it is in opposition. The system of trade unions sponsoring individual candidates was discontinued before the 1997 election,[10] but its effects will take some years to disappear.

In all parties there is a recognised route which the majority of would-be MPs are expected to follow. They must first fight a hopeless seat and, fortified by this salutary experience, they may then proceed to a marginal constituency, and later perhaps to a safe one. A fair number of lucky aspirants in both major parties succeed in bypassing this route and secure election to the House of Commons at their first attempt, but many of the most eminent Parliamentarians, including two of the last three Prime Ministers, had to undergo defeat in an unwinnable constituency before securing the nomination of the seat they represented for the rest of their career.[11]

How much security do prospective candidates enjoy? Not very much. Their relationship to their constituency parties is a delicate one. Disenchantment easily sets in on either side. This is not perhaps surprising, as candidate and constituency party have usually had only the most fleeting view of each other prior to selection.

Opportunities for disagreement abound. Parties and candidates often differ on how much work the candidate is expected to put in. It frequently happens that prospective candidates visit the constituency less often than their parties would like; less commonly, parties may decide that they see altogether too much of their candidates. Changes in the personal position of candidates may also occur. They may be offered better jobs, or their employers may prove unexpectedly difficult about allowing time off. Their health may suffer, or that of their families. They may take on other commitments which leave them less time for their candidature. Or they may wish to be considered for other, more promising, constituencies. Thus, for one reason or another, a significant number of prospective candidates withdraw 'for personal reasons' long before polling day, and the procedure for selecting a new candidate has to be gone through all over again.

The traditional culture of the two major parties is rather different. Many members of constituency Labour parties would undoubtedly like their MPs to behave as delegates of the Labour Party rather than as representatives of the constituency as a whole. Though the national party has normally set its face against this concept, it would not be alien to the spirit of the party constitution. By contrast, the Conservatives in theory adhere to the ethos of Burke:

> Your representative owes you not his industry only, but his judgment;
> and he betrays instead of serving you if he sacrifices it to your opinion
> ... authoritative instructions, mandates issued, which the Member is
> bound blindly and implicitly to obey, though contrary to the dearest
> conviction of his judgment and conscience, these things are utterly
> unknown to the laws of this land, and ... arise from a fundamental
> mistake of the whole order and tenor of our constitution.[12]

But in practice Tories, too, sometimes yearn to impose restraints on their
members' ideological freedom.

In the past, once a candidate had been elected as a Member of
Parliament he or she usually had no difficulty in retaining the support
of the party and, unless the seat was a marginal one, normally continued
to represent it, if he or she wished, until the end of his or her working
life. It was extremely difficult for a constituency party to rid itself of an
unwanted member, the required procedure for doing this in both the
Conservative and Labour Parties being heavily weighted on the side of
the member.

Labour was the first to change this. Before the 1980s, only one or two
Labour MPs had been refused re-adoption at each election. In 1981, the
party introduced new rules involving a mandatory reselection process
for all sitting MPs during the course of each Parliament. Eight MPs were
deselected before the 1983 general election, and it has been estimated[13]
that another nine would have suffered the same fate had they not defected
to the SDP. A further six were deselected before 1987, and no doubt on
each occasion some of the Labour MPs who 'voluntarily' retired from
Parliament might have fought on had they not had to face reselection.

The majority of victims of deselection were moderates, as the decision
was in the hands of the activist members of the constituency parties,
who were generally more left-wing than the membership as a whole. In
1987, Neil Kinnock attempted to widen the decisions to 'one member,
one vote' (OMOV), but was blocked by trade union opposition, and a
compromise electoral college system was used in selections for the 1992
election. However, OMOV was subsequently introduced under John
Smith, and there can be little doubt that Labour MPs are now less under
threat than they once were; but they still have far less security of tenure
than before 1981.

In the Conservative Party after the 1997 election, events paralleled those
in Labour in the early 1980s. With the leadership under William Hague
tending towards the right of the party, rule changes were introduced
which require sitting MPs to win a secret ballot of local activists if they

are to avoid fighting a new selection battle against other candidates; however, no Conservative MP has yet been dislodged in this way for deviating from political orthodoxy. (One was deselected in 2004 for non-ideological reasons, as was one Labour MP.)

Deselecting an MP carries a certain risk, of course – it may provoke him or her into resigning to call an immediate unwanted by-election, or to stand against the new nominee at the next election. However, as mentioned in the section on independents in Chapter 5, no rebel has succeeded at Westminster elections since the 1970s, though one long-standing Labour MP won a seat in the Scottish Parliament and another in the Welsh Assembly corresponding to their Westminster constituency, despite facing official Labour opposition.

It used to be the received wisdom that MPs needed to keep well in with the party whips, but could be reasonably relaxed with their constituency parties, if they wanted to have a long Parliamentary career. Now the boot is very much on the other foot. It has become a rare event indeed for a member to be dropped because of not voting with his or her party in the House (though preferment prospects may be damaged thereby). But MPs of all parties now know that their future as members may be very dependent upon the goodwill of their constituency parties or associations.

8
The Campaign in the Constituencies[1]

The announcement by the Prime Minister of an impending general election precipitates a flurry of activity in constituency and local party branches throughout the country. Emergency meetings are hastily convened to put the local party machines on a 'wartime footing' and to make arrangements for the formal adoption of Parliamentary candidates.

If the dissolution is announced unexpectedly a fair number of constituency parties may find themselves without a prospective candidate, but even when the election is anticipated a handful of parties find themselves in the same position because of the recent resignation of their previously selected candidates. A few other prospective candidates are likely to find, when the dissolution is announced, that an election campaign at that particular time would be inconvenient and they therefore withdraw from the field. All in all it is unlikely that fewer than half a dozen candidates have to be found at short notice at any general election by each of the Labour and Conservative Parties, and in such circumstances the selection procedures outlined in Chapter 7 are telescoped considerably.

In the past, the Liberal Party and each of the minor parties usually had to find a higher proportion of their candidates at this stage. In many constituencies, a decision to fight had been left in abeyance and the first question to be resolved at their emergency meetings was whether a candidate is to be put in the field at all. The Conservative, Labour and Liberal Democrat Parties now normally fight every single seat in Great Britain, except sometimes against the Speaker, as do the Nationalists in their own countries, but the smaller parties must still agonise over which constituencies to fight.

In deciding whether to put up a candidate, a constituency party will seriously consider not only its potential voting strength in the area and the availability of a suitable man or woman to stand, but also its financial position. Not only does the cost of campaigning have to be considered, but also the deposit. A deposit of £500 is required to be paid to the Returning Officer at the time of the nomination, and this is returnable only if the candidate polls more than one-twentieth of the total votes cast. Until 1986, the threshold was much higher, one-eighth of the votes cast, though the deposit was lower, at £150, a sum unchanged since deposits were first introduced in 1918. The deposit in European elections was £1000 per candidate, but with the introduction of proportional representation was altered to £1000 for each regional list. For the Scottish Parliament and Welsh Assembly, the deposit is £500 for each constituency candidate and £500 for a regional list, in each case needing 5 per cent of the vote to have the deposit returned. No deposit is required in local government elections.

As soon as the question of a candidate is resolved the election agent, who is the key figure in every campaign, is appointed. The position is a statutory one and every candidate is required to notify the name and address of the person appointed, in writing, to the Returning Officer. The election agent is legally responsible for authorising all expenditure on behalf of a candidate and his or her name must appear as the 'promoter' (the person who caused the material to be published) on all printed material, including posters and window bills, issued in support of the candidate. The agent's official duties do not end until he or she has sent in a return of election expenses to the Returning Officer after the result of the election has been declared. The amount that may be spent is strictly limited by law (see page 200), and if the limit is exceeded the candidate faces disqualification.

A candidate may act as his or her own election agent, though this rarely happens except in the case of independents and minor party candidates. When a constituency party employs a full-time agent, he or she automatically takes on the job. Otherwise it is assumed by an experienced member of the local party. Most 'amateur' agents arrange to take at least three weeks off from their regular work to devote themselves to their electoral duties. The work of an election agent is extremely arduous, beginning early in the morning and continuing far into the night, at least during the three weeks prior to polling day. An agent's family can expect to see almost nothing of him or her during this time.

Once the questions of a candidate and an agent have been settled, there is little more for a governing body of a constituency party to do. It is usual for a 'campaign committee', consisting of a handful of key workers, prepared to devote virtually all their spare time to the election, to be appointed to supervise the details of the campaign, in conjunction with the agent and candidate. A financial appeal will be issued to members and known sympathisers and the agent will be authorised to spend up to a specified sum during the campaign. The party will then pass a resolution either formally dissolving itself or suspending all public propaganda activities for the duration of the election. The purpose of this is to emphasise that all activities on behalf of the candidature during the election period are the personal responsibility of the agent.

The first task of the agent is to obtain premises suitable for use as a campaign headquarters, or central committee rooms as they are called. When the party itself owns permanent premises which are suitable for this purpose there is no problem. Otherwise a frantic search is mounted for vacant shop or office premises, preferably in a prominent position in the main street of the principal town in the constituency. Labour candidates have often experienced great difficulties in obtaining premises of this kind because of the hostility of private commercial interests, but this was partly offset by the willingness of co-operative societies to make accommodation available. A high proportion of Labour committee rooms are housed above co-operative stores. If commercial premises cannot be found or the party cannot afford to pay for them the committee rooms are likely to be established in the front room of a private house of a keen party member. The keenness of such members will certainly be put to a severe test in such circumstances, for neither they nor their families are likely to be afforded much privacy in the succeeding weeks. Subcommittee rooms in each ward or polling district will also be set up; these will nearly always be in private houses.

Once established in committee rooms, the agent is confronted with a bewildering multiplicity of duties. These come easily to the old hand, but to the inexperienced they can pose formidable problems. Fortunately the party headquarters run excellent correspondence and residential courses for those likely to be appointed as temporary agents; in case of difficulty a call to the party's regional organiser should elicit sound advice. The agent of an independent or minor party candidate is denied such help, and in practice it is he or she who is most likely to come unstuck. In the past a prudent person in such a position was well advised to swallow his or her pride and buy one of the agent's handbooks published by the major parties, but now the Electoral Commission publishes copious notes setting out clearly the legal responsibilities of election agents and giving detailed guidance as to how their duties should be carried out.

An election agent is unlikely to be short of willing helpers. The hard core of active party workers will devote the greater part of their spare time during evenings and weekends to the campaign, and they are likely to be supplemented by a larger number of normally inactive members who feel that they ought to rally round at election time. Sympathetic members of the public, too, who are unwilling to become party members, may turn up at the committee rooms and offer to lend a hand. To keep this motley array of helpers happy and purposefully occupied requires high qualities of tact and diplomacy. Nevertheless, the numbers prepared to help during elections are declining, though to some extent the increasing use of information technology can compensate. Butler and Kavanagh quote a candidate[2] comparing 1970, when he wrote 800 thank-you letters to his helpers, with 1997, when he needed to send only 170.

All the varied tasks undertaken by the election agent and his team of helpers are directed towards two main objects: to identify the party's supporters within the constituency and to build up a machine capable of ensuring the maximum turnout of these supporters on election day.

Forty years ago, one of the party's most important tasks was to familiarise the voters with the name of the candidate and underline his or her party affiliation. Before the passage of the 1969 Representation of the People Act, no mention of a candidate's party was made on the ballot paper, so it was up to parties to make sure the electors knew which candidate represented which party. Hence all election literature and posters and window bills gave great prominence to linking the candidate's name with the party. 'Jones for Labour' or 'Vote Smith, Conservative X' were slogans which became increasingly familiar to voters as polling day approached. Under the 1969 Act, however, candidates were allowed to add up to six descriptive words to accompany their names and addresses on the ballot paper. Nearly all of them utilise this facility to indicate their party affiliation, sometimes combined with a slogan, and party symbols may also now appear on ballot papers.

The ballot papers for local elections are similar to Parliamentary ones. The inclusion of a political affiliation since 1969 has certainly had a greater effect in local elections than in Parliamentary ones. The candidates' names are usually less well-known and less publicised, and when there were multiple vacancies it was evident that many mistakes were made, particularly when different candidates had the same or similar surnames.

The activities of the candidate during the election campaign are a continuation and intensification of the work which he or she has been doing in the constituency in the months and years leading up to the election. The main difference is that the word 'prospective' is at last dropped from his or her title and that the public can now be asked to 'Vote for Jones' instead of merely for the party. The transition is usually marked by an adoption meeting, held as soon as possible after the election is announced, at which the candidature is formally proclaimed. This is normally a public meeting, which every party member is strongly urged to attend as a demonstration of enthusiasm and confidence. Speeches are made by the candidate and several other speakers, an appeal for financial support is made and a resolution formally adopting the candidate may be put to the meeting. It need hardly be added that such a resolution is invariably carried with acclamation. If the candidate is the retiring Member of Parliament for the constituency he or she will by this time have dropped the title MP, having ceased to be a member since the dissolution of Parliament. During the election campaign he or she is merely a candidate with status no different from that of the other candidates in the constituency.

The adoption has no legal standing and each candidate must be formally nominated in writing. Nominations may be made on any day after the publication by the Returning Officer of the date of the election but not later than the sixth working day after the date of the Proclamation summoning the new Parliament. This gives, in practice, a period of three working days in which nominations may be made, and the final day for nominations is also the final day on which a nomination may be withdrawn.

The nomination form must be signed by a proposer and seconder and by eight other people, all of whom must be electors for the constituency in which the candidate is to stand. The nomination form contains the candidate's full name, address and 'description', and his or her proposers must sign their names in the same form in which they are listed in the election register and must also add their electoral numbers. Only one nomination form is required but it is usual for an agent to arrange for several to be filled in by different electors, partly as an insurance against one form being invalid and partly as a demonstration of support for the candidate.

The nomination form or forms must be delivered in person to the Returning Officer by the candidate or his or her proposer or seconder between the hours of 10 a.m. and 4 p.m. on one of the days when nominations may be made. The nomination must be accompanied by the £500 deposit, and by the candidate's consent in writing to nomination, which must be attested by one witness.

Provided a nomination paper has been filled in and delivered exactly as described above, it will be deemed valid by the Returning Officer. Representatives of candidates may inspect the nomination papers of their rivals and may lodge objections if they suspect them to be invalid. The

Returning Officer must then give his or her decision as soon as possible and, if it is decided that a nomination paper is invalid, the Returning Officer must endorse the paper as invalid and state on it the reasons for the decision. This does not happen at all frequently, and when it does there is normally time for the candidate to send in another nomination paper which is correctly filled in, as few candidates are so imprudent as to leave their nomination to the very last moment.[3]

In the unlikely event that by the time that nominations are closed only one valid nomination has been received, the Returning Officer declares that person elected and publishes notices to that effect throughout the constituency. Where there are at least two candidates (as has happened in every constituency at each election since 1951), the Returning Officer publishes a statement of persons nominated, together with the names of their proposers, seconders and assentors. This statement includes a notice of the poll, stating the date and time that the election is to be held, and gives particulars as to where people should go to vote.

By this time things are hotting up; it is a mere eleven days (excluding weekends and public holidays) to polling day.

Until comparatively recently, the constituency parties were mostly left to their own devices in deciding how to campaign. Advice and sometimes extra resources would be available from regional and national organisers, but a candidate and agent who knew their job and their constituency would be left to get on with it in their own way. No longer. National party headquarters now attempt to orchestrate campaigning across the country, and will send a constant stream of messages and material by fax, pager or e-mail to keep their candidates 'on message'. This can add up to a full programme of campaigning material, and pliant candidates are almost absolved from the need to think for themselves throughout the election. They will probably be instructed to give no media interviews unless cleared by the regional headquarters. But many candidates, of course, prefer not to allow themselves to be 'spoon-fed' in this way, and still insist on fighting a local campaign tailored to local issues and voters.

At least a fortnight before polling day, and probably a week or two earlier, the candidate will have moved into the constituency for the duration of the campaign. Unless the candidate normally lives there, he or she will take a room at a hotel or lodge with a supporter. A married candidate's husband or wife will normally come too, family circumstances permitting, and will be expected to take an active part in the campaign. Some idea of their daily life during the three weeks before polling day is given by the following imaginary timetable of a male candidate in a county constituency.

7.30 a.m.	Get up. Breakfast. Read all the papers – especially reports of the speeches of the party leaders and other election news.
8.30–9.30	Work in hotel bedroom on speeches to be delivered in the evening.
9.30	Meet reporter from local newspaper at hotel. Comment on speech given by rival candidate on previous day.
9.50	Arrive at main committee rooms, in car driven by wife. Dictate replies to correspondence received from electors. Quick consultation with the agent on the day's programme.
10.30	Set off with woman councillor for door-to-door canvass of housewives on new housing estate.
12 noon	Visit hospital with wife to meet patients. Talk with matron to check that arrangements for postal votes for the patients have been made.
1 p.m.	Quick lunch in café.
1.30	Drive to town at other end of constituency.
2.15	Set off on loudspeaker tour – making short speeches and answering questions at street corners.
3.15	Wife leaves to have tea with the Townswomen's Guild.
4.15	Meet a deputation of Roman Catholics to hear their case for more public money to maintain Catholic schools.
5.00	Interview with local radio station reporter.
5.30	Speak to factory gate meeting.
6.30	Return to main committee rooms, immediately set off with agent for quick tour of subcommittee rooms.
7.30	Supper at home of party chairman.
8.15	Leave for first of three village meetings.
9.45	Return to town hall for main evening meeting, which has already been addressed by a prominent visiting speaker.
10.15	Adjourn to pub with party supporters. Watch election news or party broadcasts on TV.
11.30	Return to hotel and to bed.

This kind of pace is sustained without much difficulty by nearly all candidates,[4] though elderly members who are defending safe seats tend to take it a lot easier. The constant excitement and the enthusiastic encouragement of supporters go a long way to create fresh reserves of energy which the candidate would not previously have suspected himself or herself of possessing. A major problem is to restrain the ardour of one's supporters who will quite happily keep one up talking all night. Here a firm intervention by the candidate's spouse is indicated.

It is notable how little the campaigns of rival candidates impinge on each other. The candidates may meet once or twice on neutral ground – at a public meeting for all candidates organised by a group such as Charter88, perhaps, or at an inter-denominational service held for election workers. One candidate may take up some remarks of another, as reported in the local newspaper, and reply to them at one of his meetings or challenge the accuracy of his facts. Very occasionally a candidate may make a personal attack on a rival, but this is normally regarded as bad form and is likely to do the attacker more harm than good.

The great majority of candidates, however, totally ignore the existence of their rivals throughout the campaign. If they are government supporters they will doggedly defend the record of the government with an occasional side swipe at the irresponsibility of the Opposition, but if any names are mentioned, it will be of well-known national leaders rather than the Opposition's local standard bearer. The same is broadly true, in reverse, of opposition candidates, though a former member defending a seat is more likely to be picked out by name than a newly arrived challenger.

While the candidate is making every effort to make him- or herself known to as many voters as possible, the agent is equally busy ensuring that contact is established with every potential supporter of the party in the constituency. If the party organisation is good, the agent will have started the campaign with a marked-up register covering the greater part of the constituency. In that case his or her team of canvassers will be asked to call on all the 'F' (for) voters to confirm that they are party supporters and on the 'D' or doubtful voters to see if they have moved off the fence. Those voters marked 'A' (against) are left *firmly* alone. Many agents find that no reasonably up-to-date canvassing records are in existence and they have to instruct their canvassers to call on every voter. In either case canvassing is regarded as much the most important single activity which has to be undertaken during elections, and every available person is pressed into service. It is normal for canvassing teams to go out on every evening of the campaign and in the daytime during weekends. Theoretically, parties aim to make a 100 per cent canvass of the constituency, but most agents are more than pleased if their canvassers call on 80 per cent of the voters. It is normal to begin with the most favourable parts of the constituency and move on later to the less promising areas: so if a party canvasses only 50 per cent of the voters it may have called on 75 per cent of its own supporters, though these days even that would be well-above-average coverage.

In a marginal constituency it is prudent to set a target of 2000 or 3000 more favourable promises than would be necessary to win the seat. Most canvassers, particularly inexperienced ones who are much in evidence at election time, are incurably optimistic and are liable to read into a courteous reception a promise of support. It is this rather than deliberate deception which most often leads to voters being recorded in the 'F' column by canvassers representing opposing candidates. Whatever the reason, it is certain that nine candidates out of ten receive an inflated estimate of support from their canvassers.

Canvassers are asked to undertake a number of subsidiary jobs. They are liberally supplied with window bills to offer to supporters, and they are instructed to enquire about elderly or infirm voters who might require a lift to the poll or, if there is still time, to be assisted in applying for a postal vote. Canvassers are also often given leaflets to deliver 'on their rounds'. It is important for canvassers to ask to see every voter on the register at each house at which they call, and not to assume that the person who comes to the door speaks for the whole household. More families than most people imagine are divided in their voting habits, and households containing lodgers are unlikely to be politically homogeneous. A high proportion of canvassers however, despite the instructions of their agents, take the easy way out and do not bother to interview all members of a household. This is a further source of gross inaccuracies in canvassing records, and inflates parties' estimates of the number of electors they have actually contacted.

In recent elections the scale of canvassing has fallen. The increasing reluctance of the public to answer their doors in the evening has undoubtedly played a part in this. Computer technology, making it easier for parties to link up past canvass returns with the current register, may be making up part of the shortfall, as is telephone canvassing.

In the 1992 election telephone canvassing, much in vogue in the USA, was used on a large scale for the first time in Britain, particularly by the Conservative Party. While economical in time (and in footwear), it is far from certain that it has a uniformly positive impact upon the voters. Some candidates certainly felt that it was counter-productive, being resented by many of those who were telephoned, and others thought it was illegal (during the actual campaign) because of the expense involved. However, it had spread to many constituencies by the time of the 1997 election, and it is now used by all the major parties. Its obvious advantage is the ease of concentrating resources: key marginal constituencies can be targeted from a central telephone call-centre for only the price of a long-distance call. Getting bodies physically together to knock on doors, or push leaflets through letterboxes, is a great deal more labour-intensive, however much the voters might prefer it.

After canvassing the next biggest campaign chore has traditionally been the addressing of envelopes for the candidate's election address. In the last couple of elections, though, the computer has taken over this task in most constituencies, generating printed labels from the electoral register or the party's canvass records, which much reduces the burden involved and also allows well-organised parties to target different versions of the election address to different sections of the electorate. In most constituencies some 50,000–60,000 are required and this used to place a severe strain on the weaker constituency organisations. It was usual to ask each ward or local branch to be responsible for addressing the envelopes for its own area and each active member was given a quota of anything from 50 to 1000 envelopes to address. Elderly and housebound people who were not available for canvassing and other outdoor work were often happy to volunteer to receive a large batch of envelopes; in the future, they may well be redeployed to telephone canvassing.

The election address is the traditional means by which the candidate introduces him- or herself to the electorate. It normally contains a photograph of the candidate, and perhaps also of his or her family, biographical details, a personal message promising to devote him- or herself to the service of the electors should he or she be elected, and a summary of the party's programme. It is usually also designed so that one page consists simply of a colourful advertisement for the candidate's name and party, so that with this folded to face outwards supporters can place it in their windows to proclaim their allegiance. The Royal Mail is obliged at Parliamentary elections[5] to make one free delivery to every elector on behalf of each candidate, and the great majority of candidates take advantage of this to send out their election addresses. Since 1985, candidates have been given the option of using an unaddressed service for the free delivery of their election communication, and many have taken advantage of this, thus obviating the need to address envelopes either by hand or with computer labels; but if they do so they can only send one envelope to each address, rather than one to each elector. At the 2001 election, the Royal Mail handled the delivery of 134 million election mailings.[6]

Serious doubt is often cast on whether the trouble and expenditure devoted by candidates to their election addresses is really worthwhile. With the arrival of computers, and with desktop publishing facilities, which most main party candidates in marginal seats possessed by 1992, there has been less emphasis on election addresses as such and more on the production of specialised leaflets which could be sent to target groups of voters. According to the opinion polls, more electors are reached by this means than by any other *local* form of electioneering. In 1997, 89 per cent, nine in ten, of electors said they had received leaflets through the letterbox a week before polling day, more than three times as many as had been canvassed. But, as Table 8.1 shows, the public reported a sharp fall in the number of leaflets delivered – and other forms of campaigning – in 2001.

Table 8.1   Impact of campaigning (% of voters), 1979–2001

	1979	1983	1987	1992	1997	2001
	(%)	(%)	(%)	(%)	(%)	(%)
Q. During the past few weeks have you...? *(% saying 'yes')*						
...had any political leaflets put through your letterbox?	50	78	80	86	89	69
...seen any party election broadcasts on TV?	78	83	68	71	73	58
...seen any political advertisements on billboards?	35	45	43	55	70	50
...watched the leaders debate on TV?					36	43
...seen any political advertisements in newspapers?						37
...heard any party election broadcasts on the radio?	12	27	18	18	15	16
...been called on by a representative of any political party?	25	29	32	30	24	14
...received a letter signed by a party leader individually addressed to you?			8	13	20	12
...been telephoned by a representative of any political party?					7	5
...helped a political party in its campaign?			5	6	4	3
...visited a political party's website?						2
...used the Internet to access information on candidates or parties?						2
...attended a political meeting addressed by a candidate?		2	2	1	2	1
...received a video through your letterbox from a political party?					27	1
...received an e–mail from a political party?						1

Source: MORI.

An agent who has the assistance of an able and experienced election committee, to which he or she is willing to delegate a great deal of responsibility, should find that, though it will be hard work and for very long hours, the campaign will run fairly smoothly. One who is unable or unwilling to delegate is likely to be prey to constant crises. Ideally, each member of the election committee should be allocated responsibility for one specific field of duties, allowing the agent to be freed for the general oversight of the campaign. There should be a canvassing officer, another in charge of speakers, one responsible for the addressing of envelopes, one for dealing with the press, one in charge of leaflet distribution, one for organising cars for election day and one to organise the postal vote. The agent will probably take on the planning of the candidate's timetable and it is important that a fixed time be set aside each day for consultation between the candidate and the agent.

In the past, perhaps the most significant part of the local campaign was the series of evening election meetings. Although they were rarely attended by more than 200–300 people, except when a party leader was one of the speakers, and in fact the *average* audience was probably not more than a tenth of this, public meetings normally constituted by far the most interesting and colourful events in the candidate's timetable. But nowadays, though meetings still survive in some constituencies, in most they are almost extinct or only continued with for old times' sake. In 2001, only about 1 per cent of the electorate attended election meetings addressed by a candidate (see Table 8.1); such small meetings may indeed be counter-productive, since far from enabling the candidate to put his or her message across to the uncommitted local voters, they merely draw the committed party workers who would be far better employed campaigning for the candidate elsewhere.

Planning the schedule of meetings, in constituencies where they are still held, is especially complicated in county constituencies where the candidate may easily be addressing six village meetings every evening, rounding them off with a larger meeting in one of the towns. Each meeting requires at least one or two supporting speakers, whose main qualification must be the ability to modify drastically the length of their speeches. It inevitably happens that on some evenings the candidate gets seriously held up at earlier meetings and arrives at the final meeting anything up to an hour and a half late. The supporting speaker booked to speak for 20 minutes has consequently to spin out his speech or fill in the time answering questions. On another day the candidate will arrive at the meeting just as the speaker's introductory remarks are completed and before the main body of her speech has even begun, and she must cut herself short to make way for the candidate, with as little delay as possible.

Most agents are well conversant with electoral law and are aware of the things which may or may not be done during an election campaign. A much less detailed store of knowledge is normally possessed by voluntary workers, and care must be taken that through ignorance or misguided enthusiasm they do not transgress the law. If they do, they may lay themselves open, and possibly also the agent and the candidate, to heavy penalties and even to the invalidation of the election should their candidate be elected. A summary of election offences, with the penalties involved, should be prominently displayed in all committee rooms.

In practice, people involved in electioneering in Britain have proved extremely law-abiding, and after each general election there are never more than a handful of prosecutions for election offences. The last time an election was invalidated because of an election offence was at Oxford in 1924. In Northern Ireland respect for the election laws is perhaps rather less strongly ingrained and attempts at personation (voting in the name of some other person) used to be not infrequent. However, the Electoral Fraud (Northern Ireland) Act 2002 introduced more stringent rules for identifying voters in Northern Ireland than apply elsewhere, and this may stamp out the problem.

Especially in marginal constituencies, agents make daily reports to their regional organisers, who are also likely to make at least one personal visit. The regional officers of all the main parties do their best to organise the transfer of workers from safe and hopeless into marginal constituencies so that the maximum effort can be mounted where it will have the greatest effect. This process, indeed, may have started long before the campaign: in the 1997 election, Labour's targeted campaign in 90 key marginal seats had been operating for nearly two years, with face-to-face and telephone canvassing, individual letters to voters and videos delivered to first-time voters. Potential 'switchers' were identified, and the candidates were expected to contact at least 1000 of them.

As polling day draws near, the tempo of the campaign appreciably quickens. More helpers turn up every day at the committee rooms, and enthusiasm and confidence mount. Almost all voluntary election workers and most professional ones become infected with over-optimism towards the end of the campaign, unless their own party is very obviously doing badly. It is normal to overestimate the chances both of one's candidate in the constituency and of one's party throughout the country. It would indeed be strange if it were otherwise, for so much is seen of the results of one's own campaigning and so little of the other side's that it is all but impossible to form an objective view.

A week before polling day most agents make a rapid assessment of the progress already made in canvassing and other important activities and revise their plans accordingly. Targets may be raised or lowered, or forces concentrated to recall at houses where the voters were out or 'doubtful' on the first occasion that they were canvassed. All election workers are likely to be impressed at this stage by how much remains to be done and how little time is left in which to do it.

Meanwhile, the agent's attention will be more and more concentrated on preparations for polling day. The transporting of elderly and disabled voters to the polls (and of many others who are unlikely themselves to summon up enough energy to get themselves there unaided) can add several hundred votes to a candidate's poll. Every effort is therefore made to secure the services of the maximum number of cars and drivers on election day and, especially, in the evening. It is illegal to hire transport for this purpose and party members with cars are strongly encouraged to volunteer their services. As well as compiling a roster of cars and drivers for election day, the agent will endeavour to persuade as many helpers as possible to take the day off work, so that a full-scale operation can be mounted to 'get out the vote'.

The Returning Officer also has to make arrangements to secure the services of a large number of assistants on election day. Some of them will be polling clerks, whose duty will consist of presiding over polling stations. Others will have the job of counting the votes. Unlike the parties' election workers, the Returning Officer's staff will be paid for their services. The greater number of them will be local government employees, transferred for the day from other work. They will be supplemented by others engaged specially for the day. Schoolteachers are a favourite source of labour for polling clerks, as many schools have a holiday on election day because their premises are used as polling stations. Bank clerks, for obvious reasons, are much in demand to assist in counting the votes.

Even before polling day, however, the Returning Officer has other preparations to make. Soon after the nominations are closed he or she will send out to each elector an official poll card.[7] This will notify the voters of their electoral numbers and tell them how, where and when to vote. In the presence of the candidates, or more likely their representatives, the Returning Officer will also send out ballot papers to registered postal voters. The introduction of 'postal voting on demand' in 2001 almost doubled the number of postal votes requested, and 1.75 million postal ballot papers were issued, or an average of 2668 per constituency. Each postal voter is sent, by post, four items:

- An ordinary ballot paper, duly marked or stamped.
- A form of declaration of identity.
- A small envelope for the ballot paper.
- A larger addressed return envelope.

·The postal voter must sign the declaration of identity, and have the signature attested by one witness. He or she marks an X against a candidate, seals the ballot paper in the small envelope and returns it, together with the declaration of identity, in the larger envelope. The vote can be sent back to the Returning Officer at any time after it has been recorded, but it must arrive not later than 10 p.m. on polling day. On their receipt at the office of the Returning Officer the postal votes are dropped into a special ballot box.

There were substantial dividends to be had by whichever party which was most efficient in organising its supporters to apply for postal votes, even in the past, when their availability was restricted. There is no doubt that the Conservatives used to be much more successful in registering postal voters than their opponents, and probably as a result gained between 5 and 15 extra seats at each election between 1950 and 1987 – a small number, but in closely contested elections, such as 1950, 1964 and October 1974, it may well have made the difference between a precarious and a reasonably comfortable overall majority for the Labour Party.

It was natural that the Conservatives should gain some advantage from the postal vote. Middle-class voters generally are more aware of their civic rights and more ready to claim them than are manual workers and their families. But the decisive edge which the Conservatives achieved, which used to ensure them more than 75 per cent of the postal votes in most constituencies, was a direct result of their more professional organisation. Labour greatly stepped up its efforts in marginal constituencies in the 1987 and 1992 elections, and may now have succeeded in closing the gap. This was almost certainly the case in 1992, when polling day fell during the university vacation, and much effort was put into persuading the predominantly-Labour student vote to vote by post at their term-time addresses; this probably saved several marginal seats for the party.

But the stakes are higher now. In 2001, the first general election where postal votes were universally available, 5.2 per cent of the votes counted were cast by post, more than double the proportion at previous general elections. The figure might easily rise further as the change in the law becomes more widely known, and it offers substantial dividends to any party well enough organised to use it to their advantage. Turnout levels among those who are sent postal votes are considerably higher than among those who must vote in person. Presumably this is because many electors who would not get round to voting in person are prepared to do so if they are sent a ballot paper by post and simply have to return it. This implies that a party which can persuade its supporters to apply for postal votes will see more of them vote than would otherwise be the case.

Since the application for a permanent postal vote need only be made once, and the party may hope to see it bear fruit at election after election, the efficiency of this type of effort over the traditional foot-slogging 'knocking-up' of voters at every poll is obvious. Furthermore, the effort need not be concentrated in the few weeks before a general election: the voters may forget about an election if they are canvassed months or years in advance, but the Returning Officer will not forget to send them the ballot papers. Of course, a wise party will still carry on contacting its supporters – neglected voters can quickly become resentful voters – but assuming the regulations remain as they are today it seems probable that we shall see a change in the way parties campaign, to exploit the potent possibilities of the postal vote. Indeed, there have already been some parts of the country where postal vote applications have jumped spectacularly in certain wards, almost certainly because of organisation on behalf of a particular party or candidate.

Of course, since postal voters have to post back their ballot papers in advance to make sure they arrive in time, they will already have voted before the campaign reaches its climax. Indeed, a high proportion tend to fill out the forms and return them as soon as they can after they receive them, perhaps missing a week or more of the parties' final efforts. As the number of postal votes increases, the parties will have to take this into account more, perhaps altering their campaigning strategy to allow for it.

The same considerations apply, of course, on an even greater scale when everybody votes by post. As an experiment, in a number of local elections in recent years, and in four English regions in the 2004 European Parliament elections, voters were only allowed to vote by post, ballot papers being sent out to all electors in advance with no option to vote in person at a polling station on the day. These pilot schemes have proved controversial. The aim is to increase turnout, and this has generally been achieved. However, critics have complained that, quite apart from curtailing the effective campaign, the innovation has eroded the secrecy of the ballot, and may also have made such abuses as personation and intimidation or bribery easier.[8] Some related campaigning developments, relating both to all-postal ballots and to conventional postal voting under normal rules, have also caused disquiet, notably the involvement of party representatives in collecting postal votes from voters (which the Electoral Commission has asked them to refrain from but which it has no power to ban) and the provision during the campaign by Returning Officers to parties of 'marked-up' lists of postal voters, showing which have already returned their ballot papers and which have still to do so.

Furthermore, the 2004 pilots were marred by administrative errors (not all ballot papers were printed and sent out on time, while in other cases electors reportedly received more than one ballot paper).[9] In its report on the elections, published in August 2004, the Electoral Commission (which had advised against conducting the pilot on so large a scale) recanted its earlier support for the all-postal method, and recommended unequivocally that 'all-postal voting should not be pursued for use at UK statutory elections'.[10] However, the government has subsequently indicated that it may not accept the recommendation.

9
The National Campaign

Seventy or eighty years ago election campaigns were conducted almost exclusively at a constituency level. Apart from organising speaking tours by the party leaders and other prominent personalities, the party headquarters played little direct part in the campaign. The newspapers were full of election news, but they were read only by a minority, and a far greater readership was claimed by regional and local papers than is the case today.

The irruption of mass readership national newspapers and, even more, the development of radio and television has changed all that. A general election was formerly a series of local contests to choose Members of Parliament, with the incidental effect of determining the political complexion of the next government. Now it is in effect a nationwide contest to choose a government and especially a Prime Minister, and it is fought mainly in the pages of the national newspapers and on the screens of the nation's televisions. The fact that 659 individuals are in the same process elected to represent 659 different constituencies in Parliament has become a subordinate feature.

Unlike the majority of constituency parties, which are overwhelmingly dependent on voluntary labour, the party headquarters, staffed by full-time professionals, are not likely to be caught seriously unprepared by the announcement of a general election, even if it has come unexpectedly. Much of the work on which their employees have been engaged for several years past has been designed with this very moment in mind.

In some recent elections, particularly when they have come fairly late in a Parliamentary term, the party machines (particularly the Conservatives') have concentrated on pre-electoral propaganda which has been launched well in advance of the date of the election. These have largely taken the form of colourful posters displayed on hoardings throughout the country, but particularly in marginal seats, and of advertisements in the newspapers (political advertising on television and radio being illegal). Private business interests, allied to the Conservatives, have sometimes spent even larger sums on similar campaigns. In 1983, for the first time, there was also substantial spending by interest and pressure groups on the Labour side, such as the Greater London Council (which was facing abolition under the Tories), public sector unions and animal welfare bodies. Paradoxically, the beginning of a campaign is now sometimes the cue for covering up or taking down political posters, which otherwise might be liable to be charged as election expenditure.

When the dissolution is announced the party headquarters are well prepared to produce speakers' handbooks or briefing notes outlining the party policy on a wide range of issues and documenting the failings of the opposing parties, which are quickly despatched to all Parliamentary candidates and others who are to speak on behalf of the party. These are supplemented by daily briefings on specific issues which arise during the course of the campaign, sent out to the constituencies by fax or e-mail, often within a couple of hours of the speech or press conference that prompted them. A great mass of posters, leaflets, policy statements and other propaganda material is also produced for distribution through the constituency party organisations. Some of the money subscribed to the national election funds of the parties is also disbursed to constituency parties at this stage, to ensure that even the poorest of these have some ready cash with which to finance their campaign. The Liberal Democrats have been less able to extend such monetary help to their constituency branches.

It is usual for the party leadership to depute two or three senior figures to remain in London to oversee the running of the party headquarters and to act as a campaign committee, co-ordinating the day-to-day running of the campaign and particularly to take charge of dealings with the media. It is normal to select MPs representing safe seats for this important assignment, as those with marginal constituencies could hardly be expected to leave them for the greater part of the campaign. (In 1992, the Conservatives ignored this prudent rule, leaving the organisation of the national campaign to the party chairman, Chris Patten. He successfully presided over a rather unexpected triumph for his party, but narrowly lost his own seat at Bath to the Liberal Democrats, ending his Parliamentary career.) For the same reason, leading peers are often included in the campaign committees.

Within a few days of the announcement of the dissolution, each party publishes its election manifesto. This is a statement of the issues which the party considers of the greatest importance and an indication, in more or less precise terms, of the party's policies to meet them. The Labour Party, which is strongly wedded to the idea that a party winning an election receives a mandate from the people to carry out definite policies, is normally more specific in its proposals. There is often a great deal of manoeuvring within the Labour Party's National Executive Committee and its 'Shadow Cabinet' about what items to include, which usually takes the form of a left–right struggle.

The manifestos, which can run up to 20,000 words, are given the widest possible distribution, the print orders running into millions. In addition to the large-scale distribution through constituency parties, they form the basis of the policy sections in candidates' election addresses and they are widely reported in the press and on radio and television.

Despite the prominence which they are accorded, the election manifestos are seldom notable for breaking new ground. Nearly all the major proposals will have already been published as official party policy and the function of the manifestos is to bring them together in a sharp and challenging manner and perhaps to add a few minor twists to give them an air of originality. A rare exception was Labour's offering in 1983, *The New Hope for Britain*, immediately seized on by its Tory opponents, who bought 3000 copies to use in support of Mrs Thatcher's contention that it was 'the most extreme manifesto that has ever yet been put before the British electorate'; one of Labour's senior figures, Gerald Kaufman, afterwards referred to it as 'the longest suicide note in history'. But it is rare for the manifestos to have a fraction of this impact.

The manifestos will be reported and analysed in the press and media, but the only written material the vast majority of voters will receive from the parties are the leaflets from each candidate in their constituency. Until very recently, lacking the flexibility that modern desktop publishing now allows, almost all candidates devoted their energy to a single election address. This was usually prepared before the campaign and covering all the issues expected to arise, but naturally tending to emphasise positive features rather than risk mention of issues where the party was seen to be on the defensive. With candidates increasingly abandoning the single election address for a number of differentiated leaflets, suitable for targeting at particular groups of voters, it is becoming steadily less likely that voters will receive from the parties a comprehensive statement of their policy on all the issues that may arise, and the media's role as messenger thus becomes more important still.

The issues which are discussed during election campaigns obviously differ to some extent on each occasion, but certain subjects, such as the economy, public services, education and crime, are almost certain to be raised at some stage of every election. Some issues may arise spontaneously during the campaign, but all parties attempt to divert attention to those issues where they perceive themselves to be strongest or their opponents most vulnerable, and these tactics will normally be planned in some detail. Nevertheless all will probably not go entirely as the parties expect; the focus of the campaign is unlikely to rest for long on questions where none of the parties find themselves actively gaining ground or their opponents discomfited. Thus in 1983, against most expectations, unemployment, despite running at a post-war record level of over 3 million, did not excite much interest. By contrast, defence, and particularly the divergent views of leading Labour figures, emerged as a major issue. There seems to have been an increasing tendency in recent elections that a relatively small number of issues emerge, with each of the major parties trying to force their opponents onto the defensive.

The major political exchanges during elections now take place on the television screen. The 1959 election was the first of which this was really true, as in previous elections only a minority of voters had access to a television set. But the trend had become increasingly apparent ever since the first television election broadcasts, watched by less than 10 per cent of the electorate, were screened in 1951. By 1959, 75 per cent of households possessed television sets, and by 1987 this figure had risen to 99 per cent.

Television election broadcasts are of two kinds: those for which parties are responsible, and news and other broadcasts undertaken by the BBC and the various commercial companies. The party broadcasts – for which the broadcasting authorities make time available without financial charge – have been transmitted at each election since 1951, but those for which the broadcasting companies were responsible date from the 1959 general election (before which even news bulletins avoided reporting the election campaign because it was thought that it might be illegal to do so!).

Party political broadcasts in this form are a distinctively British phenomenon. The individual broadcasters have responsibility for allocation of time for these broadcasts, though they generally reach agreement among themselves on a common formula after consultation with the parties and are now also required to have regard to any views expressed by the Electoral Commission.[1] The criterion for the apportionment of time has normally been the number of candidates in the field at the forthcoming election, though with some consideration of the number of votes achieved last time. In recent elections, the Conservatives and Labour have each normally been allocated five broadcasts and the Liberal Democrats four, though the SDP-Liberal Alliance was accorded parity with the other two in 1987. In addition the Scottish National Party and Plaid Cymru are allocated broadcasts, transmitted only in their own countries, and shorter broadcasts are offered to other parties putting up a substantial number of candidates. (In 1997, the threshold was 50 candidates and as many as eight minor parties qualified in Great Britain; it has now been raised to one-sixth of the seats, with parties contesting that proportion of Scottish or Welsh seats gaining broadcasts in those countries only. The Northern Ireland parties come under similar arrangements in Ulster.)

The parties are by no means necessarily satisfied with their share of airtime, and occasionally make attempts to remedy this, but the courts have been reluctant to interfere. In 1987 the SNP sued in an attempt to secure more airtime for themselves in Scotland, but were unsuccessful, as was Sir James Goldsmith's Referendum Party in 1997 when the broadcasters allocated them only a single broadcast despite their running 550 candidates.

The BBC and the ITV companies watch points of broadcasting or legal policy, and have the power to censor or ban altogether broadcasts they believe infringe the proprieties – an appeal for monetary contributions would be disallowed, for example, as well as any libellous content. In 1997, they insisted on changes in a broadcast by the anti-abortion Pro-Life Alliance, on grounds of taste, and also demanded cuts in the British National Party broadcast, which eventually was not shown at all on Channel 4; in 2001 the BNP complained to the Electoral Commission that the BBC had denied them access to broadcasts (and had also treated them unfairly by failing to provide a link to their website from the BBC election website, which it had done in the case of the major parties). Otherwise, in all political respects the content is the sole responsibility of the party concerned.

The programmes were relayed simultaneously on all the television channels up to and including the 1979 election. Since 1983 they have been staggered, which means that inveterate TV-watchers can avoid them altogether by switching channels throughout the evening. Nevertheless, by the final week of the 2001 campaign, no fewer than 58 per cent of the voters said that they had seen at least one party broadcast. Only leaflets delivered through the letterbox reach more electors, and almost certainly have far less impact (see Table 8.1).

When they began in the 1950s, the broadcasts could last anything up to half an hour, but this was quickly reduced to ten minutes and in recent years five minutes has been the allotment – in fact the parties often choose to make the broadcasts shorter.

The use which the parties have made of their television programmes has varied considerably, and none of them has stuck to a consistent style throughout the general elections in which television broadcasts have taken place. A wide variety of techniques has been adopted – live talks delivered straight into the camera by party leaders, filmed interviews (sometimes conducted by hostile journalists, sometimes by friendly MPs), interviews with voters in the street, specially shot film sequences, newsreel material and a great many charts, graphs and animated cartoons. By 1959 all parties appeared to have come round to the view that the party leader, whose significance to the electorate as an actual or potential Prime Minister could scarcely be exaggerated, must have the lion's share of the available time, and in all elections during the next 20 years the final broadcast of each party was reserved for a direct appeal to the voters by the leader. Since 1983, however, all the parties have occasionally felt the need to dilute their leaders' impact by including other material. In both 1997 and 2001, Labour's final broadcast was aimed at reminding their supporters to turn out, rather than winning over any waverers, with broadcasts concentrating on Tony Blair shown earlier in the campaign.

Party election broadcasts have attracted much scorn from professional broadcasters. Over the years perhaps only a few stand out in the memory as either effective or significant in the course of the election. The first was in 1987, when one Labour broadcast significantly broke with the tradition of mediocrity: a personal adulation of the party leader Neil Kinnock, thoroughly professionally produced, it was written by Colin Welland and directed by Hugh Hudson (who had collaborated on the hugely successful film *Chariots of Fire*). It immediately became one of the main talking points of the next few days, and was in many ways the outstanding incident in an otherwise rather dull election campaign. Professor Martin Harrison, who has monitored election broadcasts for the Nuffield election studies over many years,[2] called it 'a stunning invocation of the Labourism of the 1940s by the media techniques of the 1980s'.

In 1992 the Conservatives responded with a programme entitled *The Journey*, which traced John Major's progress from a Brixton boyhood to Number 10 Downing Street. Yet the broadcast in 1992 which had the most impact was again a Labour Party programme, devoted to the National Health Service. This traced the experiences of two little girls each awaiting an ear operation, one of whom was immediately treated using private medicine while the other had her NHS operation repeatedly delayed. The broadcast led to heated controversy over several days, the incident becoming known as the 'War of Jennifer's Ear', after the name of one of the children was inadvertently revealed by a Labour spokeswoman. This event, which hijacked the election campaign for the best part of a week, leading to mutual accusations of dirty tricks by Labour and Tory, probably damaged Labour by diverting attention from the substance of its case about the NHS, which should have been an important plus for them. Although the programme itself was expertly produced, and its immediate impact was striking, it was widely seen to have ultimately been an 'own goal'. A Labour broadcast also backfired in 2001, though less dramatically so: a cameo appearance by the former Spice Girl, Geri Halliwell, succeeded in generating press coverage and higher viewing figures for the broadcast, but caused subsequent embarrassment with the revelation that she would be unable to support Labour at the polls as she was not registered to vote.

The election programmes staged by the BBC and the commercial television companies were long hindered by serious doubts as to the legal standing of such broadcasts. The Representation of the People Act of 1949 had laid down that any operation 'presenting the candidate or his views' should be chargeable to election expenses. Newspapers were specifically excluded from this provision, but no mention was made of radio or television. However, the broadcasters eventually took their courage in their hands, and at the Rochdale by-election in 1958 the Granada network screened a programme in which all three candidates appeared. By 1959, fortified by legal advice, both television services had resolved to take the plunge and to embark on their own election programmes. The absence of accusations of partisanship and the high viewing figures obtained by political programmes in the 1959 election encouraged the television authorities to be much bolder in their coverage of subsequent elections.

A judgment by the Electoral Court following the 1964 general election resulted in a further lessening of their inhibitions. The Communist Party had nominated a candidate in Kinross and West Perthshire, the constituency represented by the then Prime Minister, Sir Alec Douglas-Home. Their avowed object in doing so was to claim equal broadcasting time for their nominee. The Communist claim for time was rejected, and after the election their candidate petitioned the court to declare Sir Alec's election void, alleging that expenditure on party broadcasts by the BBC and ITA was improperly incurred 'with a view to promoting the election of a candidate'. The court held that though Sir Alec may incidentally have gained some personal electoral advantage from the broadcasts, the 'dominant motive' of the BBC and ITA was 'to give information to the public and not to promote the election of the respondents'. It therefore refused the Communists' petition.

Since this judgment, the broadcasting authorities have felt free to continue to present programmes in which candidates appear as spokesmen for their parties, so long as no reference is made to the campaign in their own constituencies. But in programmes specifically concerned with constituency campaigns, including those during Parliamentary by-elections, the rule was long scrupulously adhered to that no candidate might appear unless all his or her opponents were included in the same programme. However, the restrictions were eased in 1983 and further loosened in 2000, and it is now much harder for candidates to obstruct their opponents' access to media coverage by refusing to appear themselves. The coming of regional television and of local radio has meant that participation is by no means restricted to national personalities. Hundreds, perhaps thousands, of candidates are assured of their minute, if not their hour, of glory on the airwaves.

Nowadays, not only is the election given blanket coverage in all news programmes, but there is a plethora of programmes put on by the broadcasting authorities, sometimes with a phone-in facility for the general public or a studio audience of voters, in which politicians of all parties take part. Nevertheless, in these programmes, as in the news bulletins, the broadcasters endeavour not only to be fair, but to ensure that the overall coverage conforms to the same approximate overall ratio of time which governs the party political broadcasts. (The much-derided process nicknamed 'stopwatch timing', however, by which the ratios were applied rigidly to each individual news bulletin, has been quietly dropped.)

But it is the television news programmes which have had the greatest effect on electioneering. They have led to a major change in the way that party leaders now run their campaigns. Traditionally they set off on long tours throughout the country, taking in up to a dozen 'whistle stops' per day, and aiming to cover a high proportion of at least the medium-sized towns, as well as all the major cities during the three weeks of campaigning. Now the centrepiece of each party leader's day is a televised press conference, held at the party headquarters in London. Only after that is completed will the leader venture out into the 'provinces' for a sortie which will possibly involve only one major meeting and bring him or her back to London the same evening.

Much of the remainder of the day is likely to be devoted to creating 'photo-opportunities' – incidents carefully stage-managed to provide suitable footage for the evening bulletins – and any speeches of importance will be carefully manufactured to ensure they contain 'soundbites' – moments that can be suitably excerpted to illustrate a brief news item.

Michael Foot, Labour leader in 1983, was the last who tried gamely to combine this schedule with traditional visits to a large number of constituencies, visiting 70 marginal seats during the campaign. This may have put heart into his campaign workers in the constituencies, but did not make for effective exposure on the TV screen. His opponent Margaret Thatcher made only six major speeches, and otherwise restricted her appearances to stage-managed occasions guaranteed to produce positive television coverage. It may seem a pity, but this latter strategy is far the more effective in a modern election.

At the last couple of elections, the pace has been raised still further by the advent of 24-hour rolling television news coverage. This creates a temptation of trying to continuously generate new stories to maintain momentum and avoid any risk of the viewers becoming bored or letting their attention flag. But such a strategy carries attendant risks, of course – quite apart from the danger that a constant stream of election news stories monopolising the bulletins will cause exactly the boredom it is meant to avert, too rapid a succession of topics may mean that the stories the parties really want to get across may miss getting the attention they deserve. Labour saw the perils of this in 2001, when they sent their leaders out to campaign on the same day they launched their manifesto: first the Prime Minister, Tony Blair, was accosted outside a hospital by an irate voter; then the Deputy Prime Minister, John Prescott, punched a protester who had thrown an egg at him. Both incidents were caught by the cameras and played repeatedly on the news bulletins; the manifesto launch sank without a trace. Probably the moral is that, even with 24-hour news, none but a tiny minority of 'news junkies' will watch more than one or two news bulletins in a day; the vast majority still rely on the early or late evening news from BBC1 or ITV1.

At no British general election so far has there been a direct confrontation between the party leaders on the lines of the candidates' debates which are invariably a feature of American elections, most famously the Kennedy–Nixon debates of 1960. Normally the Leader of the Opposition has been keen, but the Prime Minister of the day, unwilling to cede a position of equality, has shied away. The only exception was in 1979 when Prime Minister James Callaghan was willing to appear, but Margaret Thatcher (who was advised that her relative inexperience might be shown up), already virtually assured of victory, declined to take part. As Prime Minister, she was no more anxious to appear, declining to debate with Michael Foot in 1983 or with Neil Kinnock in 1987, as did John Major in 1992. In 1997 all the leaders seemed initially favourable, but were unable to agree a mutually acceptable format with the broadcasters; in the end there were, once again, no debates, and each party blamed the others. In 2001, the possibility was not even seriously contemplated.

There is much evidence that television has enabled voters in general elections to be better informed on the issues and to be more familiar with the personalities of leading politicians than ever before. It has often been observed that television has enabled a modern political leader to speak to more people in one evening than the total number that Gladstone or Disraeli succeeded in addressing at all the meetings during their entire careers. Television has also had its effects on other aspects of electioneering. The reporting of speeches in news bulletins enables rival political leaders to reply to each others' charges several times during the course of a day and thus the whole tempo of campaigning has been speeded up. Television has greatly increased the exposure of partisans to the propaganda of the other side and this has led to greater sophistication in the propaganda of all parties.

Radio and television programmes are widely and justifiably regarded as impartial, and are thus used as a yardstick against which newspaper reports may be measured; these, by contrast, are under no obligation to be impartial and often, especially in the case of the tabloid press, make no attempt to be. In the 1970s, it was felt that press partisanship had somewhat reduced, perhaps because editors felt discredited by the contrast with the neutral broadcasters. Expert observers felt, however, that there had been a marked increase in press partisanship in the 1983 campaign and, after a lull in 1987, in 1992 the tabloid papers, in particular, were more stridently partisan than for many years past; but the tone has been more muted at the last two elections, perhaps in deference to their readers' own impatience with politics in general and partisan politics in particular.[3]

Up to 1992, the bulk of the press in modern elections had always been on the side of the Conservative Party (see Table 9.1). Of the national daily newspapers, only the *Guardian* and the *Daily Mirror* backed Labour throughout the 1992 campaign, though the *Financial Times* also gave it reluctant backing in its final edition, while the *Independent* remained aloof and endorsed no party. On Sundays Labour had the support of the *Sunday Mirror* and the *People*, as well as the *Observer*, but the Conservatives could rely on the *Sunday Times*, the *Sunday Telegraph*, *Mail on Sunday*, *Sunday Express* and *News of the World*.

This had been the general pattern for several elections. In 1997, however, the picture was transformed, with the highest circulation daily, the *Sun*, and highest circulation Sunday, the *News of the World*, switching support to Labour, as did the *Daily Star* and the *Independent*.

The Times refused to endorse any party, advising its readers to vote for Euro-sceptic candidates, whatever their persuasion. For the first time since 1974, circulation of Labour-supporting papers was higher than that of those supporting the Tories. The same pattern of loyalties was broadly repeated in 2001 (see Table 9.2).

Table 9.1   Total readership of Conservative and Labour daily newspapers, 1964–2001

	1964	1966	1970	1974 Feb	1974 Oct	1979	1983	1987	1992	1997	2001
Per cent of adult population reading ...											
Conservative paper	60	61	54	71	31	66	75	64	50	24	18
Labour paper	49	51	52	32	32	29	24	23	22	50	50
Per cent of working-class population reading ...											
Conservative paper	–	53	44	64	23	64	74	72	48	13	11
Labour paper	–	59	61	38	39	34	30	30	24	51	58

Notes: Figures obtained by dividing Newspaper Readership Survey figures given in the Nuffield election series into the adult (15+) British population.
'Working class' is social grades C2, D and E.
Some people read more than one paper. Those who read two papers supporting the same party are counted twice, inflating the figures slightly. Newspaper partisanship is defined by its preferred election outcome.

Source: Updated and adapted from a table in David Butler and Dennis Kavanagh, *The British General Election of 1983* (London: Macmillan, 1984), p. 217.

Table 9.2   Daily newspaper partisanship in 2001 (circulations in thousands)

Conservative		*Labour*		*Neutral*	
Daily Mail	2,337	*Daily Express*	929	Independent*	197
Daily Telegraph	989	*Daily Mirror*	2,056		
		Daily Star	585		
		Financial Times	176		
		Guardian	362		
		The Times	667		
		Sun	3,288		
Total	3,326		8,063		197

* Preferred Labour victory but with increased Liberal Democrat strength to restrain the government.

Source: Compiled from figures reported in David Butler and Dennis Kavanagh, *The British General Election of 2001* (Basingstoke: Palgrave, 2002), pp. 158–9.

It is difficult to predict what may happen in the future. The national press is concentrated in the hands of a small number of proprietors, and if they change their party predilections, so may their papers. (The support of the *Sun* and the *News of the World* for Labour in 1997 was attributed by many to the sympathies of their owner, Rupert Murdoch, though his broadsheets, *The Times* and *Sunday Times*, did not follow suit.) Although the failures of several recently-introduced newspapers to become established suggest there is not much room in the market for new titles, the lower costs of modern newspaper production methods seem certain to encourage further attempts and, at the very least, to maintain the increasingly competitive climate in this field; significant changes in circulation figures are possible, and editorial attitudes may well have to alter in some cases to maintain an established title's market share. Neither party can rest assured of commanding a majority share of readership in the future.

The partisanship even of the most biased newspapers may be slightly diluted by the full-page advertisements placed by the parties or other campaigning groups – in 1987 there were over 300 pages of such advertisements, most during the final days before the election, but in 1997 it fell to under 100 pages, and in 2001 to only 30 (of which three-fifths were by trade unions or other pressure groups rather than the parties themselves). Most of the papers will accept these from any of the political parties (although in 1987 the proprietor of the *Daily Mirror*, Robert Maxwell, refused to let it carry any of the Conservatives' last week's flurry of publicity, and both the *Daily Express* and the *Sun* rejected a Labour advertisement on election day which they claimed was misleading). In most recent campaigns the Conservatives spent considerably more on this form of publicity than the other parties, reinforcing their overall advantage in the press. The gap narrowed in 1992, but in 1997 the Conservatives spent three times as much on press advertising as Labour; in 2001, by contrast, the Tories took out no national press advertisements at all, preferring to spend their budget in other ways.

The various morning, daily and evening papers published outside London are much more uniformly pro-Conservative than is the national press (with the important exception of the Scottish daily and Sunday press, which unlike other regional titles easily outsell the London papers north of the border). But, dependent as they are on sales to people of all political views within the area in which they are published, they tend to be less partisan in style. The majority of them give reasonably full coverage during and between elections to the activities and viewpoints of the anti-Conservative parties.

The influence that the press has on voters is difficult to measure, but it is clearly limited or the Conservative Party would win almost every election, as would right-wing parties in virtually every other democratic country, as in nearly all of them the press is predominantly on the side of the right. Nevertheless, it is hard to believe that the Conservatives do not draw a distinct benefit from the partisanship of the press, even though it is at least partially diluted by the potent influence of television and radio which, in Britain at least, are required by law to be neutral. Opinions are divided as to whether the pro-Tory tabloids, more partisan than ever in 1992, actually swung a closely contested election to John Major. 'It's the *Sun* wot won it', claimed a front-page headline in the paper shortly after the election, and Labour leader Neil Kinnock also expressed the view that the tabloids had deprived him of the premiership. The evidence is inconclusive, though there is a distinct possibility that the claim of the *Sun* may be justified.[4] Analysis in the 1997 election by the advertising research agency Test Research, sponsored by the PR group Shandwick, found a clear correlation between voting intention changes of the different social classes and the different balance of positive and negative coverage of the leaders and policies to which they were exposed given their different newspaper readership patterns.

The final press conferences are given on the eve of the poll and, as the campaign draws to a close, the party leaders finally set off for their own constituencies with a sense of profound relief. The extreme exertions of the preceding weeks are over, and there is now no more that they can do to influence the result. Their absence from their constituencies during the greater part of the campaign is unlikely to have caused any undue concern, for party leaders normally represent safe seats. During the last one or two days before the votes are cast they occupy themselves in much the same way as other candidates, but with the knowledge that they will soon be set apart from them, either to taste the power and responsibility of the premiership or to assume the scarcely less onerous, but infinitely less rewarding, responsibility of leading their parties on the Opposition benches of the House of Commons.

10
Polling Day

When polling day finally arrives the limelight which has shone throughout the preceding weeks on the party leaders and the national campaigns of the parties swings decisively back to the constituencies. In a general election, the morning papers carry final appeals to vote for one or other of the parties, but otherwise an uneasy quiet descends upon the national scene. The final shots have been fired on radio and television, the party headquarters have done their best or their worst, all now depends on the voter. In by-elections, local elections and European elections, the procedure is much the same, though the media coverage will usually be less comprehensive, and fewer electors will turn out to vote.

Polling day is a very long one for those most intimately concerned. The earliest risers are the Presiding Officers and poll clerks of the various polling stations. They have to be at their posts by 6.30 a.m., or thereabouts, in order to be ready to receive the first voters at 7 a.m. (In local elections the hours of polling are shorter – from 8 a.m. to 9 p.m., although when a local election is held on the same day as a general election, as in 2001, or a European election as in 2004, the longer voting hours apply to both.)

Each polling station is in the charge of a Presiding Officer, who has a number of poll clerks to help him. Many polling stations are housed in schools, but a wide variety of other premises are used in some constituencies. If no suitable building is available, a temporary prefabricated building may be erected for the occasion. Local authorities are required by law 'as far as is reasonable and practicable to designate as polling places only places which are accessible to disabled electors'. On arrival at the polling station the Presiding Officer has to satisfy him- or herself that all the necessary equipment has been installed.

Inside the polling station will be a row of voting compartments, shaped like telephone kiosks, but with a sliding curtain covering the entrance to ensure privacy. Within the compartment will be a shelf, at waist height, on which voters can mark their ballot papers. A strong indelible pencil is attached by string to the shelf. A notice giving instructions on how to vote is pinned up in each voting compartment, and is also displayed outside the polling station.

Opposite the voting compartments is a table or tables behind which the Presiding Officer and his or her assistants sit. In between, in full view of the Presiding Officer, stand one or more ballot boxes. The Presiding Officer will have been supplied with a copy of the election register for the polling district, a list of proxy and postal voters, an adequate supply of ballot papers and equipment for marking the ballot papers with the official mark. The ballot papers are printed in books, with counterfoils, rather like cloakroom tickets. Serial numbers are printed on the back of each paper and each counterfoil.

The Presiding Officer is in sole charge of the polling station. He or she and any assistants have to swear a declaration of secrecy that they will not divulge, except for some purpose authorised by law, any information as to who has or has not voted or reveal to anyone before the close of the poll the nature of the official mark. A similar declaration has to be made by the candidate and his or her agent or representatives before they may be admitted to a polling station for any purpose except to cast their own votes. It is the responsibility of the Presiding Officer to see that no unauthorised person is admitted to the polling station, that order is maintained and that the poll is conducted lawfully in every respect. At least one police constable will be on duty throughout the day at each polling station to assist the Presiding Officer to keep order.

To the surprise of many foreign onlookers, there are no provisions to allow observers, neutral or otherwise, to attend polling stations throughout the day and assure themselves that all is above board; they are not permitted. The reason though is simply that there has never been any call for them – even the more extreme or anti-establishment candidates have never seriously questioned the probity or competence of those who run British polling stations. Nevertheless, it is probable that – on the Electoral Commission's recommendation – Britain will soon fall into line with international practice, and allow observers at polling stations.

Immediately before the poll opens at 7 a.m., the Presiding Officer must show the ballot box empty to whoever is in the polling station and then lock it and place a seal on the lock. When the first voter arrives he or she will give his or her full name and address to the polling clerk; in Northern Ireland, though not in England, Scotland or Wales, photo identification[1] will also be required. The polling clerk will tell the voter his or her number, put a tick against his or her name on the register, write his or her electoral number on the counterfoil of the ballot paper, perforate the ballot paper with the official mark and hand the ballot paper to the voter. The purpose of the official mark, the nature of which is kept secret, is to prevent the forgery of ballot papers. Poll clerks must take great care to remember to perforate each paper as it is issued, or the vote will later be invalidated through no fault of the voter.[2] It is improper to perforate ballot papers in advance, because of the risk of theft.

The voter takes the ballot paper into one of the voting compartments and marks an X against the candidate of his or her choice. All that the ballot papers contain are the surnames of the candidates, in alphabetical order, and their full names and addresses and 'descriptions', which normally refers to their party allegiance and, since 1998, may also include their party emblem.

When the voter has marked the ballot paper he or she must fold it, and in the view of the Presiding Officer, drop it into the ballot box. By this elaborate procedure the secrecy of the ballot is at once protected and the possibility of forged papers being introduced into the ballot box virtually eliminated.

If a ballot paper is spoiled, the voter may obtain another one on application to the Presiding Officer, who will mark the spoiled paper 'cancelled' and put it on one side until the end of the day, when he or she has to account to the Returning Officer for all the ballot papers issued.

Blind or incapacitated voters may ask the Presiding Officer to mark their ballot papers for them, or may bring a friend with them who will be permitted to mark their ballot papers for them; alternatively they can now ask for a template, numbered in Braille, that fits over the ballot paper and enables them to cast their own vote in secret. If the election is on a Saturday, which does not normally happen in the case of Parliamentary elections though many local government elections were formerly held on that day, Jewish voters who object on religious grounds to voting in the prescribed manner may also request the Presiding Officer to mark their ballot papers for them.

By the time the first voters have cast their votes, the election agent and his or her helpers will already be in action. Outside each polling station will be 'tellers', each proudly sporting party colours, who will ask voters for their electoral numbers as they leave the polling stations. There is no obligation on voters to reveal this information but the great majority of them are normally willing to do so, at least to the tellers representing their own party. Many of the tellers are schoolchildren who are on holiday for the day and have been recruited for the job by parents who are staunch party members. Sometimes they may be paid by the party or their parents, but most of them are willing to help out for nothing. An excess of zeal may occasionally be revealed in a frosty unwillingness to co-operate with the tellers from 'the other side', but more frequently a feeling of camaraderie prevails and numbers are willingly swapped.

Each party will have established a subcommittee room near to the polling station which will contain a copy of the register on which will be marked all the voters who have promised to support the party's candidate. At hourly intervals, or possibly more frequently, throughout the day messengers will bring back from the tellers lists of the electoral numbers of those who have already voted so that they can be crossed off the register. An army of 'knockers-up' will have been recruited to call later in the day on those who have not already voted.

Soon after breakfast the candidates, usually wearing outsize rosettes, will be ceremoniously introduced – probably by their agents – to the Presiding Officer, with whom they will exchange a few light-hearted remarks. The ostensible reason for the visit is to satisfy themselves that everything is in order, though there is virtually never any question of this not being the case. During this tour the candidates will also drop into all their subcommittee rooms to give a word of encouragement to their supporters.

Throughout the day the party may have one or more loudspeaker cars touring areas where its support is concentrated, urging voters to record their votes as early as possible in the day, thus reducing the pressure on the party machine during the evening. For much of the day the candidates themselves are likely to be in charge of the loudspeaker, making a personal appeal to the voters to support them.

By 9 a.m. perhaps one elector in ten may have voted. Most of these would be people casting their votes on their way to work. During the daytime a steady trickle of retired voters and housewives make their way to the polling stations, and there may be a brief surge at lunchtime.

The result is that many party workers find themselves less than fully occupied until at least 5 or 6 p.m. In the morning and afternoon sick and elderly voters are called on and offered lifts to the poll. Knockers-up will be kept busy throughout the afternoon, but will find many houses empty and at others will be told to come back in the evening.

By 7 p.m. it is unusual for much more than half of the electors to have cast their votes and about that time begins an increasingly frantic effort by each party machine to get its supporters to the poll in the three hours remaining. This used to be especially important for the Labour Party, as a much higher proportion of Labour votes than of Conservative ones were cast in the evening, and non-political factors such as the weather and the appeal of the evening's television programmes could have an important effect on the result in closely contested constituencies; but in the last few elections there has been little difference in the time of voting of the main parties' supporters.

In the evening every available helper is mobilised to knock up voters and, wherever possible, a car is provided for every group of knockers-up, so that lifts to the poll may be offered to reluctant voters (though this is less important than it used to be, as far more voters now have their own cars than 40 or 50 years ago). Parties with a good and well-manned organisation may well be able to knock up all their supporters who have not voted earlier, as many as six times during the course of the evening. Despite this encouragement some voters remain obdurate and refuse to turn out, others delay so long that in the end it is too late to go, a few arrive at the polling station after 10 p.m. and find it closed.

Promptly at 10 p.m., the Presiding Officer must close the polling station, even if there are electors waiting to cast their votes. He or she must then seal the ballot boxes, so that no more ballot papers may be inserted, and make out the ballot paper account, which states the number of ballot papers with which he or she had been issued at the beginning of the day, the number of papers in the ballot box and the number of unused and spoilt papers. Finally the Presiding Officer must make up packages containing the marked registers, the counterfoils and the unused ballot papers and deliver these to the Returning Officer. The police, under the direction of the Returning Officer, will collect the ballot boxes and take them straight to the place where the votes are to be counted. (In European elections, although voting takes place on Thursday, the votes are not counted until the Sunday evening, as most of the rest of the EU votes at the weekend; in this case the Returning Officer has to arrange to store the boxes securely for three days.)

The count is usually held in the Town Hall or other large public hall in the constituency (although in large towns or cities with more than one constituency all the counts may be held together at one central point). In nearly all constituencies it is held on the evening of polling day; in a few remote rural seats it is postponed until the following morning. It is a crowded and lively occasion. The hall is furnished with long trestle tables at either side of which are seated the Returning Officer's assistants who are to count the votes. There is an air of expectancy as the room gradually fills up with candidates, their spouses, agents and leading supporters, whose function is to act as 'counting agents' or scrutineers of the actual counting of the votes. The number of counting agents permitted to each candidate is decided by the Returning Officer, but the total should not be less than the number of counting assistants and each candidate must be allowed the same number. All attending the count were previously required to sign a declaration of secrecy, promising not to attempt to discover how any individual has voted or to reveal such information to any other person. Since 1986 they are no longer asked to sign, but their attention is drawn to the secrecy provisions of the Representation of the People Acts and the penalties for infringing them. The press may be admitted, at the discretion of the Returning Officer, and a public gallery may also be provided. If the constituency result is of national interest, or an early result is expected, there may well be a TV crew to cover the declaration.

By about 10.15 p.m. in most boroughs the first ballot boxes will arrive from the polling stations. The ballot box containing the postal votes will be among the first to arrive. Each box is emptied of its contents, which are immediately counted to make sure that they tally with the number given in the Presiding Officer's ballot paper account. When every box has been emptied and its contents counted, the ballot papers are mixed together in one large pile, so that it is impossible to tell accurately how the voters of each polling district have recorded their votes. In the past there were often long delays in waiting for every single box to arrive before the mixing of ballot papers took place. Under the 1985 Representation of the People Act, however, it is now permissible to mix papers from several boxes at a time, providing that at least one other box is kept back to mix with the final box delivered.

The ballot papers are now sorted out into piles representing votes polled for each individual candidate. They are then counted into bundles of 100. All the time the counting agents, who will be standing behind the counting assistants, will be keeping an eagle eye on their activities – making sure that none of their candidate's papers have inadvertently been included amongst those of their opponents.

In a safe or hopeless constituency there is little tension, and the candidates and their supporters are much more concerned with whispered reports that may be coming in about the results in other constituencies, and the national trend to which they point. Some thoughtful Returning Officers go to the trouble of installing a television in an anteroom and many scrutineers spend a lot of their time popping in and out to acquaint themselves with the latest position. In a marginal constituency, however, attention is firmly fixed on the counting, and as the rival piles of votes mount so do the hopes and fears of the candidates and their supporters.

In the process of sorting the votes the counting assistants will come across a number of ballot papers whose validity is doubtful. They place these on one side and when all the other votes have been counted the Returning Officer adjudicates them in the presence of the candidates and their agents, giving reasons for accepting or rejecting them in each case. There are four categories of ballot paper which must be declared void – those which do not bear the official mark, those on which votes are given for more than one candidate,[3] those on which anything is written by which the voter can be identified, and those which are unmarked or otherwise fail to indicate a clear choice.

Papers in which the intention of the voter is unclear should be declared invalid by the Returning Officer, but where the intention is clear, even if the mark has been incorrectly made, the paper should be judged valid. Examples of incorrectly marked papers which are nevertheless valid are those where the X is placed otherwise than in the proper place, but still leaving no doubt which candidate the voter prefers; those where a tick or similar mark has been used instead of a cross and those where 'Yes' and 'No', or '1' and '2' or '1' and '0' have been written to express a preference between candidates.

When the Returning Officer has adjudicated on the doubtful votes they should be added to their appropriate pile and the total of each candidate's votes will be recorded by the chief counting assistant who will give it to the Returning Officer. The Returning Officer will then privately inform the candidates and their agents of the result of the count. If the result is close the Returning Officer may order a recount, and any candidate may claim a recount which the Returning Officer may not reasonably refuse. If the first count shows a majority of less than 500 a demand for a recount is likely, and where the majority is less than 100 several recounts may be held. It is also permissible for recounts to be demanded by candidates in danger of losing their deposits where the number of their votes is close to the minimum required, even though the majority of the leading candidate may be numbered in tens of thousands.

If after several recounts there is an equality of votes between the two leading candidates, the Returning Officer draws a lot to decide which is elected. Prior to 1948 the rule was that the Returning Officer should have a casting vote. The last occasion on which this invidious situation arose in Parliamentary elections was at Ashton-under-Lyne in 1886, but there have been a number of more recent examples in local government elections.

As soon as the result of the poll has been ascertained, the Returning Officer makes a public announcement of the votes obtained by the various candidates and declares the new member elected. It is then usual for the winning candidate to propose a vote of thanks to the Returning Officer and his or her staff for their conduct of the election, and to take the opportunity of thanking his or her own supporters, declaring that the result is a triumph for their party and the cause which it represents. The vote of thanks is seconded by the runner-up, who also gives his or her own partisan interpretation of the result, as do other candidates, who are also expected to have their say. Great demonstrations of enthusiasm are made by their supporters, especially by the winning party when the seat has changed hands.

As soon as possible after the result has been declared, the Returning Officer must publish it in writing. He or she must also attach, to the writ received from the Clerk of the Crown authorising him or her to conduct the election, a certificate naming the newly elected member. The writ is then returned to the Clerk of the Crown.

The Returning Officer must also collect up all the documents concerned with the election – the ballot papers used and unused, the ballot paper accounts and rejected ballot papers, the marked copies of the election registers and lists of proxies and the counterfoils of all ballot papers – and send these to the Clerk of the Crown. All these documents will be retained for one year and then destroyed, unless an order to the contrary is made by the High Court or the House of Commons.

The validity of an election may be challenged by a petition to the High Court, which may be presented by an elector for the constituency concerned or by one of the candidates. The court, in considering the petition, may order a scrutiny of the ballot papers and other relevant documents listed above. The High Court must report its findings to the Speaker of the House of Commons and if it has found the election invalid the House will proceed to authorise the issue of a writ for a new election.

Election petitions are rare, partly no doubt because of the great expense involved to the petitioner and partly because a member is unlikely to be unseated if only minor irregularities are proved.[4] Before 1997, the most recent election petition was that against Sir Alec Douglas-Home in 1964, mentioned in Chapter 9. At the 1997 election, three petitions were brought and one was upheld – at Winchester the narrowly defeated Conservative candidate successfully convinced the courts that he had lost only through the failure of the polling station staff properly to validate the ballot papers of some of his supporters with the official mark; the election was declared void and a new election called, the first successful petition on any matter apart from the eligibility of a candidate since 1924.

However, the aggrieved Conservative lost the by-election that followed by over 20,000 votes – presumably the electors felt his (justified) protest was merely the mark of a bad loser.

The Winchester petition was over a procedural matter, with no suggestion of deliberate wrongdoing, but the other two petitions in 1997 made more serious allegations – that the successful Labour candidate at Glasgow Govan had bribed an opponent, and that the Labour victor at Newark had made a false declaration of election expenses.[5] Thankfully for the reputation of Parliament, both candidates were cleared (though in the Newark case only on appeal, after being convicted in the court of first instance). It is perhaps worth noting that neither of these allegations was brought by the defeated candidates of the other major parties; and the eventual outcome of the Winchester by-election is also unlikely to encourage candidates to make petitions in the future. But the main reason why election petitions are seldom resorted to is the undoubted fact that major irregularities are almost unknown in modern British elections.

On election night special programmes relaying the constituency results as they become known are broadcast on radio and televised on BBC and ITV. Expert commentators, backed by computers, interpret the results and, on the basis of the trend revealed by the first contests to be counted, attempt, usually with a large measure of success, to predict what the final result will be. The computers adjust the final prediction with every constituency result that comes in.

There is lively competition to be the first constituency to declare a result, which can be a matter of considerable civic pride: a number of Returning Officers make special efforts in their preparations such as spending extra money on employing more and better skilled counting agents (such as bank clerks, for example), and even, in one reported case, printing the ballot papers on special paper which was supposedly easier to count; but all the effort may be in vain if there is a recount. In both 1983 and 1987, the safe Tory seat of Torbay won the race, with Guildford, Basildon and Cheltenham coming close behind. In 1992 and 1997 the honours went to Sunderland South, on the latter occasion smashing the record for the fastest-ever declaration by reaching a result just 45 minutes after the polls closed.[6]

Even before the first results are known, the commentators are furnished with the findings of 'exit polls', in which electors are asked how they have just voted as they leave the polling booths in a representative sample of constituencies. The first time this was attempted, in October 1974, the projected result was disastrously wrong – a Labour majority of 150, when in the event the overall Labour lead was merely three seats. At the subsequent general elections, as well as in most of the by-elections in which this technique has been employed, the predictions have been much more accurate. In 1983 the BBC exit poll, undertaken by Gallup, showed an average error in the final party vote of only 0.4 per cent. The ITN poll, conducted by the Harris Research Centre, also came very close, with an average error of 0.6 per cent. In 1987 Harris again came very close to the actual result, indicating a Conservative lead over Labour of nearly 10 per cent when the actual result put them 11 per cent ahead. The BBC did not use an exit poll in 1987; instead they asked Gallup to carry out a last-minute survey, which pointed to a Conservative lead of only 5 per cent. In 1992, national exit polls conducted for the BBC and ITN suggested a 4 per cent and a 5 per cent lead, respectively, for the Conservatives (as against an actual Tory lead of 7 per cent). The broadcasters, however, ignored these polls and relied instead on separate polls in marginal seats which indicated a much closer result. In 1997, the NOP exit poll for the BBC predicted a Labour majority of about 200 and the MORI exit poll for ITN predicted a majority of 159, neatly bracketing the actual result of 179; in 2001, MORI's and NOP's projections of Labour's second landslide were even closer, within four seats and five seats respectively (see Appendix 7).

Normally the first result is available by 11 p.m., or soon after, and by 6 a.m., when the election coverage will temporarily give way to the regular breakfast programmes, almost 600 seats will have been counted. Long before this the result of the election should be clear, unless it is extremely close, and one of the leaders will have already conceded defeat. (In 2001, Tony Blair's re-election was confirmed by 3.19 a.m., when the 330th Labour victory ensured him an overall majority.) In earlier years, when only one-half to two-thirds of the seats were counted overnight, and these predominantly the more urban ones, a misleadingly large Labour lead was often built up, which would be offset on the following day when the remaining, more rural, seats were counted. Now that television coverage has induced the great majority of constituencies to declare overnight, the 'reserve' Conservative strength on the second day of counting is much smaller than it used to be.

At about 10 a.m. the following day the count is begun in the other constituencies and from 11 a.m. onwards the results are broadcast, as they come in, to about 6 p.m., by which time all but a handful of remote Scottish constituencies have declared their results. But by this stage most of the tension has gone, the winner is known, and the victorious leader may already have been to Buckingham Palace and been formally commissioned to form (or re-form) a government to rule the country for the next four or five years.

11
By-Elections, Local Elections, Euro-Elections and Referendums

General elections are the most significant and perhaps most exciting elections which take place in Britain, but they are of course by no means the only ones. Every year there are elections to local authorities, every four years to the Scottish Parliament and Welsh Assembly and every five years to the European Parliament. Parliamentary by-elections, and indeed local government by-elections, occur haphazardly throughout the year. Occasionally, too, there is the extra diversion of a referendum.

In general terms, the arrangements for all these elections resemble those for general elections – much the same electorate is entitled to vote, in the same way and at the same polling stations, the same aspiring statesmen are eligible to stand as candidates, and the same administrators direct the elections according to the same administrative rules. Where there are significant differences between general and other elections, we have endeavoured to indicate in the text.

However, the different elections each have their own particular political significance, and it is that, together with more detailed consideration of what each actually involves, which is discussed in this chapter.

By-elections[1]

Casual vacancies in the House of Commons are filled through by-elections in the constituency concerned. Such vacancies may be occasioned by the death of the sitting member, his or her expulsion from the House or becoming disqualified from sitting. This can happen, for example, when an MP is elevated to the House of Lords. MPs also became disqualified if they inherited a peerage, although this provision is now redundant, hereditary peers having lost their right to inherit a seat in the Lords. MPs can also lose their seats through bankruptcy (it last happened to C. W. J. Horam, MP for Ashton-under-Lyne in 1928; these days an MP would only be disqualified if put under a bankruptcy restrictions order by the courts), and will be expelled if convicted of a serious crime (as when John Stonehouse, MP for Walsall, was convicted of fraud in 1976). Even rarer, but still possible, is for an MP to be deprived of a seat for lunacy, as happened to C. Leach, MP for Colne Valley, in 1916.

Much the most frequent cause of by-elections apart from deaths, however, is for an MP to forfeit his or her seat by being appointed to an 'office of profit under the Crown', listed in the House of Commons Disqualification Act. This is because, technically, there is no means by which an MP can resign; therefore an archaic legal fiction is maintained by which any MP who wishes to resign is appointed to one of two entirely nominal offices, the posts of Steward of the Chiltern Hundreds and Bailiff of the Manor of Northstead.

Between the general elections of 1945 and 2001 there were, in total, 452 by-elections. During the whole period there have been, on average, 8.1 by-elections per year, or one every six weeks; but as Table 11.1 shows, the overall figure conceals a fall of two-thirds in the incidence of by-elections. Though the number of deaths of MPs has remained generally steady, the proportion who resign or are made peers has fallen sharply as governments have learned not to risk the unnecessary loss of seats by appointing their Parliamentary supporters to official posts or offering them peerages. Such preferments are now more often saved up until the end of Parliaments in order to avoid this risk, as the casualty rate in by-elections has steadily risen.

In place of the Royal Proclamation authorising a general election, the Speaker of the House of Commons issues a writ instructing the Returning Officer in the constituency concerned to make arrangements for the poll to be held. Polling day is fixed between three and four weeks after the receipt of the writ (see timetable in Appendix 4). The writ is issued following a motion approved by the House of Commons, but when the House is in recess the Speaker may issue the writ on receipt of a certificate signed by any two Members of Parliament.

By tradition the party holding the seat chooses the date on which the by-election is held, and it is the party whips who move the appropriate motion in the House, which is normally agreed without discussion. Tactical considerations clearly influence the choice of date, but if it is unduly postponed there is likely to be an adverse reaction within the constituency and the opposing parties will seek to capitalise on the unwillingness of the defending party to face a contest. Since the early

Table 11.1 By-elections 1945–2001

Parliament	Government	Total number of by-elections	By-elections per year	By-elections included in calculations*	Change in government party percentage of vote		
					By-elections (average during Parliament)	Subsequent general election	Improvement for party in office
1945	Lab	52	11.5	43	-3.3	-2.0	1.3
1950	Lab	16	10.1	14	-2.0	+2.5	4.5
1951	Con	48	13.7	44	-0.6	+1.5	2.1
1955	Con	52	12.1	49	-8.9	-0.5	8.4
1959	Con	62	12.6	61	-14.3	-5.9	8.4
1964	Lab	13	9.6	11	-1.4	4.0	5.4
1966	Lab	38	9.2	37	-17.3	-4.9	12.4
1970	Con	30	8.1	27	-12.4	-7.4	5.0
1974: Feb	Lab	1	1.9	0	–	+2.2	–
1974: Oct	Lab	30	6.7	26	-9.5	-2.4	7.1
1979	Con	20	5.0	17	-11.6	-1.4	10.2
1983	Con	31	7.9	15	-14.3	-0.2	14.1
1987	Con	24	5.1	19	-12.3	-0.5	11.8
1992	Con	18	3.6	16	-19.6	-11.4	8.2
1997	Lab	17	4.2	13	-11.0	-2.3	8.7

* By-elections are excluded from the calculations on the right if the governing party was not in first or second place in the constituency at the preceding general election, or did not run a candidate in the by-election. By-elections in Northern Ireland and university seats are also excluded.

1970s there has been an informal agreement between the main parties that by-elections shall normally be held within three months of a vacancy arising. With very minor variations, the legal provisions concerning a by-election are the same as in a general election. However, the limit on expenditure by candidates in a by-election is a flat rate of £100,000 per constituency, many times the general election limit.

This higher expenditure limit is recognition that although a by-election campaign closely resembles that within an individual constituency at a general election, it frequently excites a great deal more interest. There is normally far stronger competition to be selected as a candidate, even for the minority party in a hopeless seat, as the publicity given to the by-election might well result in subsequent invitations from constituency parties in more attractive seats. At a general election an individual contest is merged in the national campaign and little note is taken of it outside the constituency concerned. At a by-election it holds centre stage.

For this reason, too, it is more likely to attract intervention by a minor party or independent candidates, including a few who have no serious political interests and put themselves forward purely for exhibitionist reasons. For example, a total of 111 candidates contested the 16 by-elections held in Great Britain during the 1983–7 Parliament, an average of 6.9 per contest. In the general election of 1987, 2325 candidates contested 650 seats, an average of 3.6 per constituency. In 1985 the deposit required from candidates was increased from £150 to £500. This appears to have led briefly to a slight reduction in the number of fringe candidates in by-elections, but, as in general elections, the number is now increasing again.

In fighting a by-election a constituency party can normally depend on help from outside. The party's regional organiser will probably move into the constituency for several weeks to supervise the campaign, and professional agents from other constituencies will be borrowed to undertake important specialist tasks. Other professionals from the national party headquarters may also be seconded, while voluntary workers from neighbouring constituencies can also be expected to lend a hand. In the case of key contests in highly marginal seats, helpers may travel from all parts of the country to support their party's nominee.

Traditionally, the Prime Minister sends a personal message of support to the government party's candidate, which is useful for attracting press publicity, and the leaders of the opposition parties also send similar letters to their standard-bearers. Prominent Cabinet ministers, and their counterparts in the other parties, descend on the constituency to speak at election meetings and MPs are drafted in to lead canvassing and loudspeaker drives.

The personality of the candidate in a by-election is more important than in a general election campaign. Freed from the awesome responsibility of helping to choose a government, voters are more prepared to cross party lines and to vote for the most attractive candidate. Electors also appear to be more inclined to engage in 'tactical' voting at by-elections, that is to say to vote for their second preference party if it appears to be better placed than their first preference, in order to try to defeat the party to which they have the greatest objection. This is perhaps the major reason why, in the recent past, Liberal Democrat candidates have consistently polled better in by-elections than in general elections. Tactical voting can be greatly stimulated by opinion polls in by-elections if, as is often the case, they demonstrate that one of the two largest parties has no chance of winning. This can lead to a stampede of a high proportion of its supporters towards the Liberal Democrat candidate. Conversely when, as in the Fulham by-election in March 1986, the polls clearly showed the SDP-Alliance candidate to be in third place they probably had a depressant effect on his vote.

It may seem surprising that rather more seats do not change hands at by-elections. One reason is that relatively few of them take place in marginal seats. Even those caused by death are disproportionately in safe seats, as, generally speaking, it is the younger members who represent the more marginal seats. By-elections caused by resignations or elevation to the peerage are the consequence of voluntary decisions, and political parties are normally more cautious than to put their marginal seats at risk, especially when they are going through a period of unpopularity.

Governments may sometimes appear to take by-elections more seriously than their effects would warrant. It is true that it is only rarely that a government's fate can be directly affected by the result of a by-election, but the Labour government elected in October 1974 did eventually fall through losing too many seats in by-elections. Its original overall majority was only three seats, and it lost seven in all, leaving itself in a minority for the last two years of its existence. Prime Minister James Callaghan prolonged its life, by negotiating the Lib-Lab pact, but when this expired in July 1978 it became vulnerable to the threat of all the other parties combining in a vote of no confidence. This eventually occurred, in March 1979, and the government was pitched into a general election at a time not of its own choosing and lost disastrously. The disaster was largely self-inflicted, as Callaghan had recklessly provoked a by-election in Workington by awarding a peerage to Fred Peart (who became Leader of the House of Lords) at a time when the anti-Labour swing in the immediately previous by-election was more than enough to ensure a Labour defeat at Workington, which duly occurred.

But it is not just the *loss* of seats which governments fear. By-elections have long been used as a means of gauging public opinion, and a disappointing result, even if it does not involve the loss of a seat, can have a disastrous effect on party morale, while boosting that of the Opposition. The results of by-elections can have an influence out of all proportion to their intrinsic importance. Before the Second World War, when there were no opinion polls and by-elections were the only available thermometer of the national mood, this was perhaps inevitable; but even today their results are taken very seriously, and this can best be shown by discussing briefly some of the more significant results in the post-war period.

During the Parliament of 1945–50 there was no single by-election result which had more than a passing effect. But, cumulatively, the by-elections contributed in no small measure to the standing of the then Labour government. Although the Conservatives gained ground in the great majority of the 52 contests, and won three seats from minor parties, their failure to win a single seat from Labour was constantly invoked as evidence that the government was still enjoying wide support, despite other indications to the contrary.

During the course of the 1951–5 Parliament the Conservative government actually won a seat – Sunderland South – from the Labour opposition. This was a rare feat indeed – the great majority of by-elections have invariably shown a swing against the government in office, and it was almost 30 years since a government had actually picked up a seat in a by-election. The consequence was that pressure on the government eased perceptibly, and most observers concluded, correctly, that the Conservatives would win the subsequent general election.

In the period from the spring of 1962 to the summer of 1964 an almost unbroken succession of by-election disasters did immense damage to the reputation of the governments of Harold Macmillan and Sir Alec Douglas-Home, and provoked them into taking a number of ill-considered actions. The most sensational result, in March 1962, was at Orpington, hitherto regarded as an extremely safe Conservative seat. The by-election resulted in a Liberal victory: a Conservative majority of 14,760 was turned into a Liberal one of 7855. Although the Liberal revival which it appeared to foreshadow did not immediately materialise, this result largely transformed the terms in which electoral strategy was discussed. During the succeeding two years the Conservatives lost a further three seats to Labour, and suffered the further humiliation of seeing their candidate forced into third position in six Labour seats, and into fourth place in a seventh. The dismissal by Harold Macmillan, in July 1962, of one-third of his Cabinet, and the postponement by Sir Alec Douglas-Home of the general election until the last possible moment in 1964, were both plausibly attributed to this series of setbacks.[2]

In the 1964–6 Parliament, by-elections continued to have an important influence on the fortunes of the Labour government. The completely unexpected loss of Leyton to the Conservatives in January 1965 (when a Labour majority of 7926 was turned into a Conservative one of 205) not only led to the immediate resignation of the Foreign Secretary (Patrick Gordon Walker, who was the defeated Labour candidate), but reduced the government's precarious Parliamentary majority from five to three. It also deterred the Prime Minister, Harold Wilson, from calling an early general election, which he might otherwise have been tempted to do by the favourable opinion poll findings.

A year later, in January 1966, in a keenly contested by-election at North Hull, Labour achieved a swing of 4.5 per cent – the largest swing to the governing party in any by-election in a marginal seat in 32 years. This result confirmed other evidence (from opinion polls) that an early general election would produce an increased Labour Parliamentary majority, and the North Hull result certainly appears to have clinched the Prime Minister's decision to go to the country in March 1966.

The 1966–70 Labour government created a post-war record in losing 15 seats in by-elections, though as it had a large Parliamentary majority these losses did not put its existence in jeopardy. Twelve of these seats were gained by the Conservative Party, but perhaps the greatest impact was made by two other by-elections, at Carmarthen and at Hamilton, where Labour defeats brought Plaid Cymru and the Scottish National Party into Parliament.

The Conservative government elected in 1970 had a less bumpy ride, losing five seats, four of them to the Liberals. Yet much the most striking by-election of this Parliament hardly affected the government at all. This occurred at Lincoln, where the sitting Labour MP, Dick Taverne, resigned his seat after being dropped as Labour candidate by his constituency Labour Party. Running as Democratic Labour, he routed both the official Labour and Conservative candidates, winning 58.2 per cent of the poll in what has been described as 'the greatest *personal* election victory in British political history'.

Taverne's victory foreshadowed the series of by-election successes in 1981–2, following the launch of the Social Democratic Party in March 1981, which enabled it to make an immediate impact in national politics and made it clear the SDP-Liberal Alliance would be a force to be reckoned with at the general election. The first of these was at Warrington in July 1981, when Roy Jenkins won 42.4 per cent of the vote (against a Liberal score of 9 per cent at the previous general election) and almost won a safe Labour seat. This was followed by three striking gains in Tory-held seats, by a Liberal (William Pitt) in Croydon North West and by Social Democrats Shirley Williams, at Crosby, and Roy Jenkins, at Glasgow Hillhead. The Falklands War brought an abrupt end to the sequence, but late in the Parliament there was a further Liberal gain at Bermondsey, a former Labour stronghold where the Labour Party was seriously split over its choice of candidate. Despite the Alliance's disappointment at failing to make a decisive breakthrough at the 1983 general election, its strong showing in by-elections was repeated in the 1983–7 Parliament, when it won three seats from the Conservatives, and, in a virtual re-run of the Bermondsey episode, captured Greenwich from the Labour Party.

After the Conservatives were re-elected in 1987 they began confidently, but then embarked on a string of improbable defeats in their heartland which charted their increasingly tenuous hold on the electorate's affections. Labour won Conservative seats with notable swings at Vale of Glamorgan in 1989, at Mid-Staffordshire in 1990, and at Monmouth and at Langbaurgh in 1991. In October 1990 the Liberal Democrats captured Eastbourne from the Conservatives, in a by-election caused by the murder of the local Conservative MP, Ian Gow, by the IRA. The swing was 20.1 per cent, and the result was interpreted both as an indication that the Liberal Democrats, who since the Liberal–SDP merger that founded the new party had been trailing badly in the opinion polls, might be back in business, and, more certainly, that a general election was now unlikely to be held during the first half of 1991. A month later poor Tory performances in two Labour-held seats, Bootle and Bradford North, contributed to the pressures which led to the ousting of Margaret Thatcher as Tory leader and Prime Minister shortly afterwards. In March 1991, a further striking Liberal Democrat victory in the Tory-held seat of Ribble Valley hastened a government decision to abandon the unpopular poll tax.

In the 1992 Parliament, the 18 by-elections produced the worst results ever experienced by a government. The Conservatives lost all eight of the seats they were defending, with massive swings of up to 35.4 per cent. There were four Liberal Democrat gains, three for Labour and one for the SNP, and with some Conservative MPs temporarily abandoning the whip over policy differences, the government at one point technically lost its majority.

Since 1997, there have been fewer such dramas. In the 1997 Parliament, only one seat changed hands between the major parties – Romsey, gained by the Liberal Democrats from the Conservatives, a very rare instance of the main Opposition party losing a seat. Other big swings were seen at the 1997 Winchester by-election, caused by the invalidation of the original general election result on a counting irregularity, where the margin by which the aggrieved Tory was defeated increased from 2 votes to over 20,000; and at Hamilton South in 1999 where Labour's majority was cut from nearly 16,000 to under 600 by the Scottish Nationalists, a 22.6 per cent swing. Since 2001, by-elections of any sort have been few and far between, but the Liberal Democrats made a dramatic gain from Labour at Brent East in the autumn of 2003, on a 29 per cent swing, which was taken as confirming the government's loss of support over the invasion of Iraq. A year later they repeated their success by gaining Leicester South with a 21.5 per cent swing, but narrowly missed taking another Labour stronghold, Birmingham Hodge Hill, on the same day, despite an even bigger (27.7 per cent) swing in their favour. Yet although the government were severely embarrassed, they were arguably strengthened rather than weakened because of the humiliation of the Conservatives, pushed into third place in all three cases; Brent East contributed to the ousting of Iain Duncan Smith as Conservative leader, and the 2004 defeats were a severe blow to his successor, Michael Howard.

Despite the influence which by-elections such as these undoubtedly had, there is a serious risk of reading too much into individual by-election results. In fact the result of any particular by-election may be wildly misleading as a reflection of the national strength of the parties. Regional and local issues which tend to cancel out in a general election may assume disproportionate importance; the turnout, which at a general election is normally around 75 per cent, fluctuates widely (in the 1992–7 Parliament, for instance, from 33.6 to 74.2 per cent, and hitting a record low for a peace-time election of 19.6 per cent at Leeds Central in 1999); the personal qualities of candidates have a greater effect than in a general election; and minor party and independent candidates are more likely to intervene and their influence, though marginal, is difficult to interpret.

The fallacy of drawing too many conclusions from the result of a single by-election can easily be illustrated. In November 1960 six by-elections were fought on the same day. In one of these, Carshalton, there was a swing to the Conservatives of 3.8 per cent; in another, Bolton East, there was a swing to Labour of 2.0 per cent – a difference of 5.8 per cent. In the not quite so distant past, on 28 April 1977, by-elections were held at Ashfield and Grimsby. One showed a pro-Tory swing of 20.9 per cent, the other 7.1 per cent, a difference of 13.8 per cent.

Single by-election results, then, are clearly unreliable guides to the state of public opinion, but experience has shown that groups of by-elections, held over a period of several months, do give a reasonably accurate idea of the *trend* of opinion, if their results are averaged out. They are nevertheless inherently likely to understate the actual level of support for the government. Year in, year out, the great majority of by-elections show a swing against the government in power.

There may be several reasons for this, but it seems probable that by-elections are often used as a means of registering a 'protest vote' against particular government policies, without incurring the risk of actually overthrowing the government. The turnout at by-elections is almost invariably lower than at a general election, and it may also be the case that government supporters are rather more inclined to be complacent, and to stay at home on such occasions.

In any event, Table 11.1 above clearly shows that at every general election since the war the governing party has done better than the previous by-election results had indicated. In considering the significance of by-election results therefore, whilst it is usually justifiable to assume that the trend revealed by a series of by-elections over a period of time is probably correct, it would be prudent to conclude that the government's standing is a little higher than the results indicate.

Local elections[3]

Apart from Parliamentary by-elections, the most frequent subsidiary elections held in Britain are those of representatives on local authorities. These are held each year in the spring, normally on the first Thursday of May.[4] Councillors are elected for a four-year term. England is divided into counties, and in 34 of these counties there is a county council, of 60–100 councillors re-elected every four years (county council election years are 1997, 2001, 2005 and so on). These counties are subdivided into districts. In each of the other three years in a four-year cycle, the lower-tier or *district* councils are elected (some of these may be dignified by the title of borough or city council, but they all have the same powers, and consist of 30–80 councillors). The 238 non-metropolitan district councils have a choice: the whole council can be re-elected together once every four years (which is the case in 149 districts), or one-third of the council is re-elected in each of the non-county election years (in 83 cases), or half the council may be elected every other year (the remaining 6). If they choose whole council elections, these are held in the mid-year of the county cycle – 1999, 2003, 2007 and so on.

However, since the mid 1990s, Scotland, Wales and some parts of England are governed by *unitary authorities*, combining the powers and functions of county and district councils, and having 40–70 councillors. (Some of these unitary authorities have the title county council or county borough council.) In Scotland (32 councils), all are elected on a four-year cycle, the years being 1999, 2003, 2007; Wales (22 councils) was on the same cycle, but this was interrupted when the Welsh Assembly postponed the elections from 2003 to 2004, and the next elections will be in 2008. In England the 46 Unitary Authorities may choose either to be elected as a whole every four years, in which case the election years are the same as in Scotland, or may be elected by thirds. In London and in England's six metropolitan counties (Tyne and Wear, West Midlands, Merseyside, Greater Manchester, West Yorkshire and South Yorkshire), the boroughs were converted to unitary status earlier, in 1985. The 32 *London boroughs* and 36 *metropolitan districts* form single-tier authorities; in all the London boroughs members are elected *en bloc* every four years (cycle: 1994, 1998, 2002 and so on), but the Metropolitan District Councils are elected by thirds.

In Northern Ireland local government is now on a single-tier basis, with 26 *district* councils elected for four-year terms on the basis of proportional representation, using the Single Transferable Vote (see Appendix 9). The electoral cycle is 1993, 1997, 2001 and so on.

Except in Northern Ireland, the districts are subdivided into a number of wards, most of which elect three councillors, one of whom retires each year if the council has decided to be elected by thirds. The counties are divided into electoral divisions returning one member each.

In most other respects the legal provisions for the conduct of local elections are the same as for Parliamentary contests, and, on a more restricted scale, the candidates run a similar type of campaign. But there are a number of important differences. At general elections between 70 and 85 per cent of the registered voters go to the polls, at local elections the figure seldom rises above 50 per cent, and the average is not more than 40 per cent – less in recent years. At a general election virtually all seats are contested by Labour, Conservative and Liberal Democrat candidates, while in local elections this is not the general rule, except in the main urban areas. In the past there were relatively few contests on party lines in the more rural areas, and even in towns there was a fairly large number of unopposed returns. The reorganisation of local government into larger units, which took place in 1973–4, had the effect of politicising local elections in many parts of the country where previously they had been held on non-party lines, and this has greatly reduced the incidence of unopposed returns. It is still the case, however, that regular three-party competition is far from being universal and, indeed, there are still local councils where independents or other non-party groupings hold the majority.

Nevertheless, the results of local elections are closely scrutinised as guides to political trends. On rare occasions, when a particularly outstanding change in political control is registered, it can have a substantial impact on the national political scene. It is clear that many voters use local elections as a means of passing judgement on the performance of the national government, and to 'send a message' to Westminster, rather than voting on the basis of which parties and candidates they would prefer to run their local council.

More generally, the total gains and losses each year in the district and county elections are taken as a barometer of the parties' standing in the country, though account has to be taken of the fact that the seats contested were last fought four years previously. With this proviso, there is much evidence that these results do give an accurate reflection of public opinion, though, as in the case of by-elections, there is a tendency to exaggerate the swing against the government party. As political barometers, however, local elections have been regarded as being unsatisfactory, as they take place only once a year. In recent years this has focused attention on the previously unregarded trickle of local government by-elections, which take place throughout the year. The results of these are now carefully collected and scrutinised, and there are several regularly updated websites which track them month by month. When taken in clusters, these have proved to be extremely sensitive though sometimes misleading indicators of movements in party support, and they are a useful check against opinion polls which record statements of intention rather than actual votes. In 1986 the Conservatives devoted resources to an extensive computer analysis of the local election results which played a significant role in deciding the timing of the following year's general election.

There have been some changes in the arrangements for local government elections in recent years, and others may follow. This may affect their political significance. Following the example of London, a number of other towns and cities have been given directly-elected mayors, who are likely to be more significant and higher profile figures than are council leaders at present. Proportional representation will also be introduced in Scotland in 2007, though not, for the moment, in England and Wales.

One particular feature of local government elections in recent years has been the very poor turnout – often hovering round 30 per cent – and reforms to make their executives directly accountable to voters are seen as one possible way of arresting this trend. Because many councils under 'first past the post' are virtual 'one-party states', it has been suggested that many voters see no point in voting each May. Another change with the same aim has been experimentation with alternative methods of voting, which have been used at some local elections in recent years. Such minor innovations, if successful, may possibly be extended to general elections in due course.

More change may be on the way in some parts of England. The present government is committed to regional devolution provided the public approves, and a referendum was held in the North-East[5] in autumn 2004, both to determine whether a regional assembly should be set up and, if so, how local government should be rearranged to accommodate it. If the voters were to approve regional devolution, the two tiers of councils now existing in some of the affected areas would be replaced by unitary authorities – the referendums would determine whether it was the county councils, district councils or a compromise between the two which would survive in each region. However, the North-East voted heavily against a regional assembly, and referendums in other regions now look unlikely in the near future.

European elections

A new type of election was introduced into Britain in June 1979, with the first direct elections to the European Parliament. Eighty-one British Euro MPs (or MEPs) were elected, at the same time as 329 other members in eight different countries, making 410 members altogether. Five years later, in June 1984, in the second direct election, 434 MEPs were elected from ten countries, and they were later joined by a further 84 members from Spain and Portugal, who joined the European Community on 1 January 1986, making a total membership of 518. The third direct election, in which twelve countries voted simultaneously to fill the 518 seats, took place on 15–18 June 1989. The fourth was on 9–12 June 1994, when the twelve countries elected an enlarged Parliament of 567 members (including 87 from the United Kingdom); subsequent partial elections were held for the representatives of the three new member states of Austria, Sweden and Finland. The fifth direct election, in which Britain elected 87 of the 626 members of the Parliament, was held on 10–13 June

1999. With the most recent expansion of the European Union to 25 states, Britain now has 78 of 732 members, elected on 10–13 June 2004.[6]

Three of the 78 British MEPs are elected from Northern Ireland in a three-member constituency which comprises the whole of the province. They are elected by proportional representation, under the STV system (see Appendix 9), which ensures in practice that two Unionists and one Nationalist will be elected. The remaining members were before 1999 elected in single-member constituencies, under the 'first past the post' system, just as in elections to the House of Commons. From the 1999 election, however, they have been elected by a regional 'closed list' system of proportional representation. Voters choose between parties rather than candidates, and in each region (which range in size from the North-East of England with three MEPs to the South-East with ten) the seats are shared out between the parties in proportion to their votes using the D'Hondt formula (see Appendix 8). The candidates elected are the highest on their party's list for that region – for example, the Conservatives won three seats in London, and therefore the first three candidates on their list were elected; the system is called a closed list because voters have no opportunity to choose between candidates of any party, but must accept the list in the order in which the party has chosen to present it.

European elections in Britain have been much more low key than general elections. The parties produce election manifestos which relate to European issues, and in some cases are drawn up jointly with like-minded parties in the other member states. However, the elections have essentially been fought as part of the continuing battle of British domestic politics, with the main objective being to register support for, or opposition to, the government of the day. Opinion polls confirm that more voters determine their Euro-vote on domestic issues than on those matters which are actually within the competence of the European Parliament.

So far the British public has not shown enormous interest in these elections, and the turnout has been low (31.8 per cent in both 1978 and 1984, rising to 35.9 per cent in 1989 and 36.1 per cent in 1994, but falling to just 23.1 per cent, the lowest in any national election in Britain, in 1999). In 2004 it rose to 37.2 per cent,[7] but perhaps only because the election was held in tandem with the local elections, and in some regions was conducted with an all-postal voting system. In Northern Ireland the turnout has been much higher (64.4 per cent in 1984, 57 per cent in 1999 and 51 per cent in 2004). The absence of proportional representation (PR) in Great Britain meant that British representation before 1999 was much more unbalanced than that of any other member state. No Liberal or SDP member was elected in any of the first three elections, despite the fact that the Alliance polled nearly one-fifth of the votes in 1984. In 1994 the Liberal Democrats, however, succeeded in electing two members. With the introduction of PR, seven different parties secured seats in Great Britain in both 1999 and 2004, as well as the three in Northern Ireland. The results of the elections are shown in Appendix 2.

Devolved assemblies[8]

In May 1999, elections to the Scottish Parliament and National Assembly of Wales were held for the first time. Of these bodies, the Scottish Parliament ('Holyrood') is the more powerful, with considerable legislative and limited taxation powers, though still ultimately subservient to the Westminster Parliament. The Welsh Assembly ('Cardiff Bay') has fewer powers, but is still considerably more than merely a new tier of local government. How devolution will work in practice, and how these new bodies will fit into the overall political scene in Britain, may take several years to emerge, but their immediate effect has been to introduce, for the first time in modern peacetime Britain, coalition politics at Parliamentary level.

Both the Scottish Parliament and Welsh Assembly are elected by the Additional Member System (AMS), 129 members at Holyrood and 60 at Cardiff Bay. This is a hybrid system that combines the traditional single-member, 'first past the post' constituencies with 'top-up' seats that compensate the parties whose votes are too evenly spread to win their fair share of constituencies. Each elector has two votes. The first vote is a constituency vote for an individual candidate, using (for the moment) the same constituencies as in Westminster elections.[9] In both Scotland and Wales, Labour has won the vast majority of these seats, even though they won much less than half the votes in both countries. The second vote is for a party, and is used to distribute the top-up seats; it is not in any sense a second-best or second-choice vote, and most voters supported the same party with both their votes. On the basis of these second votes, the parties in each region that are most under-represented are awarded extra seats. (The system is discussed in more detail in Appendix 8.) The system is not fully proportional because there are too few top-up seats to entirely correct the exaggerative effects of the 'first past the post' element, but the biggest party's advantage is greatly reduced, and both Parliaments were left 'hung' by the 1999 elections. In each case Labour was the largest party but short of a majority, and the Nationalists the second largest party. In Scotland, Labour formed a coalition administration with the Liberal Democrats; in Wales, where they missed a majority of seats much more narrowly, they opted for a minority government, hoping to secure sufficient opposition support for each measure on its merits.

One effect of using the AMS system, which has often been criticised by its opponents, is that in effect it creates two classes of members – those who have been directly elected to represent constituencies, and the top-up members elected from the party list who, because they are elected by party rather than personal votes, might be thought to be 'second class' members. Although there were assurances before the first elections that all members would be considered equal, there was considerable debate during the Parliament's first session whether the top-up members, not having constituencies, should be entitled to the same level of secretarial support and similar expenses. The top-up members argued that, far from not needing such assistance, since they represented whole regions rather than constituencies, they were actually more in need of such back-up. The issue is a controversial one, because almost all the Labour MSPs sit for constituencies whereas most of the SNP and Conservative members hold top-up seats.

The governing coalition is headed by a First Minister and his Cabinet, who direct the Scottish executive, and although the different spheres of responsibility of Holyrood and Westminster are theoretically distinguished and delineated, it is plain that tension may – and in practice no doubt will – arise between the two executives, especially when they are in the hands of different parties. Some commentators have suggested that the government may have entirely underestimated the political implications of the constitutional revolution they have set in motion by establishing legislative devolution. The Liberal Democrats hold the balance of power in both assemblies, and Labour's local leaders have been forced to accept some compromises. This can leave the implementation of Westminster policy a hostage to fortune – devolution applies not only to institutions but to the political parties that operate in them, and the Scottish and Welsh Labour parties have proved less amenable to control from Old Queen Street than Labour's national election strategists might wish. The SNP and Plaid Cymru are in a powerful second place, and as official Oppositions will be able to act as a focus for resentment in the coming years, a new consideration for Prime Ministers to bear in mind in future general elections.

Opinion polls show that many Scots already believe that, even assuming Scotland does not move to full independence, the Holyrood rather than Westminster Parliament will be the most significant influence on their lives within a few years. This may well affect the character of future Westminster elections in Scotland, perhaps even diminishing their importance in the public mind so that turnout is affected; certainly, by providing a new platform for the parties to put their case on a regular basis and perhaps indeed participate in government, it will affect the terms of the electoral battle.

The 108-member Northern Ireland Assembly was elected under the terms of the Good Friday Agreement in June 1998, but the mutual distrust of the Unionists and Republicans over the issue of terrorist arms decommissioning delayed the handover of devolved power until December 1999. Its 12-member executive is designed on a power-sharing basis to ensure representation of all the main parties, and a system of weighted majority voting in the Assembly prevents any section of the community from dominating power. However, this forces bitterly opposed parties to work together and arguably exacerbates the tensions between them. The Assembly was suspended in October 2002, executive power reverting to the Secretary of State, and remains inactive at the time of writing although elections were nevertheless held in November 2003.

For details of the election results for all of these bodies, see Appendix 2.

Greater London Authority

Since spring 2000, the body for local government at strategic level in London has been the Greater London Authority (GLA), directed by a directly elected Mayor and the London Assembly of 25 members elected by a system of proportional representation. Both Mayor and Assembly are elected for four-year terms, so the second elections were in 2004 and the next will be in 2008. The GLA has responsibility for those functions of local and regional government better handled at county level than by the various London boroughs, notably transport, but also economic development, planning and the environment. London had no elected local government body above borough level between 1986 and 2000; previously the Greater London Council (1965–86) and, covering only inner London,[10] London County Council (1888–1965) had been London's county council, but some responsibilities which elsewhere had fallen on the county council were in London retained by Parliament (notably, overseeing of the Police).

The Mayor of London is Britain's first directly-elected governmental chief executive (similar positions have now been set up in a number of towns and cities). The electoral system is a unique one, called the Supplementary Vote. Each elector has two votes, one for a first and one for a second choice, cast at the same time; the two candidates who receive the most first preferences qualify for the second count, at which they add to their first-choice votes all the second choices they received from voters whose first choice was one of the unsuccessful candidates.

The Mayoral election of 2000 was won by the left-wing MP Ken Livingstone, who had been Labour leader of the former Greater London Council at the time of its abolition, and who ran as an independent after being denied the Labour nomination. His victory was an undoubted personal triumph, and the Labour government's embarrassment was increased by the Conservative candidate, Steven Norris, pushing its own nominee into third place.

Mr Livingstone has proved, as expected, to be a high-profile political figure. In 2003 – in breach of a strict interpretation of party rules – he was readmitted to the Labour Party and adopted as its candidate for 2004. (The candidate already selected, Nicky Gavron, stood down.) The decision was a mark of Mr Livingstone's success in establishing his position, and a virtual admission that Labour had no conceivable chance of defeating him if he ran for re-election as an independent. In the event, as the Labour candidate, he was re-elected though more narrowly than in 2000, Steven Norris again being his opponent in the final count.

The Assembly has 25 members, elected by the two-vote Additional Member System (AMS), in 14 constituencies (each consisting of two to four London boroughs) with 11 additional members. There is a 5 per cent 'threshold': no party securing less than 5 per cent of the total vote will be entitled to top-up seats. In the 2000 elections, Labour and the Conservatives each won 9 seats, the Liberal Democrats 4 and the Greens 3. The key power of the Assembly is its ability to veto certain decisions by the Mayor (including his budget), for which it requires a two-thirds majority. Therefore what was most significant about the result in 2000 was not that no party has a simple majority, but that either Labour or the Conservatives had enough seats to block a veto if they so chose; from 2004, when the Conservatives held their 9 seats but Labour could secure only 7, only the Conservatives have that power. (See Appendix 2 for the detailed results.)

Referendums[11]

Apart from local polls on such issues as the Sunday opening of cinemas and public houses, referendums were unknown in Britain before the 1970s. They still form no part of the regular decision-making process, but have been used on a number of occasions to settle constitutional decisions, and will doubtless continue to be so used in the future.

The first referendum was confined to Northern Ireland, and was boycotted by the great majority of Roman Catholic voters. Only 58.7 per cent of the electors voted on 8 March 1973, and of them 98.9 per cent wanted Northern Ireland to remain part of the United Kingdom, while 1.1 per cent supported union with the Republic of Ireland.

A much more significant development was the referendum held on 5 June 1975, in all four parts of the United Kingdom, on continued British membership of the EEC (Common Market). All four countries voted in favour, the overall vote being 67.2 per cent, on a turnout of 64.5 per cent. During the course of the campaign a small amount of public money was made available to the 'umbrella' organisations which ran the 'Yes' and 'No' campaigns – £125,000 for each side. The Labour government, which had called the referendum, agreed to suspend collective responsibility so that Cabinet ministers could campaign on both sides – 16 members supported the pro-EEC and 7 the anti-EEC cause.

The 1975 referendum was supposed to be a one-off affair, but four years later, on 1 March 1979, the people of Scotland and Wales were asked to vote on whether they wanted separate elected assemblies for the two countries. The Welsh voted decisively against, and the Scots narrowly in favour, though they failed to achieve the minimum level of 40 per cent of registered voters in favour that the House of Commons had required.

No further referendums were held under the Conservative governments of 1979–97, but since 1997 there have been referendums in Scotland and Wales on devolution, in London on establishing the Greater London Authority and in Northern Ireland on the Good Friday peace agreement. Further referendums have been promised on the European Union constitution, on joining the Single European Currency (when the time comes to make a decision, which will probably not be until the government feels confident of winning) and, in some parts of England, on regional devolution. The government was also initially committed to a referendum on electoral reform, but little has been heard of this in the last few years.

The electorate for national referendums has consisted of the Parliamentary electorate plus peers. With so little established precedent, though, there is scope for much controversy here. Should EU citizens living in Britain, who can vote in local elections, have a vote on joining the single European currency, for example? Supporters will argue that it is an issue directly affecting their everyday life and economic wellbeing as British residents, and they have a right to a voice; opponents that this is a vital question of the future of the UK as a nation state, and the right of British nationals to make their own independent decision must not be abridged. Whatever the government's (or Electoral Commission's) decision, it will be controversial – especially if the eventual result is very close.

The arrangements for referendums have so far been on an *ad hoc* basis with the main details settled by an Act of Parliament in each case, but under the Political Parties, Elections and Referendums Act 2000 (PPERA), such matters now fall within the remit of the Electoral Commission, who not only have a statutory duty to comment on the proposed wording of the question in any future referendum, but must also police campaign spending.

It seems likely that referendums will continue to be used only to decide on (or ratify the government's decision on) major constitutional changes. There have been spasmodic demands for a referendum on capital punishment, but Britain seems unlikely to move towards using referendums to determine matters of government policy, as is the case in Switzerland and some US states, even though opinion polls have found the idea to be popular.

12
Opinion Polls[1]

Apart from television, the most important new factor which has influenced elections in the post-war period has been the public opinion polls. No politician worth his salt is now ignorant of the latest state of the parties, as revealed by any one of half a dozen polls; and at closely fought by-elections the predictions of the pollsters receive incomparably more attention than the pronouncements of the candidates. At first the polls were used purely by the media, for publication in their reporting. But the political parties quickly caught on to their potential and started to commission private polls for their own use to plan their strategy and test their ideas (with the results kept confidential unless there is any benefit in releasing them). The private polls have been a feature of British elections for around 50 years, but suddenly came to greater public notice in 1997 when Labour's campaign appeared to be more poll-driven than hitherto.

This is all a comparatively recent development. On the eve of the 1945 general election the Gallup poll reported in the *News Chronicle* a Labour lead over the Conservatives of 6 per cent. Nobody took the slightest notice of this, least of all the *News Chronicle*. So far from predicting a runaway Labour victory, the political correspondent of that paper wrote that 'the final result may well prove very near a stalemate'. The most popular prediction in the other papers was a Conservative majority of 'around one hundred', and none of them mentioned the Gallup poll forecast. The lack of interest in the Gallup predictions in 1945 is in itself a commentary on British insularity, for nine years previously the methods of public opinion polls had been sensationally vindicated in an American presidential election (see below).

It is a mistake, though a common one, to think of opinion polls as purely intended for predicting election results. In fact that is only a subsidiary purpose, although it is the one on which their worth tends to be judged and the one which the editors who commission the polls consider most valuable.

As well as the regular questions on voting intention, other questions examine the underlying motivations, attitudes to the political issues of the day, the images of the parties and their leaders, and all other factors that may contribute to the voters' decisions on how to vote. A large number of further questions of a socio-political nature are included in questionnaires, which often yield valuable evidence of changing public attitudes over the years. The political polling is only a small part of the polling companies' work, though as it is so prominently publicised it acts as a standing advertisement for the commercial market research which they undertake, which is likely to account for more than 90 per cent of their turnover.

The man who introduced opinion polling into Britain was Dr Henry Durant. In 1937 he set up the British Institute of Public Opinion, later known as the **Gallup** poll, under the sponsorship of the *News Chronicle*, which published its findings from 1938 to 1960. Gallup carried out surveys of political opinion nearly every month from October 1938, has predicted the result of every general election since 1945 and of some 100 by-elections. After the demise of the *News Chronicle* in 1960, Gallup findings were published in the *Daily Telegraph* and the *Sunday Telegraph* until late 2001. Gallup are no longer active in opinion polling.

Several other organisations now produce regular polls between elections, published in their client newspapers and often, in more detail, on their websites;[2] and each polls weekly, or even more often, for its clients during election campaigns. Three have been established for decades. The longest standing of these is **NOP** (National Opinion Polls), founded in 1958 as a subsidiary company of Associated Newspapers, but now belonging to United Business Media. In 1997 and 2001 it also did the fieldwork for the private polling directed by Philip Gould for the Labour Party and also conducted the BBC's election night exit polls. **ICM** Research was formed as a breakaway by the political research team of Marplan, a subsidiary of McCann Erickson Advertising, which started political polling in 1968. ICM's polls appear regularly in the *Guardian*, and the company handled the Conservative Party's private polling at the 1997 and 2001 elections. Possibly the most widely-known British polling organisation over the past 30 years has been **MORI** (Market & Opinion Research International), founded in 1969 by Robert Worcester. MORI polled for the Labour Party in the elections of 1970–87, and conducted ITN's election night exit poll in 1997 and 2001. MORI also worked for Times Newspapers from 1975 to 2001 and now polls for the *Financial Times*.

Three new players have entered the field of regular polling since the last election. **Populus** now polls for *The Times*, **Communicate Research** for the *Independent*, while **YouGov** fills Gallup's former place at the *Daily Telegraph* as well as polling for the *Sunday Times* and *Mail on Sunday*; YouGov differ significantly from their rivals in that they poll on the Internet rather than by telephone or face-to-face.

Other pollsters have come and gone from the polling scene, including **Harris** Research (formerly ORC, Opinion Research Centre), a familiar name for many years who formerly polled for the Conservative Party and for ITN. Other market research organisations conduct one-off polls from time to time when they are commissioned to do so. In addition to the national polls, there are regular polls of Scottish opinion and less frequently of opinion in Wales. Apart from the companies already mentioned, **TNS System Three** and **Scottish Opinion** both poll for the Scottish newspapers, and the Cardiff-based **Beaufort** Research publishes occasional polls in Wales.

For the man in the street, the main interest in opinion polls is in whether they can succeed in picking the winner at a general election. Table 12.1 shows the polls published in the final week of the 2001 general election.

The polls have a better record than they are often credited with. It has only been in 1970 and 1992 that most of the polls have gone wrong. In February 1974, a hideously close contest, all the last-minute polls predicted that the Conservatives would win the most votes. They did, but owing to the vagaries of the British electoral system the Labour Party won more seats and formed the new government. Some polls try to avoid translating their vote predictions into seats, which (as discussed in Chapter 4) is not a calculation which can be made with precision as predictive models have to be based on assumptions of uniform swing, though the press reports of their findings tend to make it routinely in any case.

The pollsters themselves do not claim that their polls should be any more accurate than plus or minus 3 per cent for each party's support at best, which means that in measuring the *gap* between two parties the error should not be more than 6 per cent. Of course, in practical terms this is a big difference – especially since two polls taken at the same time might err in opposite directions. It may be that given these admitted limitations, opinion polls are not actually especially useful in reporting the day-by-day course of the election. Most pollsters would agree, and decry the concentration on the 'horse-race' as opposed to the more sophisticated analysis that the details of the polls, and the questions apart from voting

Table 12.1 Polls in the final week, 2001 election

Pollster: Client:	ICM Evening Standard	ICM Guardian	Rasmussen Independent	MORI Economist	MORI The Times	Gallup Daily Telegraph	Average poll finding	Final result*
Fieldwork	2–3 June	2–4 June	2–3 June	4–5 June	5–6 June	6 June		7 June
Party	(%)	(%)	(%)	(%)	(%)	(%)	(%)	(%)
Con	30	32	33	31	30	30	31.0	32.7
Lab	47	43	44	43	45	47	44.8	42.0
Lib Dem	18	19	16	20	18	18	18.2	18.8
Others	5	6	7	6	7	5	6.0	6.5
Av. error	2.5	0.6	1.4	1.1	1.8	2.5		

* The polls measure the share of the vote in Great Britain (i.e. excluding Northern Ireland), and it is this 'final result' with which they are compared. For this reason the figures differ from those in Appendix 1, where the totals and percentages include Northern Ireland.

intention, can show. But it is probably inevitable that media and as a result the public will expect the polls to be more precise than is realistic, and blame them if they fail.

Table 12.2 shows that in 11 out of the last 13 elections the *average* final forecast by the polls fell within the declared margin of error. In 1970 it was exceeded, and in that election four out of the five final polls finished up predicting the wrong winner. In 1992 the average error was considerably greater, and three out of the five polls put the 'wrong' party ahead; but in terms of the substantive result all five would have indicated a hung Parliament, which would have been the outcome had the gap between the parties been just 1 per cent narrower.

Table 12.2   Accuracy of final election polls

Year	Error of the average of all polls ('poll of polls')		Average error of all the individual polls		
	Average error in lead (%)	Average error in party share (%)	Average error in lead (%)	Average error in party share (%)	Number of polls
1945	3.5	1.5	3.5	1.5	1
1950	3.6	1.2	3.6	1.2	2
1951	6.0	2.0	6.0	2.1	3
1955	1.3	0.7	1.3	0.7	2
1959	1.1	0.4	1.1	0.7	4
1964	0.6	1.4	1.2	1.4	4
1966	3.9	1.3	3.9	1.3	5
1970	6.5	2.1	6.5	2.2	5
1974: Feb	1.6	1.2	2.4	1.6	6
1974: Oct	5.0	1.5	5.0	1.6	6
1979	1.2	0.5	1.7	0.9	4
1983	4.5	1.2	4.5	1.4	6
1987	3.6	1.3	3.7	1.4	6
1992	8.7	2.5	8.7	2.7	5
1997	3.2	1.3	4.4	2.1	5
2001	4.2	1.4	4.2	1.6	4
Average 1945–2001	*3.7*	*1.3*	*3.9*	*1.5*	*4*

Sources: Calculated from details of the final polls 1945–92 given in *The Opinion Polls and the 1992 British General Election: A Report to the Market Research Society* (London: Market Research Society, 1994); for 1997 in Robert Worcester and Roger Mortimore, *Explaining Labour's Landslide* (London: Politico's Books, 1999) and for 2001 in Robert Worcester and Roger Mortimore, *Explaining Labour's Second Landslide* (London: Politico's Books, 2001).

In some respects, the 1970 British general election was a re-run of the 1948 experience in America (when the polls predicted Dewey to beat

Truman in the presidential election!). The Labour Party was continuously ahead in the polls from the beginning of the campaign, and the almost universal expectation was that it was going to win. All except one polling organisation (ORC) completed their interviewing at least two days before polling day. ORC re-interviewed some of its respondents on election eve, and found clear evidence of last-minute switching to the Conservatives (which may have been caused by the unexpected defeat of England in the football World Cup or the publication of misleadingly bad monthly trade figures). It adjusted its figures accordingly, and forecast a Conservative win by 1 per cent: their actual lead over Labour was 2.4 per cent.

In 1992 the polls again failed to pick the winning party. Throughout the campaign they indicated a close result, mostly so close that a hung Parliament seemed the most likely outcome, but a clear majority of the polls (38 out of the 50 published during the campaign) showed the Labour Party ahead. In the event, the Conservatives led Labour by 7.6 per cent, and finished up with an overall Parliamentary majority of 21 seats. On average the five final polls had given Labour a lead of 1.1 per cent, which meant that the mean gap error was 8.7 per cent, easily the largest in British polling history (see Table 12.2). The reasons for the polls' errors were exhaustively investigated, notably in an inquiry undertaken by the Market Research Society.[3] No single cause was found, but several factors emerged, each of which was likely to result in an underestimate of Conservative support. These were deficiencies in the sampling frame and population profile adopted by the pollsters, reluctance by Conservative voters to reveal how they intended to vote, a high turnout by Conservative voters and a late swing towards the government (possibly the most important factor). However, all the polling companies introduced changes in their procedures in the light of the MRS inquiry findings, and the polls in the 1997 and 2001 elections were much nearer to the mark.

Apart from occasionally failing to pick the winner, the other main cause for scepticism over the polls is that on occasion different polls produce strikingly different findings in surveys which are published on the same day or in the same week. This is often because apparently comparable polls did not interview at the same time (public opinion can be very volatile) or (with polls of opinions rather than election polls) because the wording of the questions was different and they were not in fact measuring the same thing at all. But it is also true that the various companies sometimes have different opinions on how best to measure voting intention, and consequently use slightly different methodologies which can affect their findings. There is no obviously best way to compensate for one party's supporters being more reluctant to talk to the pollsters, nor a natural level of turnout which should be assumed for a future election when the real turnout is only a matter of conjecture and yet will have a partisan effect.

There are two established methods of constructing a polling sample. A *random* or *probability* sample consists of taking every hundredth or thousandth name from the election register or address from the Postcode Address File and calling on voters in their own homes. With a *quota* sample, interviewers are instructed to contact so many voters of each sex, age group, occupation and social class, worked out in proportion to the total population. The random sample, which involves contacting named individuals and calling back several times if they are out, is much more expensive than the quota system but, more crucially, is also much slower so its findings will be more out of date. The consensus of opinion used to be that random samples were more reliable, as in theory they certainly should be. In practice, however, their results were worse, and they were abandoned for election polls at the end of the 1970s. (They are still used for other research where time and cost are less of an object – for example in government-sponsored social surveys.)

A newer method in Britain, though longer established elsewhere, is *telephone* polling, with the telephone numbers more or less randomly selected; this may or may not be combined with quotas to control the representativeness of the sample. Telephone polling was used on a small scale, without conspicuous success, by specialist companies in elections during the 1980s, but after the embarrassment of 1992 two of the five main polling companies, Gallup and ICM, switched to telephone sampling for their main polls in the 1997 election. MORI also used telephone polling for some of its campaign and constituency polls, but retained face-to-face interviews and quota sampling for its main election polls, and its monthly Political Monitor is now the only regularly published poll conducted by the older method.

The normal national sample of each poll, whether by telephone or face-to-face, includes between 1000 and 2000 respondents, though larger samples may be used for the final poll in an election. In theory the larger the sample the smaller the margin of error should be; but the mathematics dictates that doubling the sample size only makes the margin of error half as good again, and there is a point beyond which the extra expense of larger samples is wasted. It should perhaps be stressed that the size of the sample is less important than its representative nature. A badly drawn sample of 2 million can be much less accurate than a well-constructed one of a thousand or so, as was demonstrated in the 1936 presidential election in the USA, when the unscientific *Literary Digest* poll, with 2,376,533 respondents, predicted a landslide victory for the Republican candidate, while George Gallup and his rivals – using their newly developed method of polling with nationally representative samples – accurately forecast an easy win for Roosevelt. In practice, when the polls have proved inaccurate in Britain, other factors were to blame and larger samples would not have helped. (In fact, both in 1987 when the polls were substantially correct and in 1992 when they were not, there was one poll conducted with a 10,000 sample, but its results were right in line with all the other polls based on samples of 1000 or 2000.) One legitimate reason for larger samples is to allow small subgroups of the population (first-time voters, for example, or readers of a particular newspaper) to be examined and compared.

In the last couple of years, YouGov has introduced a third methodology to British polling: polling Internet users. Unlike the established polls, which approach a freshly drawn sample of the public for every survey, YouGov depends on a 'panel' who have volunteered to take part and agreed to be approached for a number of polls; its samples are usually a little bigger than those of the other polls, between 2000 and 2500. The new method is controversial, but YouGov claims a good record of election prediction since its establishment.[4]

Arguably, there is more strength in diversity of methodologies than in a consensus. When there are consistent differences it may be safer to be guided by the *average* of several reputable polls, so long as the dates of fieldwork are similar, rather than to depend exclusively on any one of them. Much the greatest stimulus to the polls to improve their methods is the fact that there are several of them. Competition keeps polls on their toes: this is one field where monopoly could be very dangerous.

The margin of error for polls in by-elections and for individual constituencies in general elections is sometimes much larger, and there have been several examples of poll predictions being far out of line with the actual result. One example was the Brecon and Radnor by-election of July 1985, where the polls had shown the Labour candidate to be well in the lead, but the Liberal captured the seat.[5]

There are good reasons why it can be more difficult to get an accurate result in a single constituency than in a national sample. If the poll is conducted face-to-face rather than by telephone, it must inevitably involve shipping in teams of interviewers unfamiliar with the local area or, much worse, using local but untrained interviewers. (For this reason, among others, most constituency polls by the major companies these days are conducted by telephone.) Furthermore, in a by-election turnout can be unpredictable, and if one party's supporters are more likely than others to vote, of course it will distort the result; although the pollsters naturally attempt to allow for this, they cannot always do so successfully.

Things are made worse by the reluctance of most newspapers that sponsor local polls to fund a large enough sample (made more difficult because the cost of a reputably designed local poll will usually be, head for head, more expensive than a national one). Superficially, it might seem that if a sample of 1000 is adequate for a poll of the whole 40 million electorate of the country, then a much smaller sample should do equally well for the 70,000 or so electors of the typical constituency. In fact this is a fallacy – the mathematical formulae that determine the statistical margins of error of a perfect poll are the same whether the universe is 70,000 or 40 million, and a 1000 sample would still be needed to achieve the standard ±3 per cent margin of error. Most constituency polls today make do with a 600 or 800 sample, and accept a consequently wider level of inaccuracy.

Nevertheless, in recent years the vast majority of polls conducted by the major polling companies have performed satisfactorily. Indeed, a MORI poll in the Wirral South by-election just before the 1997 general election campaign opened, which predicted Labour's swing to capture the seat to an accuracy of 0.4 per cent, was taken by alert commentators as an early confirmation that the pollsters had, as they claimed, solved the problems that led to inaccuracies in their 1992 election predictions. Of the 16 constituency polls conducted by ICM for publication in the Sunday papers the weekend before the 1997 election, 11 were within four points of the final percentage share for each of the main parties (and in some of the remainder, late swing and tactical voting caused by the publication of the poll itself may well have been a factor in the discrepancy). However, this goes only for polls conducted professionally by the major polling companies: beware the amateur poll by the local paper or radio station run by journalists or enthusiastic non-specialist academics, and often using students or other cheap untrained labour for interviewing.

Worse still (and by no means confined to constituency polls) are the entirely spurious 'phone-in' polls, which some pollsters characterise as 'voodoo polls' or 'phone(y) polls'. Because the participants are entirely self-selecting (and usually not prevented from voting several times), they cannot hope to be representative of the electorate, and their results normally bear no relationship to reality. Nevertheless, they are often reported as if they were reputable polls, especially by the tabloid press, and many naive readers no doubt take them seriously – sufficiently so, at any rate, that political parties have on occasion organised volunteers to phone-in systematically and 'rig' the results.

Although the opinion polls have established such an important role for themselves in British politics, in one respect they have until recently played a smaller part in Britain than in the USA and some other countries. This is in the use of privately commissioned polls by the parties and by individual political leaders. The national party headquarters have been using polls since the 1950s. However, both because of the absence of primary elections and the financial restraints imposed by legal limits on election expenditure, the commissioning of polls by individual politicians has been almost unknown in Britain. The election of a Mayor of London in 2000, though, to all intents and purposes introduced primary elections to Britain for the first time, and some of the hopeful candidates commissioned polls to help their campaigns; this is probably a development that is here to stay, though perhaps only the Mayoral election in London will be on a large-enough scale for it to be useful.

Private polling differs a little from the public polling published in the newspapers, though it may use many of the same techniques. Some of the private polls may, like the newspaper polls, measure the current state of the contest (and may occasionally be 'leaked' if it seems to the party's advantage to do so) but their real purpose is to show the party how it can win the election. The parties also now make considerable use of qualitative research or focus groups, in which small groups of voters are brought together to discuss aspects of the election in greater depth. The parties' use of focus groups drew little media attention before 1997, and many commentators have mistakenly assumed that they are a new departure in British elections; but, in fact, they have been part of the scene for many years, certainly back to the 1960s. Focus groups cannot produce quantitative findings (measurements of *how many* electors think in a particular way), and perhaps for that reason are rarely commissioned by newspapers in their election reporting, but they can offer vital insights for skilled analysts into how the mind of the electorate works, and are an essential part of a modern political polling programme.

Even the parties themselves were long cautious in their use of opinion polling, and they used it mainly to test propaganda themes and for copy-testing of posters, newspaper advertisements and other visual material.

The first campaign to be based to any significant degree on material gleaned from the polls was that launched by the Conservatives before the 1959 election. Labour was slower off the mark, but relied to a similar extent on privately commissioned polls for its run-up campaign to the 1964 election. From 1964 the Conservatives retained the services of Opinion Research Centre, later part of the Harris Research Centre, which originally worked almost exclusively for them. Its former co-director, Humphrey Taylor, one of the wisest heads in the polling world, interpreted the polling findings to Tory leaders during each election campaign.

The Tories used to show a highly professional attitude to polls, and integrated the use of their privately commissioned polls, as well as the analysis of the mass of material available from the public polls, into all their election planning. But during the 1980s and 1990s, especially during John Major's leadership, the party became increasingly sceptical, put less energy into its polling programme and paid less attention to the results or to their pollster.

The Labour Party, despite having retained the services of MORI's shrewd director, Robert Worcester, and of his organisation, during each election from 1970 to 1987, tended to make less effective use of their private polls. This was partly due to the suspicion with which Labour leaders such as James Callaghan and Michael Foot (but not Harold Wilson) regarded polls, and partly due to the more amateur and internally divisive nature of the Labour organisation. In 1987 and 1992 there was a distinct improvement, and Labour not only spent much more money than previously on its private polls but made much more intelligent use of their findings; and since Tony Blair's election to the leadership in 1994 the polling programme, and especially the focus groups run by the party's political consultant, (Lord) Philip Gould, have played a dominant role in forming the election strategy and undoubtedly contributed to the scale of Labour's victories.[6]

The former Alliance parties were enthusiastic followers of the polls, but lacked the resources to commission many private polls for their own use. Whereas the Conservatives were spending some £100,000 a year on polls in the 1980s, and the Labour Party about £85,000, and both parties spent an extra £120,000 during the 1987 election campaign, it is doubtful if the Alliance spent as much as one-tenth of these amounts.[7] In the 1992 election the Conservatives spent about £250,000 on private polls, Labour about £200,000 and the Liberal Democrats about £40,000;[8] in 1997 Labour certainly spent more, while the Conservatives spent around £600,000.[9] In 2001, the parties were required for the first time to submit detailed accounts to the Electoral Commission (see Table 14.2), but, unfortunately, market research was combined as a category with canvassing; while telephone canvassing might seem superficially similar to polling it has an entirely different purpose, and comparable figures to those from earlier elections are not available.

Private polling has been unfavourably received in some quarters, and allegations have been made that politicians have subordinated their principles to the desire to win votes. Such critics appear to be ignorant of the manner in which politicians make decisions. It is in fact a totally unrealistic view that polls can tell a politician what policies to adopt. Any political leader who allowed them to do so would soon develop a reputation for irresolution and lack of consistency. The most that a poll can do for a politician or a party is to help them put over, in an effective way, the policies on which they have already decided, and to determine which policies should be stressed to particular target audiences. It is difficult to see anything improper or dishonourable in this.

There has from time to time been well-merited criticism about the simplistic ways that some newspapers have presented poll findings, and of the deliberately misleading partial leaking of private polls by political parties. To protect themselves from such criticism, and to force their clients to behave more responsibly, the leading polling organisations drew up a code of practice in May 1970, which was revised in January 1974. This stipulated that all published poll reports should include details of the sampling method used, the sample size and the dates of the fieldwork. It further provided that if private poll findings were leaked, details of the poll should be made publicly available. In November 2004, eight leading polling companies (including all those regularly publishing political polls in the national press) formed the British Polling Council, to 'ensure standards of disclosure designed to provide consumers of survey results that enter the public domain an adequate basis for judging the reliability and validity of the results'.[10]

Some critics of opinion polls have suggested that they may create a bandwagon effect in favour of the party which they report to be in the lead. Others, rather more plausibly, have hypothesised an underdog effect, arguing that some voters may be put off voting for a party which seemed to be well in the lead, and suggesting that they may discourage people from bothering to vote if they suggest that the result of the election is a foregone conclusion, though the evidence that this has happened to any significant degree is at best weak.[11] Such an effect, if it exists, could have influenced the results of the two narrowly contested elections in 1974, depriving the Tories of a victory in February and reducing to a minimal level the predicted Labour majority in October. The polls in the 1992 election, most of which showed Labour in the lead but pointing to the probability of a hung Parliament, may have motivated hesitant Conservatives to record their votes and induced some would-be Liberal Democrats to switch to the Tories to avoid such a result.[12] The polls may also guide voters on tactical voting, especially in the case of constituency polls.

Most pollsters would agree that some voters, at least, may be influenced by poll results. However, assuming that the information given by the polls is reasonably accurate, this is not necessarily pernicious. It should not be up to the state, or anybody else, to tell voters in a democracy what information they may take into account in deciding how they will vote.

There have been periodic attempts to ban the publication of opinion polls during election campaigns. In 1968 the Speaker's Conference on Electoral Law recommended that 'There should be no broadcast, or publication in a newspaper or other periodical of the result of a public opinion poll or of betting odds on the likely result of a parliamentary election during the period of seventy-two hours before the close of the poll.' The then Labour government refused to act on this recommendation, but 17 years later, in October 1985, the House of Commons rejected a Private Member's Bill to impose a ban, by the narrow margin of 128 votes to 124. A further Bill, introduced under the Ten-Minute Rule, was actually approved by 116 votes to 103 in February 1987, but made no further Parliamentary progress. However, foreign experience has shown that such bans are unworkable,[13] as well as being objectionable in principle as being designed to deprive voters of information which would in any case be available to promoters of private polls, including the political parties themselves. The former Liberal MP, Clement Freud, aptly commented on the 1985 proposal: 'the effect of the bill would be rather like banning meteorologists from forecasting the weather a week before a garden party in case anyone might be put off from going'. Any such ban could be seen as a restriction on the freedom of the press, and might now be challenged under the Human Rights Act; in both Canada and India in recent years similar bans were ruled unconstitutional by the supreme court.[14]

One restriction which has been imposed, however, is a ban on 'exit polls' (those which ask voters how they *have* voted rather than how they are going to vote) being published before the election is over. At the 2004 European election, *The Times* was threatened with prosecution for publishing a poll that included reports by some electors of how they had voted by post, days before the ballot boxes for the majority of voters had opened. At the time of writing it is unclear whether the case will reach court, but if it does it seems likely the journalists will vigorously protest against the attempt to restrict their reporting of the election.

Whether the polls to any great extent affect the way in which people vote, they clearly influence the morale of party activists, though even here the effect it has on their efforts cannot easily be predicted. A disappointing poll may lead to a slackening of effort *or* to gestures of defiance which give a sharper edge to a party's campaign – a favourable one may equally lead to complacency or renewed dedication. More importantly, polls have a very considerable influence on the behaviour of politicians. The importance of polls in informing the Prime Minister of favourable occasions for holding a general election, and even more importantly, warning him or her off unfavourable ones, has already been stressed in an earlier chapter.

The whole tenor of recent election campaigns has been dominated by opinion poll findings, especially as the great majority of voters now have a reasonable idea of what the polls are saying. The 1979, 1983 and 1987 election campaigns were all fought in the knowledge that the Conservatives were a long way ahead and were virtually certain winners, and those of 1997 and 2001 in the expectation of a Labour victory (though in 1997 there was widespread scepticism that Labour would achieve as convincing a landslide as the polls seemed to indicate). In 1983 the battle for second place, in terms of votes if not in seats, between Labour and the Alliance attracted disproportionate attention solely because of the steady flow of poll findings. Indeed the Alliance parties, and before them the Liberals, have been peculiarly dependent on the polls for their credibility: the better their standing in the polls the more likely are they to attract votes. Conversely, adverse poll findings, as in the 1987 election, normally have a depressant effect on their prospects. In 1992 the polls predicted a close result, which probably contributed to the rise in turnout. The perceived failure of the polls to predict the result in 1992 may have lessened their influence in the 1997 campaign, but in 2001 they were attracting almost as much interest as ever. It is difficult to imagine a modern election without them.

13
How People Vote, and Why Some Don't

The British voter is subjected to a heavy barrage of propaganda from all the major parties – and to occasional salvoes from minor groups and independents – during election campaigns, and to a lesser degree at other times. Earlier chapters of this book have sought to describe the various ways in which the parties seek to influence public opinion. This chapter will attempt to discern whether all this activity makes much difference to the way that people vote.

The traditional answer has been 'not much'. The dominant theories of voting behaviour in Britain have been mostly sociological, and rest on the idea that most voters identify with one or other of the parties. This identification may follow from the voter's fixed social characteristics, such as class or region, or it may be developed through social interaction with other people; it affects the way individuals understand political issues and assimilate political arguments, and predisposes them to vote in a particular way. Most voters, it is argued, are set in their ways, and are not much influenced by what happens in election campaigns, making up what is often referred to as the parties' 'core votes'.

This belief has been based on the assumption that most voters are profoundly influenced by social class factors, and in particular by the political views of their parents, which in the great majority of cases are bequeathed to their children along with their more worldly possessions. These voters would be likely to vote the same way for most of their lives; but the minority of 'floating voters', who are prepared to switch their support between parties from one election to another, generally hold the balance of power between the parties so that election campaigns still matter and either of the major parties can hope to win the election. On this assumption, explaining the result of a British general election therefore involves two separate factors – both the explanation and evolution of the long-term, underlying pattern, and the shorter-term factors such as the government's performance or the election campaign itself affecting the decisions of the floating voters.

For many years this belief was largely based on conjecture, and inference from the relatively small movement in the party share of votes recorded at each successive general election. Over the past four decades, however, a great deal of harder evidence has become available, partly from opinion polls but more particularly from a series of election studies, based on in-depth interviewing, sponsored by the Social Science Research Council (now renamed the Economic and Social Research Council) since 1963, and directed by various teams of political scientists.

This series, known as the British Election Studies (BES), has involved interviews with more than 30,000 voters during eleven general elections, and has produced a series of major studies,[1] as well as a substantial amount of secondary literature.[2] Much of the argument in this chapter is based on the successive findings of these surveys,[3] but also draws on MORI surveys from the 1997 and 2001 elections to confirm how far the findings of the earlier BES surveys are still true. In general, these have supported traditional beliefs, but have also suggested that though there is a stable pattern to the electorate's voting behaviour, it is by no means static.

One of the first findings of the BES was an emphatic confirmation of the belief that most children voted the same way as their parents had done. Respondents were asked if they could remember how their parents had voted during their own childhood and were then asked their present voting intention. The result is shown in Table 13.1.[4] David Butler and Donald Stokes, who were the authors of the first of the BES studies, published in 1969, constructed on the basis of their detailed findings on parental influence on voting a theory of political generations. This implied a long-term shift from Conservative to Labour as a result of demographic changes. The reasoning behind this was that it is only since 1945 that the number of Labour voters has been approximately equal to the number of Conservative voters. People who started voting before 1945 were much more likely to have Conservative-voting than Labour-voting parents. As these older voters died off, the proportion of 'hereditary' Conservatives in the electorate was bound to decline, while new generations of voters entering the electorate at the age of 18 were much more likely to be the offspring of Labour-voting parents.[5]

Table 13.1 Party preference by parents' Conservative or Labour preferences, 1960s

	Parents' partisanship		
	Both parents Conservative	Parents divided	Both parents Labour
Respondent's own present preference	(%)	(%)	(%)
Conservative	75	37	10
Labour	14	49	81
Liberal	8	10	6
Other	–	–	–
None	3	4	3
Total	100	100	100

Source: Reprinted by kind permission from David Butler and Donald Stokes, *Political Change in Britain*, 2nd edition (London: Macmillan, 1974), p. 48.

If this 'generational' effect was the only factor at work, it is clear that Labour would have done better at every succeeding election until the 1990s, and the Conservatives worse, which has not been the case. The later BES studies have concentrated more on probing what other factors have played a part, and in particular whether the traditional link between social class and voting is becoming weaker. Substantial evidence was produced to suggest that this was in fact the case, and that the simple dichotomy of middle-class Tory and working-class Labour was being attenuated.

Bo Särlvik and Ivor Crewe, who produced the second major BES study, in 1983,[6] argued not only that the working class was becoming more Tory and the middle class more Labour, but that long-term partisan commitments were getting weaker for a large number of voters. Table 13.2 shows how support among Labour identifiers for Labour principles had declined over the ten-year period 1964–74, while Table 13.3 revealed a strikingly high level of support for professed Tory objectives among Labour voters in 1979. Särlvik and Crewe found that the strength of partisan commitment among both Tory and Labour identifiers was weakening during this period. Later studies by the same authors showed this trend continuing up until 1983. Särlvik and Crewe described this process as one of 'dealignment', and suggested that it was a reason behind the much larger swings in by-elections which have occurred in the period since 1966. The authors of the third BES study,[7] Anthony Heath, Roger Jowell and John Curtice, challenged the thesis that class divisions are becoming less important as a factor in voting. They argued that what has happened is not so much a decline in class influence as a change in

Table 13.2　Falling support for Labour principles, 1964–74

	All Labour identifiers			Core Labour identifiers		
	1964 (%)	Feb 1974 (%)	Change 1964–74 (%)	1964 (%)	Feb 1974 (%)	Change 1964–74 (%)
In favour of nationalising more industries	57	50	–7	64	50	–14
In favour of spending more on social services	89	61	–28	92	57	–35
In favour of retaining close ties between trade unions and the Labour Party	38	29	–9	50	34	–16
Whose sympathies are generally for strikers	37	23	–14	33	25	–8
Who do not believe that the trade unions have 'too much power'	59	44	–15	74	52	–22
Perceiving 'a great deal' of difference between the parties	49	33	–16	62	41	–21
Average (mean)	55	40	–15	63	43	–20

Source: *The Economist*, 11 March 1978.

the relative size of the different classes. Once account is taken of this, the class connection with voting is as strong as ever, they asserted.[8] Table 13.4 shows the substantial changes in class sizes that occurred between 1964 and 1983, with the salariat increasing by half, and the working class declining from nearly half the electorate to barely a third. Table 13.5 shows how people in these five different class categories voted in 1983. The Conservative Party held a large lead in the four higher groupings (particularly the petty bourgeoisie, defined as 'farmers, small proprietors and own-account manual workers' or 'independents'), while Labour remained well ahead in the residual working class. (The Alliance support was more evenly distributed.)

Table 13.3   Labour voters on Tory aims, 1979

Should the next government attempt to achieve these objectives?	*Should (%)*	*Should not (%)*	*Don't know (%)*
Reduce violent crime and vandalism	95	3	2
Reduce Supplementary Benefit for strikers, on assumption that they are getting strike pay from their unions	63	30	7
End secondary picketing by strikers	78	14	8
Reduce income tax, especially for the higher paid	52	45	3
Give council house tenants the right to buy their homes, with discounts for people who have lived in them for three years or more	75	20	5
	75	20	5
Reduce the number of civil servants	70	22	8
Sell off parts of some state owned companies	40	49	11

Source: RSL poll in the *Observer*, 22 April 1979.

Table 13.4   Class composition of the electorate 1964 and 1983

	1964 (%)	*1983 (%)*
Salaried	18	27
Routine non-manual	18	24
Petty bourgeoisie	7	8
Foremen and technicians	10	7
Working class	47	34
Total	100	100
	(N = 1,475)	(N = 3,790)

Source: Reprinted by kind permission from Anthony Heath, Roger Jowell and John Curtice, *How Britain Votes* (Oxford: Pergamon Press, 1985), p. 36.

Table 13.5   Head of household's class and vote, 1983

Head of household's class	Conservative	Labour	Alliance	Others		
Salariat	54	14	31	1	100%	(N = 923)
Routine non-manual	49	24	25	2	100%	(N = 495)
Petty bourgeoisie	69	13	17	1	100%	(N = 291)
Foremen and technicians	45	28	26	1	100%	(N = 266)
Working class	30	48	21	1	100%	(N = 1,089)

Source: Reprinted by kind permission from Anthony Heath, Roger Jowell and John Curtice, *How Britain Votes* (Oxford: Pergamon Press, 1985), p. 27.

It should be noted that the class categorisation adopted by Heath *et al.* is different from that used in the great majority of voting studies, which is based on standard market research designations used by the opinion polls. This classification, known as social grade, divides the population into six occupational categories, as follows:

A   Higher managerial or professional
B   Lower managerial or administrative
C1   Skilled or supervisory non-manual, lower non-manual
C2   Skilled manual
D   Unskilled manual
E   Residual, on pension or other state benefit.

Table 13.6 shows how the 2001 vote divided, according to this classification. All studies agree that occupational differences are more significant politically than differences in income, as such, though there is a considerable overlap, the more prestigious occupations being normally, but not invariably, better paid. Heath *et al.* hypothesised also that the actual working situation was of importance, in particular whether a

Table 13.6   Social grade and vote, 2001

Social grade	Conservative	Labour	Liberal Democrat	Others		
Grade A	52	23	22	3	100%	(N = 431)
Grade B	37	31	26	6	100%	(N = 3,189)
Grade C1	36	38	20	6	100%	(N = 5,318)
Grade C2	29	49	15	7	100%	(N = 4,041)
Grade D	23	55	13	9	100%	(N = 2,742)
Grade E	24	55	14	7	100%	(N = 2,845)

Source: MORI.

voter was in a position of authority over others and whether he or she was directly exposed to market forces in earning his or her livelihood. In both cases this proved likely to sharply increase the probability of voting Conservative. Hence the 'petty bourgeoisie' class in their findings, which is drawn effectively from among the B, C1 and C2 categories, but contains a much higher incidence of Conservative voters than any of these three groupings.

Any division of the population into social classes is somewhat artificial, and may not coincide with the population's own perceptions. In fact, many voters do not think of themselves as falling into the class in which political scientists or market researchers put them on the basis of their occupation. Butler and Stokes found that subjective class feelings were a clearer indication of political partisanship than a voter's objective position in the social system. That is to say that people with 'middle-class occupations' who regarded themselves as working class were much more likely to vote Labour, while the reverse was the case with voters in 'working-class occupations' who regarded themselves as middle class. This was perhaps unsurprising, especially as the terms of the party political debate in the 1960s were still strongly tied to the issue of class, and it is possible that voters' ideological beliefs were as much a cause of their class self-image as vice versa; but the relationship still survives today. In 2002, a MORI survey asked the public whether they agreed or disagreed with the statement 'At the end of the day, I am working class and proud of it'; 60 per cent agreed, including 45 per cent of those who would normally be classified as middle class (A/B/C1). Previous studies had found that those in each class who agreed with the statement were much more likely to support Labour than those who disagreed. As Table 13.7 shows, this seems to be no longer true for the ABs, though the relationship still holds for the other classes.

Table 13.7   Support for Labour by social grade and class self-image, 2002

		Social grade			
		AB	C1	C2	DE
% (of those who expressed a voting intention) that supported Labour					
'At the end of the day, I am working class and proud of it'	Agree	41%	47%	55%	60%
	Disagree	41%	40%	42%	48%

Base: 1,875 British adults aged 15+.

Source: MORI, July 2002.

Another important factor is trade union membership, with members being much more likely to vote Labour than non-members (Table 13.8), although with the decline of the size of the union movement in recent years, it may be that the decision to join a union these days is as much caused by Labour sympathies as a cause of them. Again, whereas this relationship was previously clear-cut for all occupational classes, the most recent survey shows it breaking down in one class, in this case the DEs. While not too much weight should be given to the evidence of surveys at a single election, it may be that some of the factors that previously drove adherence to Labour have weakened in their effects.

Table 13.8 Support for Labour among union and non-union members by social grade, 2001

	Social grade			
Proportion voting Labour	*AB*	*C1*	*C2*	*DE*
Among union members	46%	46%	57%	57%
Among non-union members	24%	37%	47%	58%
Difference	+22%	+9%	+7%	−1%
	(N = 717)	(N = 895)	(N = 608)	(N = 759)

Base: Those who voted.

Source: MORI.

Another significant influence on voting, according to many studies, is housing, with owner-occupiers being more likely to vote Tory and council tenants Labour, irrespective of class differences. Table 13.9 demonstrates this was still true in 2001. This factor was of considerable political significance in the 1980s, as the Tory government's sale of council houses to their tenants increased the size of the owner-occupier class, consolidating the party's electoral base.

Where they live also seems to be a factor in influencing how people vote. As everybody knows, there are profound regional differences in voting patterns, with the Conservatives and the Liberal Democrats being much stronger in the south of England, and Labour in Scotland, Wales and the north. Figures for 2001 illustrate this point (Table 13.10). To a large extent, these figures can be explained by social class differences between the regions, but this is far from being the whole story. There is, apparently, a 'neighbourhood effect', which means that even working-class voters in the south are more inclined to vote Conservative, and middle-class voters in the north and in Scotland and Wales to vote Labour.

Table 13.9   **Housing, class and vote, 1997**

		Conservative	Labour	Liberal Democrat	Others		
AB	Owner-occupiers	41	29	25	5	100%	(N = 2,121)
	Private tenants	25	32	39	4	100%	(N = 68)
	Council / housing association tenants	19	45	30	6	100%	(N = 75)
C1	Owner-occupiers	39	37	19	5	100%	(N = 2,446)
	Private tenants	32	35	26	7	100%	(N = 203)
	Council / housing association tenants	22	51	17	9	100%	(N = 355)
C2	Owner-occupiers	32	46	16	7	100%	(N = 1,599)
	Private tenants	23	50	22	6	100%	(N = 72)
	Council / housing association tenants	20	59	13	8	100%	(N = 480)
DE	Owner-occupiers	30	49	15	7	100%	(N = 1,241)
	Private tenants	29	49	13	10	100%	(N = 153)
	Council / housing association tenants	17	64	12	8	100%	(N = 1,441)

Source: MORI.

Table 13.10   **Region and voting, 2001**

	Conservative	Labour	Liberal Democrat	Others
Scotland	16%	43%	16%	25%
Wales	21%	49%	14%	17%
North	28%	52%	17%	3%
Midlands	38%	42%	16%	4%
South	38%	34%	24%	4%

Source: Calculated from Tables 4 and 5 in Electoral Commission, *Election 2001: The Official Results* (London: Politico's Publishing, 2001), pp. 224–7.

Similarly, there is a marked urban–rural division, with urban voters, irrespective of class, being more likely to vote Labour, and rural voters more inclined to vote Conservative. People living in predominantly middle-class neighbourhoods are more likely to be Tory voters, whatever their own class background. The separate effects of region and neighbourhood are indicated in Table 13.11, based on the 1983 election.

Table 13.11   Class, neighbourhood, region and vote, 1983

| | Percentage voting Conservative | | | |
	North		South	
Salaried individuals				
in salaried wards	54	(78)	54	(269)
in mixed wards	51	(40)	60	(140)
in working-class wards	40	(81)	–(14)	
All salaried individuals	48	(199)	57	(423)
Intermediate-class individuals				
in salaried wards	56	(87)	63	(251)
in mixed wards	60	(79)	53	(236)
in working-class wards	39	(142)	40	(28)
All intermediate–class individuals	49	(308)	57	(515)
Working-class individuals				
in salaried wards	46	(22)	49	(106)
in mixed wards	31	(57)	40	(145)
in working-class wards	20	(235)	19	(40)
All working-class individuals	24	(314)	40	(291)

Note: Figures in brackets give cell sizes.

Source: Reprinted by kind permission from Anthony Heath, Roger Jowell and John Curtice, *How Britain Votes* (Oxford: Pergamon Press, 1985), p. 83.

Education is a more complicated factor, as its effect seems to vary according to social class. Among the working class, the better somebody is educated the more likely they are to vote Conservative. In the middle class, the better educated, and particularly those who have benefited from higher education, are less likely to vote Conservative (see Table 13.12). Heath *et al.* surmise that this may be because higher education exposes people to 'liberal values' (on such issues as the death penalty, free speech, defence expenditure, the common market and stiff jail sentences) which are more likely to lead to people voting Labour or Alliance (now Liberal Democrat) rather than Conservative.

For many years polls and electoral studies showed women to be more Conservative than men. This is still generally true, but only marginally so – the 'gender gap' has narrowed in the last few decades. Nevertheless, there are still very sharp differences between the voting behaviour of the sexes within each age group and, furthermore, the pattern of the voting differences is not uniform. In fact, young women are far *less* likely to be Conservative than their male counterparts; but above the age of 30 the position is reversed. Table 13.13 shows the figures from the aggregates of MORI's polls in each of the last five elections.

Table 13.12   Class, education and vote, 1983

		Conservative	Labour	Alliance	Other		
Salaried	degree	42	16	41	1	100%	(N = 131)
	'O' level or above	54	12	33	1	100%	(N = 501)
	below 'O' level	60	17	22	2	101%	(N = 231)
Intermediate	degree	–	–	–	–	–	(N = 21)
classes	'O' level or above	57	17	25	1	100%	(N = 441)
	below 'O' level	49	25	24	2	100%	(N = 748)
Working	degree	–	–	–	–	–	(N = 4)
class	'O' level or above	40	36	22	2	100%	(N = 169)
	below 'O' level	28	52	20	1	101%	(N = 815)

Source: Reprinted by kind permission from Anthony Heath, Roger Jowell and John Curtice, *How Britain Votes* (Oxford: Pergamon Press, 1985), p. 67.

Table 13.13   The 'gender gap' in voting, 1983–2001

	1983	1987	1992	1997	2001
All	+8	0	+6	+2	+1
18–24	+5	–17	–18	–14	–12
25–34	+14	–4	0	+3	+4
35–54	+9	+11	+10	+9	+2
55+	+5	0	+12	+2	+2

Base: c. 13,000–25,000 adults at each election.
Note: The 'gender gap' in each group is measured as the difference in the Conservative percentage lead over Labour among men and among women; a positive gender gap means that the Conservatives do better among women than among men, a negative gap the reverse.

Source: MORI aggregate surveys. Cited in Robert Worcester and Roger Mortimore, *Explaining Labour's Second Landslide* (London: Politico's Books, 2001), p. 201.

One fact that stands out concerning all the factors discussed so far is that the correlation between any one of them, or even the combination of all of them, and voting intention is a lot less than 100 per cent. Although each factor may predispose an individual to vote in a certain way, large numbers of people do not in fact do so. Should they therefore be regarded as 'deviants', or is there another important countervailing factor at work which in large measure cancels out these particular influences? Heath *et al.* had no doubt that there is, and that this factor is ideology, or the settled opinions of voters.

In other words, voters are thinking animals, who are not the mere creatures of economic determinism. If their own values or beliefs or perceptions conflict with their social circumstances they are fully capable of giving them priority. If no conflict arises, their beliefs naturally reinforce the social influences, and people to whom this applies form the bedrock support for the Conservative and Labour Parties. Where there is a conflict, however, one is likely to encounter less extreme partisanship, a willingness to consider the claims of the other side, perhaps to vary one's vote from one election to the next, and a greater propensity to support alternatives, such as the Liberal Democrats, or the SNP in Scotland. No researcher has been able to demonstrate mathematically the relative strength of economic and ideological factors, but Anthony Heath asserts categorically that 'values and perceptions explain much more of the variance in vote than does social class, but then they always have done'.[9] All the factors discussed so far, insofar as they influence consciously or unconsciously the actions of voters, are permanent or long-term and are therefore likely to affect the orientation or identification of voters over a long period. Other factors, such as the impact of individual candidates or party leaders, the effect of campaign techniques, the success or failure of governments in dealing with transient issues, may well affect actual decisions on how to vote in particular elections. These factors may confirm or challenge the long-term identification of voters. Moreover, a voter who consistently votes contrary to his or her long-term identification because of short-term factors may well end up by changing identification as well.

The greater volatility of voters – in other democracies as well as in Britain – suggests that long-term identification may be becoming weaker, a thesis strongly supported by the Särlvik–Crewe study which showed a declining number of voters who identified with one or other party, and a diminishing sense of commitment even among identifiers.[10] This weakening sense of identification provided an opportunity for the Liberal-Social Democratic Alliance, without guaranteeing its success.

It has been suggested that rising living standards and improved educational opportunities have resulted in fewer voters being influenced by class considerations. According to this theory a new generation of 'post-materialist voters' has arrived, 'people who have been brought up in an economically secure environment ... who will grow up to place greater emphasis on higher needs such as freedom of speech and a humane society'. Heath *et al.* credit the American writers Ronald Inglehart and Abraham Maslow with this concept:

Maslow postulates that man has a hierarchy of needs: needs for food and shelter come at the bottom of the hierarchy and tend to receive highest priority until they are satisfied. Once they are satisfied people move on to higher needs culminating in ones such as 'self-actualisation'. Inglehart claims to follow this account and argues that people who experienced 'formative affluence' will grow up to place more emphasis on values such as democracy and freedom of speech.[11]

Heath *et al.* see the development of 'post-materialist values' as a countervailing factor to the advantage that the Conservative Party might otherwise expect to gain from the numerical decline of the working class.

Not all theorists, however, accept the sociological model of voting behaviour. The authors of the latest BES study, Harold Clarke, David Sanders, Marianne Stewart and Paul Whiteley,[12] argue instead for an individual-rationalistic model, where preferences are potentially more fluid and based on perceptions of the parties' characteristics and their relative desirability to the voter. An influential early theory along these lines was that developed by an American author, Anthony Downs,[13] which sees the parties as competitors in a market place, modifying their offerings in response to the preferences of the customers (voters). This theory is also explored by Heath *et al.*, in particular the evidence that the Labour Party had in the 1980s wilfully refused to modify its policies in the direction indicated by voter preferences,[14] and more recently a number of researchers have argued that modern parties do modify their policies in this way, becoming more 'market-oriented' in their policy formation as well as their campaigns.[15] If so, this might be undermining the sense that the parties have a continuing ideological identity, and weakening the loyalty of their adherents.

Clarke *et al.* argue for a more complex individual-rationalistic model, depending on what they call 'valence', the relevance of particular considerations to each voter. Unlike the Downsian model, which assumes a single 'left–right' dimension, they suggest voters judge the parties' relative competence on multiple issues, but that to help them make these judgements voters rely on 'shortcuts', notably their perceptions of the leaders and image of the parties. They expound their theory primarily in their analysis of the 2001 election, but also find support for it at earlier periods in a re-analysis of the data from previous BES surveys.

Whichever model is more accurate, it seems plain that a growing number of voters are becoming more susceptible to short-term influences. A perceptive analysis of the electorate was made by Dr Mark Abrams as long ago as 1964. Referring to the Labour and Conservative Parties, he wrote:

> Each party can rely upon the unwavering support of approximately one-third of the electorate. Their devotion is unaffected by any shortcomings in party leadership, party programme, constituency, candidate or party organisation ... The remaining uncommitted one-third of the electorate do not form a homogeneous group. Its members are drawn from both sexes, all social statuses, and all age groups ... no more than half of them will usually vote.

This final third of the electorate (sometimes referred to as the floating vote) was made up of a number of overlapping subgroups. These were Liberal voters, abstainers, lukewarm supporters of either party and genuine floaters. Liberal voters were a much more heterogeneous collection than their Labour or Conservative counterparts. A large proportion of both Labour and Conservative voters were regular supporters of their party. It is doubtful if more than a third of the electors who voted for Liberal candidates regarded themselves as Liberals. The remainder were mostly disgruntled supporters of the larger parties or those who voted Liberal at a particular election because of the personal qualities of the candidate.[16] Now, over 30 years later, Abrams's analysis is probably still essentially valid, except that the number of unwavering supporters of both the largest parties has undoubtedly declined.

Of most interest, and most elusive, are the people who actually switch their votes from one major party to the other. These can be particularly difficult to study, because answers to surveys about how a respondent voted at a previous election are notoriously inaccurate. (For example, surveys of recalled past vote in Britain have consistently, over more than 30 years, found a reported Liberal vote far lower than the actual Liberal vote.) One way of getting round this problem is a panel study, where the same group of voters would be interviewed at successive elections; one such is the British Election Panel Study (BEPS). But panels have problems of their own – in particular, those who agree to take part will tend to be those more interested in politics, and further there may be a conditioning effect, by which being a panel member actually stimulates a respondent's interest. This means that a panel is likely to under-represent uninterested and apathetic citizens, who are probably the most likely to be abstainers or floating voters.

To understand the dynamics of change, an election like 1997 (when there had been a big shift since the previous election) is naturally more helpful than an 'as-you-were' election like 2001. The BEPS data suggested that a quarter of those who voted Conservative in 1992 switched parties in 1997, while one in ten abstained, and that only 6 per cent of Liberal Democrats and 2 per cent of Labour voters switched in the opposite direction. However, the panel overall considerably underestimated the number of abstainers, and may have also underestimated the number of switchers. It is certainly normally the case that, even in an election where the country as a whole has swung decisively in one direction, there will be a significant number of voters who have swung in the other.

Despite the increasing interest which sociologists have, since 1945, shown in elections and in voting habits, relatively little is agreed about what actually causes people to change their voting allegiances. There is evidence that many more people switch over between elections rather than during election campaigns, and this has led the parties to begin their campaigning at a much earlier stage than was once the case; indeed, in some respects the campaign never really stops. Even so, very many voters do not make up their minds until the last minute, and panel studies show that an increasing number of electors are in fact changing their minds during the few weeks of the formal campaign. The MORI/*Evening Standard* panel in 1997 found that more than a quarter of the electorate changed their minds during the six-week campaign. (This figure includes those who had been undecided but made up their minds, and those who had changed their minds whether to vote at all.) In the corresponding MORI panel in the 1979 election, the proportion changing their minds had been just half this number, 12.5 per cent, with an increase at each subsequent election.

The voters' own judgement is usually that the media coverage of the election has more effect on their voting decisions than any elements of the parties' direct campaigns (see Table 13.14).

Undoubtedly, one longer-term factor which influences voters is their perception of the government's performance. Often they are particularly swayed by the state of the economy, and in the elections of the 1980s there was a very close correlation between the public's economic optimism as measured in opinion polls (often referred to as the 'consumer confidence index') and the poll rating of the governing Conservatives. However, this relationship broke down in the 1990s and has not yet been re-established.

If the national campaigns of the parties appear to have had only a limited effect on people's voting, what of the campaigns in the constituencies? In the period before the First World War many voters were probably directly influenced by these campaigns. But as we have seen, the growth of the mass media has shifted attention overwhelmingly away from the individual candidates towards the party leaders. The result has been that neither the personality of the candidate nor the quality of his or her campaign apparently has much effect on the average voter. Yet the difference it does make can be significant, and this has been recognised by the parties in recent years by increasing the targeting of their national campaigns and resources on key seats, reversing an earlier trend towards a nationally uniform campaign. Studies of the last three elections[17] have shown a clear link between the level of campaigning in a constituency and a party's electoral performance, although less so for the Conservatives than the other parties. Earlier studies comparing performance with the level of each party's campaign spending in the constituency also found a clear link.

Table 13.14   Campaign's effect on vote choice, 2001

Q. Please tell me how much influence, if any, each of the following had on your decision about what you would do on the day of the General Election?	*A great deal (%)*	*A fair amount (%)*	*Not very much (%)*	*None at all (%)*	*Don't know (%)*
Election coverage on TV	13	36	20	30	1
Election coverage in newspapers	8	30	22	39	1
Leaflets or letters delivered by the parties	4	22	25	49	*
Party election broadcasts on TV	6	16	20	57	1
Election coverage on radio	5	17	18	58	3
Views of friends or family	6	14	20	60	*
Opinion polls	2	11	21	65	1
Political advertisements on billboards	2	8	17	72	1
Personal calls from representatives of the parties	2	6	9	80	3
Election coverage on the Internet	1	3	5	87	4

Base: 1,162 British adults, 9–18 June 2001.
* Indicates a figure of less than 0.5 per cent but greater than zero.

Source: MORI/Electoral Commission.

Nearly all authorities agree that virtually no candidate, however outstanding, is worth more than 500 extra votes to his or her party from one election to the next, and the great majority of candidates are clearly worth much less. This is not true of by-elections, where voters are relieved of the responsibility of helping to choose a government and more of them feel freer to give weight to personality factors. It is also less true of Liberal Democrat and Nationalist candidates than of those representing the two larger parties. But it remains true that in the great majority of constituencies, the most distinguished of statesmen can hope to win very few votes more than would the most mediocre of the party hacks. Evidence does suggest, however, that the *cumulative* effect of a sitting Member of Parliament, measured over several successive elections, may be rather greater than had been imagined. Good constituency members may build up personal support over the years, which means that they will poll markedly better than the normal support for their party. Conversely, unpopular members may do substantially worse, especially if they are elderly and have outstayed their welcome.[18]

Much more than the actual policies on which political parties fight elections, or the local candidates or issues, voters may also be influenced by such factors as the personalities of the party leaders, the perceived degree of unity or disunity within a party, its general air of competence or its absence, and the extent to which its approach fits in with the voters' sense of fairness.[19] The voters are also aware of general images, whose roots may go back far into the past. These party images evolve over time, of course, but particular aspects – especially negative ones – may linger for years, long after the events and personalities that caused them are no more than history. In the late 1980s the Labour Party was still associated by many voters with the industrial unrest (the 'Winter of Discontent') that was instrumental in the fall of the Callaghan government in 1979, and with the influence of the extreme left over the party in the early 1980s. The strenuous efforts of its more recent leaders – Neil Kinnock, John Smith and Tony Blair – to cast off this damaging legacy took many years to bear fruit. Similarly, the Conservatives today still seem handicapped by the persistence of many voters in associating them with the 'sleaze' and incompetence seen as the characteristic failings of John Major's government during the 1992–7 Parliament.

An earlier edition of this book noted that 'Nevertheless, a large proportion of voters, though they remain committed to one party or the other, are willing to admit that their opponents have many virtues. Extreme partisanship is rare.' It is still rare for voters to vilify one party through excessive loyalty to another; but it is, unfortunately, clear that far more people than was once the case take the attitude 'a plague o' both your houses!', tarring all parties and all politicians with the same brush as unworthy of their loyalty.

This is undoubtedly a factor in the sudden plunge in turnout which has afflicted recent British elections, and which has thrown the spotlight very distinctly on the remaining group of the population, the abstainers. Allowing for inaccuracies in the election register, for removals and for people who are sick or away from their homes on election day without having arranged to vote by post, the proportion of electors who actually vote in Parliamentary elections is traditionally rather high. Between 1950 and 1997 it ranged from 71 per cent to 84 per cent, which suggests that the proportion of avoidable abstentions was probably not usually much more than 10 per cent (see Appendix 1 for the figures). As recently as the 1992 general election, 78 per cent of the registered electorate voted. However, in 2001 the figure was only 59 per cent, and in other elections similar low points have been reached (notably the 1999 European Elections when only 23 per cent voted). Indeed, recent turnout in Britain, whether in Parliamentary, European or local elections, has been the lowest of any of the major Western European countries, and has sparked considerable concern. Although some commentators have argued that this is only a transient phenomenon, based on the political conditions of the time, others believe the problem is more deep-rooted and more dangerous to the health of our democratic system. Consequently in recent years, but especially since 2001, there has been a great deal of research aimed at understanding why people fail to vote, and what can be done to persuade them to turn out.[20]

One of the clearest characteristics of non-voters – which was equally true in the past, when they were considerably fewer in number – is that they consist predominantly of the least discriminating of electors – those who have the least interest in and the smallest knowledge of current political issues. They tend to be concentrated amongst the poorest and least educated sections of the population, the very old, the very young and more among women than among men. Abstention is also highest among ethnic minorities. But studies have also repeatedly suggested[21] that the current problem does not arise from apathy, but from 'disengagement' – many of those who fail to vote feel strongly about political issues but do not see voting as an efficacious expression of their opinions, or associate political decision-making with the solution of the problems that most concern them.

This also seems to be being affected by an evolution in the British public's civic values. In the past, the vast majority of adults believed that it was their duty to vote, a part of their responsibility to society. While this is still overwhelmingly true among older generations, many of the young – especially those aged 35 and under – no longer subscribe to this; though they may value their *right* to vote, they feel no duty to do so unless they are interested in the outcome. Indeed, they may often feel that if they have no preference between candidates they should leave the choice to be taken by those who do. Whether this change in values, which has only recently been studied, is a permanent rather than a transient one it is too early to tell, but if permanent it may have a profound effect on British elections. Of course, it is not essential to the workings of democracy that the public should vote, even if they do not care who wins; the more fundamental requirement is that they should be taking sufficient interest so that they *do* care who wins. But elections such as 2001, when fewer voted for the winning party than decided not to vote at all, raise uncomfortable questions about the strength of the government's mandate to govern.

Low turnout raises other questions. If the most deprived and marginalised groups fail to vote, how are their interests to be expressed and represented politically? Their further marginalisation will naturally follow and soon lead to a permanent 'underclass' and perhaps eventually to a breakdown in the entire system as the underclass resorts to extra-democratic and possibly unconstitutional means to defend its interests. Such considerations are one of the strongest arguments for compulsory voting, which exists in some other countries including Australia and Belgium.

Of course, low turnout is also capable of affecting the election result. Successive polls have shown that among non-voters a higher proportion are sympathetic to Labour than to the Conservatives and it is generally considered that a high turnout favours Labour, while a low one is to the advantage of the Tories. Although Labour's lead in the last two general elections was so large as to be immune to this risk, the same is not true of many local elections and of the European elections, and the Conservatives can almost certainly thank the low turnout of Labour supporters for the scale of their 1999 victory in the European Parliament.

Solving the turnout problem – if it really is a problem, which not everybody agrees – is perhaps the hottest question concerning elections at the moment. As already mentioned, in Chapter 8, the apparently promising expedient of making voting easier by 'all-postal' ballots has already come to grief, though the government seems reluctant to abandon it. Other new initiatives seem certain to follow.

14
How Much Does it Cost – and Who Pays For it?[1]

The cost of fighting elections, and the means by which the political parties raise money to pay for it, has become perhaps the most controversial aspect of Britain's electoral arrangements over the last few years. In the mid-1990s a Committee on Standards in Public Life was set up, originally under the chairmanship of Lord Nolan and subsequently under Sir Patrick (now Lord) Neill, with a wide remit to examine all aspects of political life in which concerns were being raised (whether justified or not) of corruption, undue influence or abuse of office. One of the areas they investigated was the funding of political parties, and the recommendations in their report led to a considerable shake-up in the way British elections are run. The report was by far the most comprehensive investigation for many years into party financing and spending.[2]

The cost of elections is less in the United Kingdom than in many other democratic countries and, in particular, substantially less than in the USA. But total election expenses do amount to a considerable sum.

Restriction of expenditure is highly desirable if money is not to talk at election time. The amount of money which may be spent on behalf of a *candidate* during the actual election campaign has been strictly limited by law since 1883, but until 2001 there was no restriction on the amount that could be spent by a *party* nationally, provided it was not directed to helping any particular candidate. As the parties became more centralised and better organised through the twentieth century, the amounts spent nationally began to dwarf the total sums spent on behalf of all candidates.

While constituency spending, constrained by the legal limits, stayed at roughly the same level, there was an exponential increase in national spending during the 1980s and 1990s. As recently as 1979, the three main parties spent only £4 million between them on the election, but by 1997 the total spent by the three main parties touched £56 million (to say nothing of the millions spent by the Referendum Party); even allowing for inflation, this was five times as much as had been spent just 18 years before. However, new laws cut this by half in 2001.

In 2001, each party was limited to spending £15,384,000. Only Labour and the Conservatives came, or are likely to come, close to these limits. In the past, access to information about spending in general elections was a little haphazard. In each constituency, the Returning Officer was required to publish a summary of expenses in at least two local newspapers within ten days of the deadline for returns, and eventually – sometimes more than a year after the election – a Parliamentary Paper would be published, pulling together the figures from across the country. But for spending at national level there was often no reliable information.

At the 2001 general election, for the first time, the Electoral Commission published a comprehensive report covering all expenditure, local and national, both by the political parties and others.[3]

Table 14.1   General election expenditure at national level 1979–2001

	Conservative (£m)	Labour (£m)	Lib/Alliance/ Lib Dem (£m)	Total* (£m)	Total at 2001 prices (£m)
1979	2.3	1.6	0.2	4.0	12.2
1983	3.6	2.2	1.9	7.7	15.7
1987	9.0	4.4	1.9	15.3	26.0
1992	11.2	10.2	1.8	23.2	29.0
1997	28.3	26.0	2.1	56.4	62.1
2001	12.8	10.9	1.4	25.1	25.1

* Only includes spending by the three named political parties. Spending by 'recognised third parties' was regulated in 2001 for the first time and amounted to a further £1.2m, while spending by other political parties totalled £1.6m.

Sources: For 1979, the figures are as given in an article by Michael Pinto-Duschinsky in *The Times*, 14 April 1998. For 1983–97, figures reported in *The Funding of Political Parties in the United Kingdom*, Fifth Report of the Committee on Standards in Public Life, Cm. 4057 (London: The Stationery Office, 1998), tables 3.10 and 3.11. For 2001, *Election 2001: Campaign Spending* (London: Electoral Commission, 2002), table 2.

In the past, the Tories hugely outspent the other parties, but in the last three elections Labour has been almost able to match Tory spending. The figures are given in Table 14.1.

By far the biggest element of this expenditure is on advertising, even though paid advertising on television (a prime feature in countries such as the USA) is banned in Britain; in 2001 it constituted 46 per cent of Labour's spending and 35 per cent of that by the Conservatives, as Table 14.2 shows. The cost will mostly be split between press and poster advertising, though the balance between the two will depend on party tactics: in 1997 for instance, the Tories spent over £11 million on posters and £3 million on press advertisements, while Labour spent £5 million on posters and less than £1 million in the press; but the balance is not always in that direction – in 1987 the main parties spent three times as much on newspaper as poster advertising. The cost of tours of the country by leading politicians of each party and mass rallies, especially in the last few days of the campaign, add millions more to the bill. Less costly than this, but by no means insignificant, is the cost of opinion research, as discussed in Chapter 12, and the new practice of canvassing by telephone.

Table 14.2 Breakdown of campaign spending, 2001

	Con (£m)	Lab (£m)	Lib Dem (£m)
Advertising	4.4	5.0	0.2
Rallies and other events	2.0	1.3	0.1
Transport	1.5	0.8	0.6
Market research/canvassing	1.7	0.9	0.1
Unsolicited material to electors	1.2	1.5	0.1
Manifesto/policy documents	1.0	0.5	0.1
Party political broadcasts	0.6	0.3	0.1
Media	0.4	0.8	0.2
Total	*12.8*	*10.9*	*1.4*

Source: *Election 2001: Campaign Spending* (London: Electoral Commission, 2002), pp. 53, 59 and 61.

But it is not only the parties who may spend money campaigning – both interested groups and individuals may take advertising space, commission polls, and participate in other ways. Trade unions have often spent their political funds in this way, as have employers and industry pressure groups on occasion. Since 2001, this 'third party' spending has also been restricted by law, and any organisation or individual spending more than £10,000 in England or £5000 in Wales, Scotland or Northern Ireland must register with the Electoral Commission. Ten bodies were registered as 'recognised third parties' in 2001.[4]

At constituency level, the campaign is usually regarded as dating from the announcement of a dissolution in the case of a general election or the date that the vacancy occurs in the case of a by-election, though the law is woolly on this point. It may be that only the shorter period following the actual dissolution (or issue of a writ) is in fact covered by the law. On the other hand, the campaign might be held to date from the announcement of a candidature, and this is why all parties are careful to describe their standard-bearers as *prospective* candidates until the announcement of the dissolution. The point has never been contested in the courts and, in practice, all candidates play safe and return their expenses for the longer period.

Though the electorate greatly increased and the value of money depreciated, the level of permitted local expenditure was lowered both in 1918 and in 1948. The effect of this was that the actual money expended in the constituencies was lower in the 1966 general election (£1,130,882) than in 1906 (£1,166,858). Since then the rate of inflation has been so high that the actual amount expended grew by over eleven times between 1966 and its peak in 1997. Yet in real terms the expenditure level in the constituencies is still far lower than in the early years of this century.

The level of permitted expenditure used to be formally laid down by Act of Parliament, which meant that a new Act needed to be passed whenever an increase was considered desirable because of the erosion in the value of money. Since 1978, however, the Home Secretary has been permitted to enact new limits by an order in council, subject to an affirmative vote by both Houses of Parliament. In 2001 the maximum expenditure permitted for each candidate was £5483 plus 6.2p per elector in county constituencies, and £5483 plus 4.6p per elector in borough constituencies. The average maximum for county constituencies is about £9700 and that for boroughs around £8600, but as the former often contain widely scattered areas of population difficult to organise, the differential can easily be justified. Candidates' personal expenses are excluded from the limitation. Until 1989, the same limits also applied to by-elections; in that year the permitted expenditure at a by-election was quadrupled, and has subsequently been raised to a flat rate of £100,000 per constituency.

There is also a statutory limit to the amount of expenditure which a candidate may incur in non-Parliamentary elections. For the Scottish Parliament and Welsh Assembly in 2003, constituency candidates were allowed to spend no more than £5761 plus 6.5p (counties) or £4.8p (burghs/boroughs) per elector, with further restrictions on nationwide party spending. (The limit was £1,516,000 in Scotland, £600,000 in Wales.) In local government elections the basic limit is £242 plus 4.7p per elector; where there are two joint candidates the maximum expenditure for each is reduced by a quarter, and if there are three or more joint candidates the maximum is reduced by one-third. Unlike Parliamentary candidates, few candidates in local elections spend anything near the limit laid down. In the 2004 elections to the European Parliament each candidate could spend £45,000 multiplied by the number of MEPs to be returned for the electoral region. (For example, the limit for individual candidates in the East Midlands region, which elected six MEPs, was £270,000, or 6 × £45,000.)

The introduction of national spending limits finally forced a change which some experts have been advocating for many years: the setting up of an Electoral Commission, as exists in other countries such as Australia and Canada, which in the past has been resisted, mainly on grounds of cost. The Commission was needed to police the spending limits (there being no existing national body to do so, since constituency spending is reported to the local Returning Officer), and to oversee the registration of parties, without which there would be too many loopholes for the regulations to be enforceable. The Commission is an independent though publicly funded body, headed by a board of neutral commissioners approved by all the political parties. It also inspects the parties' accounts and is responsible for a number of other functions: supervising the administration and funding of elections, establishing best practice and keeping the effectiveness of electoral law under review, functions previously spread between local authorities, the Home Office, Scottish Office, Welsh Office and other government departments. It will also eventually absorb the present role of the Boundary Commissions.

All political parties, small as well as large, must now submit their accounts annually to the Commission. At constituency level, the agent of each candidate in an election has to submit to the Returning Officer a complete statement of expenses incurred, together with the relevant bills and receipts, within 35 days after the declaration of the result.

The amounts expended by all candidates and by those of the three main parties in general elections since 1945 are given in Table 14.3.

Only a minority of candidates spend anywhere near the limit – in 2001 only 702 (one-fifth of the total) exceeded 80 per cent of the permitted maximum while more than half spent less than 30 per cent of the maximum. Spending is highest by the major parties and, naturally, in the more marginal constituencies. In 2001 Conservative candidates spent on average 69 per cent of the permitted maximum, Labour candidates 64 per cent and Liberal Democrat candidates 32 per cent. Minor party and independent candidates spent a great deal less.

Table 14.3   **Expenditure by Parliamentary candidates, 1945–2001**

Year	Candidates	Total expenditure* (£)	Average per candidate (£)	Con (£)	Lab (£)	Lib/Alliance /Lib Dem (£)
1945	1,683	1,009,256	600	780	593	532
1950	1,868	1,106,092	592	777	694	459
1951	1,376	894,868	650	773	658	488
1955	1,409	852,420	605	735	611 ·	423
1959	1,536	990,211	645	761	705	532
1964	1,757	1,158,577	659	790	751	579
1966	1,707	1,070,746	627	766	726	501
1970	1,837	1,392,796	758	949	828	525
1974: Feb	2,135	2,008,660	941	1,197	1,127	745
1974: Oct	2,252	2,168,514	963	1,275	1,163	725
1979	2,576	3,557,441	1,381	2,190	1,897	1,013
1983	2,578	6,145,463	2,384	3,320	2,927	2,520
1987	2,325	8,039,174	3,458	4,400	3,900	3,400
1992	2,948	10,433,407	3,539	5,840	5,090	3,169
1997	3,724	12,929,207	3,472	6,211	6,011	3,144
2001	3,319	11,885,785	3,581	6,474	5,860	3,062

* Excludes personal expenses not subject to legal maximum.

Sources: Compiled from *Election 2001: Campaign Spending* (London: Electoral Commission, 2002), table 7 and pp. 101–51, and *Election Expenses* (London: The Stationery Office, 1999), p. 160, and David Butler and Gareth Butler, *Twentieth Century British Political Facts 1900–2000* (Basingstoke: Macmillan, 2000), p. 260.

Table 14.4 shows the returns made in 2001 by the five candidates in a marginal county constituency, Selby, where the maximum permitted expenditure was £10,281.24.

All parties consistently spend more money in respect of their successful candidates than on behalf of their unsuccessful nominees, but it is in the highly marginal seats that candidates of all parties tend to spend very near the maximum permitted. Evasion of the law had apparently been fairly widespread in marginal constituencies, according to David Butler and Richard Rose, who wrote after the 1959 election:

> Agents quite often admitted to subterfuges, some plainly legal, some more dubious, by which they kept their official expenses down. Sympathetic printers could undercharge, knowing that no objection would be raised to a compensating overcharge outside election time. Equipment needed solely for the campaign could be bought in advance and then hired to the agent at a very low notional figure. Although the

likelihood of either side scrutinising its rivals' accounts or launching a petition is very small, it is unfortunate that the law should be so much circumvented.[5]

Table 14.4   Election expenses in Selby, 2001

	John Grogan (Lab) £	Andrew Michael Mitchell (Con) £	Jeremy David Wilcock (Lib Dem) £	Helen Mary Nightingale Kenwright (Green) £	Graham Robert Lewis (UKIP) £
Agents	–	1,200.00	–	–	–
Clerks	–	180.00	–	–	–
Printing, stationery, tele- communications etc.	8,083.57	7,765.45	1,813.81	300.00	785.00
Public meetings	–	–	–	–	–
Committee rooms	532.13	150.00	–	–	–
Miscellaneous matters	1,165.15	907.38	23.50	500.00	–
Total subject to legal maximum	9,780.85	10,202.83	1,837.31	800.00	785.00
Personal expenses	450.00	–	–	–	–

* The maximum permitted expenditure, not including personal expenses, for this constituency was £10,281.24.

Source: *Election 2001: Campaign Spending* (London: Electoral Commission, 2002).

Little may have changed in the subsequent 40 years. The limit for by-elections was quadrupled in 1989 as it was universally recognised as unrealistic, and has since been raised much further. With regard to general elections the *Observer*, reporting the prosecution of a winning candidate at Newark in 1997 (initially successful but overturned on appeal – see page 142), stated that 'The *Observer* has discovered widespread evidence of a Faustian pact between political parties, with candidates of all sides using ingenious ruses to keep within the limits'.[6] The Newark case made it clear that, at the very least, a more precise legal definition of how declarable expenses are defined is desirable, and preferably one that is more up to date. (The legal status of spending on telegrams, years after their abolition, remained on the statute book, while telephone calls were entirely unmentioned in the regulations.) However, it is possible that the advent of the Electoral Commission, with all returns now being professionally scrutinised, may force candidates to comply in the future. The present guidance to candidates issued by the Commission makes quite clear that the return of expenses must include any 'notional expenses', that is the full commercial value of any goods or services provided free or at a discount.

As at the national level, non-party bodies and individuals are also restricted in what they may spend to influence an election at constituency level. Until 1998, it was a criminal offence to spend more than £5 supporting or opposing the election of any candidate (except as authorised by a candidate's agent and duly reported as an election expense). In that year, the European Court of Human Rights condemned as illegal the prosecution of a campaigner, Phyllis Bowman, who had distributed 25,000 leaflets in Halifax at the 1992 election about the candidates' views on abortion, ruling it a breach of her right to free speech. The permitted limit has, as a result, now been raised to £500.

In recent elections, it has become customary for the two major parties to spend far in excess of their available resources, running up a huge deficit that has to be paid off in subsequent years. As a result both parties have needed, and been grateful for, some very substantial individual donations. Traditionally, the Conservative Party has had much the highest income. In the 1980s, members' subscriptions and other local fundraising figured as much the largest items in the incomes of the Alliance parties, but donations, mostly from business firms, provided 80 per cent of the Conservative income, while trade union and other affiliations accounted for 78 per cent of Labour's. The Conservatives used to be able to raise additional funds, through special election appeals to companies, which were substantially greater than the amount provided by the trade unions for Labour, and were often able to further ease the situation with interest-free loans; even so, they were generally heavily in debt. The mid-1990s were rife with reports that companies who had previously been generous donors were withdrawing their support, and the Conservative Party is probably now far more dependent on wealthy individuals that at any time in the recent past. Of the central party's £13.6 million income in 2003, £7.6 million was derived from donations and fundraising, and less than £500,000 from party membership fees. Grants of public money added £4.1 million, of which £3.6 million was 'Short money' (the grant paid each year since 1975 to meet the specifically Parliamentary expenses of opposition parties, who lack the Civil Service assistance available to the government). That left a £2.4 million deficit for the year, the outgoings being almost entirely running costs (including £6.7 million staff costs), but this was probably partly because of the party's failure to find a buyer for their old offices in Smith Square; other reports have suggested that the Conservatives have been generally solvent since the turn of the century.

Labour's financial position was turned on its head in the 1990s, as it successfully attracted a wide range of both individual and corporate donors, and at the time of the 1997 election had expanded its membership to over 400,000. Some, at least, of these donations were from companies that had previously donated to the Conservative Party, and Labour currently has the highest income of the parties. Labour's accounts for 2003 show that, of an annual income of £27 million, £9 million came from donations and another £10 million from membership and affiliations; a third of the remainder was commercial income, while fundraising activities contributed only £850,000 and public money (a policy development grant) just £439,000. Running costs account for two-thirds of the party's £24.2 million expenditure, half of which are staff costs. However, 2003 is one of the quietest years in the electoral cycle, with campaign expenditure less than £1 million; in a general election year income must rise to meet the huge extra liabilities.

The Liberal Democrats' more meagre £4 million income included £1.4 million of donations, of which half was specifically to the campaign fund. Membership and subscription fees added £680,000, and their share of public money amounted to £445,000.

The potential influence of party donors caused increasing disquiet throughout the mid-1990s, especially in the case of the Conservatives who, until recently, did not reveal their identities. It was known, however, that some individual donations were in excess of £1 million, that foreign businessmen were among the donors, and there were accusations that at least one of the donors had obtained the money illegally in the first place. Questions were raised as to whether such donations might not be intended to buy improper influence over the Conservative government – although the party always emphasised that its fundraising and policy-making functions were entirely separate and divided by 'Chinese walls'.

Various changes in the law have now been implemented, including mandatory disclosure of details of party financing, a national campaign expenditure limit, and a ban on donations from foreign citizens. Nevertheless, many concerns still remain, and after the Labour government's election in 1997 several cases of £1 million-plus donations to Labour were taken up by the press, with similar insinuations that they might be suspected of aiming at improper influence over government policy.

Therefore, although there is for the moment less need to fear that disparity between the funds available to the major parties may give the Conservatives an unfair advantage, the reliance of all parties on their donors is still a potential cause for concern. A tighter rein on total expenditure through a national spending limit will help, but it is only a partial solution. A further measure advocated by some is to limit by law the amount that may be donated, but this would exacerbate the parties' financial problems, and the experience of other countries suggests such restrictions would probably be simply evaded by those who abuse the existing arrangements, increasing rather than reducing the influence of those whose money gets through the net.

One alternative suggestion – which the senior author of this book was the first to articulate[7] – is for the election expenses of British political parties to be partially reimbursed from public funds. This now happens in a majority of democratic countries in Europe, as well as in Australia, Canada and the United States (presidential elections only, so far). An independent committee of inquiry, under Lord Houghton, looked into this problem and reported in 1976: a majority of its members were in favour of introducing such a system in Britain, with both annual grants to the national party organisations and limited reimbursement of candidates' election expenses, in both cases dependent on their electoral support.

The Houghton report was not acted on: although the Labour Party, then in power, was broadly in favour of its proposals, the Leader of the House of Commons, Michael Foot, to whom the report was presented, was unenthusiastic. The Thatcher government, elected in 1979, was openly hostile, but Labour and the Liberal Democrats subsequently endorsed the principle of public funding. An earlier edition of this book considered that 'legislation may be expected to be introduced by the next non-Conservative government'. However, opinion polls have consistently suggested that the public would resent such a change,[8] and although the possibility has been much discussed in the last few years the present government has taken no steps to implement it.[9] In the meantime, the only public money available to the parties is the 'Short money', mentioned above, and some small grants for policy development.[10]

But the state already makes a considerable contribution in kind, if not in cash. The administrative costs of running the election are, of course, met by the taxpayer – though it was not always so. Until 1918, the whole of the Returning Officers' expenses in each constituency were chargeable to the candidates, and this constituted a considerable extra burden, especially for poorer candidates and parties. Now they have only to meet the cost of campaigning and of the £500 deposit.[11]

There are three categories of election expenditure chargeable to public funds – the cost of printing and compiling the register, the Returning Officers' expenses, and the cost of the public facilities made available free of charge to candidates and political parties (the free postal delivery of electoral communications, the free hire of meeting halls and the provision of free broadcasting time for party election broadcasts on television and radio).

The cost of the election register is borne equally by the Treasury and the local authorities. It is of course an annual charge and the cost across the country is estimated at £52 million. As the register is used annually for local government elections, and every five years for elections to the European Parliament, it would be unrealistic to count the whole cost of maintaining the register as part of the expense of a general election.

Returning Officers' expenses are lower, but not negligible. The total expense reported in 1987 was around £2 million, an average of £3100 per constituency. This included the cost of publishing the notice of the election, receiving and publicising the nominations, and of sending out poll cards to all electors. The actual cost to the local authorities is in fact much greater than this sum suggests, as no account is taken of the cost of the temporary diversion of local government staff from other work during elections, nor of the cost of employing polling-station clerks on election day and of people to count the votes after the poll has closed.

The Post Office is reimbursed by the Treasury for the cost of the free postal delivery, at a cost of £20.2 million in 2001. No precise figures are available for the cost to local authorities of making halls available free to candidates, or to the broadcasting authorities (who are not reimbursed) of the provision of free air time. Estimates[12] by Michael Pinto-Duschinsky in the 1979 election put the subsidy to the Labour and Conservative Parties at £62,000 each for the free hire of halls and £2.7 million for party political broadcasts; allowing for inflation would more than treble these figures for 2001. Given this context, perhaps the proposal of a direct grant to subsidise the parties' campaigning is less radical than it appears on the surface. Overall, the Electoral Commission has estimated[13] that the annual cost to the public purse of running elections can vary from £14 million to £122 million depending on the number and type of elections, not including the cost of upkeep of the register. The 2001 general election alone cost £56 million.

15
An Evolving System

In 1254 the Sheriff of each county was ordered to send two knights, chosen by the county, 'to consider what aid they would give the King in his great necessity'; eleven years later the Parliament summoned by Simon de Montfort contained not only two knights from each county, but also two citizens from each city and two burgesses from each borough. The Parliaments of the thirteenth century were very different from those of today, and no doubt there were even greater differences in the manner of their election. Nevertheless, a statute approved by the Parliament of Edward I, in 1275, stipulating that the elections should be 'free' is still in force today, and the gradual evolution of the present system can be traced back through hundreds of Acts of Parliament spanning the centuries in between.

This evolution is a continuing process. In 1985 alone, for instance, three important changes were made – postal voting was extended to holiday-makers, British citizens who had been living abroad for five years or less became eligible to vote, and the deposit for candidates was increased from £150 to £500, while the qualifying limit for its return was reduced from one-eighth to one-twentieth of the votes cast. In fact, the two most distinctive features of the British electoral system are its antiquity and its capacity to absorb changes. More substantial changes introduced since 1997 include the setting up of the Electoral Commission, registration of political parties, national election spending limits and even a whole new tier of elections; but the system as a whole remains recognisable and fundamentally the same. While some parts of the electoral law remain intact for centuries, others are liable to be amended at virtually any time. The great majority of amendments are of a minor character.

The period of most significant change was, of course, the hundred or so years following the passage of the Great Reform Bill of 1832 when, as described briefly in Chapter 3, the struggle for universal suffrage was fought and won. Almost as important as the extension of the franchise was such legislation as the Ballot Act of 1872, which secured the secrecy of the ballot, and the Corrupt Practices Act of 1883, which effectively eliminated bribery from British elections.

The advances won in the nineteenth and early twentieth centuries were consolidated in the Representation of the People Acts of 1948 and 1949, and subsequently again in the 1983 Act, which forms the basis of the present system, but is still basically nineteenth century in form. The legal provisions relating to elections are in many respects similar to those in force over a hundred years ago. What has transformed election campaigns out of all recognition in the past century has primarily been not the change in the law but the technological and sociological developments which have taken place. It would be pointless to elaborate on them in a work of this kind, but it may be useful just to list the four changes which appear to have had the greatest effect upon British elections.

First there has been the revolution in transportation, which has enabled politicians to travel rapidly round the country – the growth of railways in the mid-nineteenth century and, even more important, the spread of the motor car, which has also greatly affected local campaigning. In a densely populated but geographically small country, however, the aeroplane and the helicopter have so far made little impact upon electioneering, their use being effectively limited to the party leaders.

Second has been the development of mass media of communication – newspapers with national circulation, telegraphs, radio and, later, television. More humbly, the telephone has also made an incalculable contribution and the Internet is just beginning to make an impact. Third has been the spread of education, even if the growth in higher education has been slower than in some other developed countries; and, finally, the development of highly centralised party machines.

In a number of respects electoral law has tended to lag behind these developments, and for many years failed, for example, to take account of the consequences of broadcasting for electoral campaigning. A comparatively recent tradition has been established that an attempt at all-party agreement should precede any important changes in electoral law, and inter-party conferences under the chairmanship of the Speaker of the House of Commons preceded the Representation of the People Acts of 1918, 1948 and 1969 (though in each case the Act did not exactly follow the recommendations of the Speaker's Conference). Other Speaker's Conferences sat in 1929–30, 1972–4 and 1977–8. These conferences, which were made up entirely of Members of Parliament, met in private under the Speaker's chairmanship. They heard evidence from interested parties and from expert witnesses before considering their recommendations. The initiative for convening them was taken by the government, which consulted the Opposition about the terms of reference before the members were appointed.

The recommendations of the Speaker's Conferences were by no means followed slavishly by governments, which of course had to frame the legislation to put any changes into effect. For instance, the government introduced the 1969 Representation of the People Act after receiving the final report from the 1965–6 Conference. Several of its recommendations – including votes at 18 and the exemption of broadcasting as an election expense – were reflected in its provisions, but others were not. The Act did provide for party labels to be included on ballot papers (which the Conference had recommended against), but it included no provision to restrict the publication of opinion polls, which the Conference *had* suggested. It also extended the time that polling stations remain open in Parliamentary elections, from 9 p.m. to 10 p.m., which had not been recommended by the Conference.

More recently, the development of the system of departmental select committees in the Commons meant that, in the Home Affairs Select Committee, there was a permanent body with all-party representation, independent of the government, which had the consideration of electoral law as part of its remit. Over the years the committee has on several occasions taken evidence and produced a report on aspects of the electoral system and it seems likely that this rather than a Speaker's Conference is perhaps now the most convenient Parliamentary forum where any future major reforms of the electoral system can be debated.[1]

The 1998 Home Affairs Committee investigation and report offers a good example of how the system works. Their remit was to investigate possible improvements to the electoral system in seven respects:

(a) Increasing participation and turnout
(b) Improving the accuracy of the register
(c) Making it easier to cast a vote
(d) Electoral fraud
(e) The franchise
(f) Parliamentary candidates
(g) Administrative machinery and an electoral commission.

The items discussed ranged from fundamental matters of principle (should EU citizens living and paying taxes in the UK be entitled to a vote?) to minor improvements in the practical details (how can the official guidance to Returning Officers be revised to persuade them to improve accessibility of polling stations to the disabled?). The committee took evidence from interested parties (such as representatives of the political parties and pressure groups campaigning for particular changes), from electoral administrators and from academic experts, among others. They produced a lengthy report of recommendations, including some radical changes such as a rolling register and the introduction of 'early voting' polling stations, by which voters who expected to be unable to turn out on polling day could vote at some time in the week before. The report was welcomed by the Home Office and some of its recommendations, notably the rolling register and the establishment of an Electoral Commission, have been put into practice.

But the Parliamentary committee may now have been superseded by external bodies. The changes to the law brought in before the 2001 general election were mostly derived from the recommendations of the Committee on Standards in Public Life (Neill Committee), nearly all of which were implemented. Since then, the Electoral Commission has come into existence with a permanent remit to monitor and report on the workings of the electoral system, and to recommend changes where appropriate. Nevertheless (as with the Speaker's Conference and Home Affairs Committee) the government has preferred on occasion to reject the Commission's recommendations.

The system is likely to continue to evolve in an unspectacular way, with one or two minor changes being introduced each year. Indeed, the Electoral Commission has already produced one report recommending a raft of modernisations,[2] and its continuing series of consultations suggest more to come; probably most, at least, will be implemented. But any substantial change in the system – such as the introduction of proportional representation, or even the payment or partial payment of election expenses out of public funds – will be an essentially political decision, and is unlikely to result in this way – more likely it will be a manifesto commitment of an elected government, to be implemented when the time seem seems ripe to the Prime Minister. Many confidently predicted changes have never materialised. If British elections in the twenty-second century were as recognisable to us as today's system would be to those who voted a hundred years ago, perhaps nobody should be entirely surprised.

Appendix 1
British General Election Results, 1945–2001

Year	Parties	Candidates	MPs elected	Unopposed returns	Lost deposits	Total vote	Percentage vote
1945	Conservative	624	213	2	6	9,972,010	39.6
	Labour	604	393	1	2	11,967,746	48.0
	Liberal	306	12	–	64	2,252,430	9.0
	Others	148	22	–	91	903,009	3.4
Turnout: 72.7%		1,682	640	3	163	25,095,195	100.0
Swing* 11.3%							
1950	Conservative	619	298	2	5	12,502,567	43.5
	Labour	617	315	–	–	13,266,592	46.1
	Liberal	475	9	–	319	2,621,548	9.1
	Others	157	3	–	137	381,964	1.3
Turnout: 84.0%		1,868	625	2	461	28,772,671	100.0
Swing* –2.9%							
1951	Conservative	617	321	4	3	13,717,538	48.0
	Labour	617	295	–	1	13,948,605	48.8
	Liberal	109	6	–	66	730,556	2.6
	Others	33	3	–	26	198,969	0.7
Turnout: 82.5%		1,376	625	4	96	28,595,668	100.0
Swing* –0.9%							
1955	Conservative	623	344	–	3	13,311,936	49.7
	Labour	620	277	–	1	12,404,970	46.4
	Liberal	110	6	–	60	722,405	2.7
	Others	56	3	–	36	321,182	1.2
Turnout: 76.7%		1,409	630	0	100	26,760,493	100.0
Swing* –2.1%							
1959	Conservative	625	365	–	2	13,749,830	49.4
	Labour	621	258	–	1	12,215,538	43.8
	Liberal	216	6	–	55	1,638,571	5.9
	Others	74	1	–	58	255,302	0.9
Turnout: 78.8%		1,536	630	0	116	27,859,241	100.0
Swing* –1.1%							

Year	Parties	Candidates	MPs elected	Unopposed returns	Lost deposits	Total vote	Percentage vote
1964	Conservative	629	303	–	5	12,001,396	43.4
	Labour	628	317	–	8	12,205,814	44.1
	Liberal	365	9	–	53	3,092,878	11.2
	Others	134	1	–	121	348,914	1.3
Turnout: 77.0%		1,756	630	0	187	27,649,002	100.0
Swing*	3.1%						
1966	Conservative	629	253	–	9	11,418,433	41.9
	Labour	621	363	–	3	13,064,951	47.9
	Liberal	311	12	–	104	2,327,533	8.5
	Others	146	2	–	121	452,689	1.7
Turnout: 75.8%		1,707	630	0	237	27,263,606	100.0
Swing*	2.6%						
1970	Conservative	628	330	–	10	13,145,123	46.4
	Labour	624	287	–	6	12,179,341	43.0
	Liberal	332	6	–	184	2,117,035	7.5
	Others	253	7	–	208	903,299	3.2
Turnout: 72.0%		1,837	630	0	408	28,344,798	100.0
Swing*	–4.7%						
Feb 1974	Conservative	623	297	–	8	11,872,180	37.8
	Labour	623	301	–	25	11,646,391	37.1
	Liberal	517	14	–	23	6,058,744	19.3
	Others	372	23	–	265	1,795,590	5.7
Turnout: 78.7%		2,135	635	0	321	31,372,905	100.0
Swing*	1.3%						
Oct 1974	Conservative	623	277	–	28	10,464,817	35.9
	Labour	623	319	–	13	11,457,079	39.3
	Liberal	619	13	–	125	5,346,754	18.3
	Others	387	26	–	276	1,920,528	6.6
Turnout: 72.8%		2,252	635	0	442	29,189,178	100.0
Swing*	2.1%						
1979	Conservative	622	339	–	3	13,697,923	43.8
	Labour	622	268	–	22	11,532,218	36.9
	Liberal	576	11	–	303	4,313,804	13.8
	Others	756	17	–	673	1,697,503	5.4
Turnout: 76.0%		2,576	635	0	1,001	31,241,448	100.0
Swing*	–5.2%						
1983	Conservative	633	397	–	5	13,012,316	42.4
	Labour	633	209	–	119	8,456,934	27.6
	Liberal-SDP	633	23	–	10	7,780,949	25.4
	Others	679	21	–	605	1,420,938	4.6
Turnout: 72.7%		2,578	650	0	739	30,671,137	100.0
Swing*	–4.0%						

Year	Parties	Candidates	MPs elected	Unopposed returns	Lost deposits	Total vote	Percentage vote
1987	Conservative	633	376	–	0	13,760,935	42.3
	Labour	633	229	–	0	10,029,270	30.8
	Liberal-SDP	633	22	–	1	7,341,651	22.6
	Others	426	23	–	288	1,398,348	4.3
Turnout: 75.3%		2,325	650	0	289	32,530,204	100.0
Swing*	1.7%						
1992	Conservative	645	336	–	3	14,093,007	41.9
	Labour	634	271	–	1	11,560,484	34.4
	Liberal Democrat	632	20	–	11	5,999,606	17.8
	Others	1,038	24	–	888	1,960,977	5.8
Turnout: 77.7%		2,949	651	0	903	33,614,074	100.0
Swing*	2.0%						
1997	Conservative	648	165	–	8	9,600,943	30.7
	Labour	639	418	–	0	13,518,167	43.2
	Liberal Democrat	639	46	–	13	5,242,947	16.8
	Others	1,798	30	–	1,571	2,924,227	9.3
Turnout: 71.4%		3,724	659	0	1,592	31,286,284	100.0
Swing*	10.0%						
2001	Conservative	643	166	–	5	8,357,615	31.7
	Labour	640	412	–	0	10,724,953	40.7
	Liberal Democrat	639	52	–	1	4,814,321	18.3
	Others	1,397	29	–	1,171	2,470,494	9.4
Turnout: 59.4%		3,319	659	0	1,177	26,367,383	100.0
Swing*	–1.8%						

* Swing (between the Conservative and Labour Parties) shown here is calculated on the total national vote, *not* on the average of the swings in all constituencies contested. Positive figures represent a swing from Conservative to Labour, and negative from Labour to Conservative.

Note: 'Others' include the Speaker when standing for re-election as a non-party candidate.

Appendix 2
Other British Election and Referendum Results

British elections to the European Parliament

1979:

Great Britain (78 seats) Turnout: 32.1%

Party	Votes	%	Seats
Conservative	6,508,492	50.6	60
Labour	4,253,247	33.0	17
Liberal	1,690,638	13.1	0
Scottish National Party	247,836	1.9	1
Plaid Cymru	83,399	0.6	0
Others	90,318	0.8	0
Total	12,873,930	100.0	78

Northern Ireland (3 seats)

STV system of PR Turnout: 55.6%

Party	First preference votes	%	Seats
Democratic Unionist Party	170,688	29.8	1
Social Democratic & Labour Party	140,622	24.6	1
Official Unionist Party	125,169	21.9	1
Others	135,760	23.7	0
Total	572,239	100.0	3

1984:

Great Britain (78 seats) Turnout 32.1%

Party	Votes	%	Seats
Conservative	5,426,866	40.8	45
Labour	4,865,224	36.5	32
Liberal/SDP Alliance	2,591,659	19.5	0
Scottish National Party	230,594	1.7	1
Plaid Cymru	103,031	0.8	0
Others	95,524	0.7	0
Total	13,312,898	100.0	78

Northern Ireland (3 seats)

STV system of PR Turnout: 64.4%

Party	First preference votes	%	Seats
Democratic Unionist Party	230,251	33.6	1
Social Democratic & Labour Party	151,399	22.1	1
Official Unionist Party	147,169	21.5	1

Provisional Sinn Féin	91,476	13.3	0
Alliance Party of Northern Ireland	34,046	5.0	0
Others	30,976	4.6	0
Total	685,317	100.0	3

1989:

Great Britain (78 seats) — Turnout: 35.9%

Party	Votes	%	Seats
Conservative	5,224,037	34.1	32
Labour	6,153,604	40.2	45
Liberal Democrat	986,292	6.4	0
SDP	75,886	0.5	0
Scottish National Party	406,686	2.6	1
Plaid Cymru	115,062	0.7	0
Green	2,292,705	15.0	0
Others	39,971	0.3	0
Total	15,353,154	100.0	78

Northern Ireland (3 seats)
STV system of PR — Turnout: 48.8%

Party	First preference votes	%	Seats
Democratic Unionist Party	160,110	29.6	1
Social Democratic & Labour Party	136,335	25.2	1
Official Unionist Party	118,785	22.0	1
Provisional Sinn Féin	48,914	9.1	0
Alliance Party of Northern Ireland	27,905	5.2	0
Others	42,762	7.9	0
Total	534,811	100.0	3

1994:

Great Britain (84 seats) — Turnout: 36.1%

Party	Votes	%	Seats
Conservative	4,248,531	27.8	18
Labour	6,753,863	44.2	62
Liberal Democrat	2,552,730	16.7	2
Scottish National Party	487,239	3.2	2
Plaid Cymru	162,478	1.1	0
Green	494,561	3.2	0
Others	568,151	3.7	0
Total	15,267,550	100.0	84

Northern Ireland (3 seats)
STV system of PR — Turnout: 48.7%

Party	First preference votes	%	Seats
Democratic Unionist Party	163,246	29.2	1
Social Democratic & Labour Party	161,992	28.9	1
Ulster Unionist Party	133,459	23.9	1
Sinn Féin	55,215	9.9	0
Alliance Party of Northern Ireland	23,157	4.1	0

Others	22,798	4.0	0
Total	559,867	100.0	3

1999:

Great Britain (84 seats)

D'Hondt regional list system of PR   Turnout: 23.1%

Party	*Votes*	*%*	*Seats*
Conservative	3,578,217	35.8	36
Labour	2,803,821	28.0	29
Liberal Democrat	1,266,549	12.7	10
Scottish National Party	268,528	2.7	2
Plaid Cymru	185,235	1.9	2
Green	625,378	6.3	2
UK Independence Party	696,057	7.0	3
Pro-Euro Conservative Party	138,097	1.4	0
Others	440,388	4.2	0
Total	10,002,270	100.0	84

Northern Ireland (3 seats)

STV system of PR   Turnout: 57.0%

Party	*First preference votes*	*%*	*Seats*
Democratic Unionist Party	192,762	28.4	1
Social Democratic & Labour Party	190,731	28.1	1
Ulster Unionist Party	119,507	17.6	1
Sinn Féin	117,643	17.3	0
Alliance Party of Northern Ireland	14,391	2.1	0
Others	43,775	6.4	0
Total	678,809	100.0	3

2004:

Great Britain (75 seats)

D'Hondt regional list system of PR   Turnout: 37.2%*

Party	*Votes*	*%*	*Seats*
Conservative	4,397,090	26.7	27
Labour	3,718,683	22.6	19
Liberal Democrat	2,452,327	14.9	12
Scottish National Party	231,505	1.4	2
Plaid Cymru	159,888	1.0	1
Green	1,028,283	6.3	2
UK Independence Party	2,650,768	16.1	12
British National Party	808,200	4.9	0
Others	996,656	6.1	0
Total	16,443,400	100.0	75

* Turnout 38.2% including spoilt and invalid papers

Northern Ireland (3 seats)
STV system of PR   Turnout: 51.2%*

Party	First preference votes	%	Seats
Democratic Unionist Party	175,761	32.0	1
Sinn Féin	144,541	26.3	1
Ulster Unionist Party	91,164	16.6	1
Social Democratic & Labour Party	87,559	15.9	0
Others	50,252	9.1	0
Total	549,277	100.0	3

* Turnout 51.7% including spoilt and invalid papers

Elections to the Scottish Parliament, 6 May 1999

Additional Member System (AMS)
Turnout: 58%

	Constituency votes	%	Constituency seats	Regional votes	%	Top-up seats	Total seats
Conservative	364,225	15.6	0	359,109	15.4	18	18
Labour	908,392	38.8	53	786,818	33.6	3	56
Liberal Democrat	331,279	14.2	12	290,760	12.4	5	17
Scottish National Party	672,757	28.7	7	638,644	27.3	28	35
Scottish Green Party	0	0.0	0	84,024	3.6	1	1
Scottish Socialist Party	23,654	1.0	0	46,635	2.0	1	1
Others	63,770	1.7	1	132,921	5.7	0	1
Total	2,342,462	100.0	73	2,338,911	100.0	56	129

Elections to the Scottish Parliament, 1 May 2003

Additional Member System (AMS)
Turnout: 49%

	Constituency votes	%	Constituency seats	Regional votes	%	Top-up seats	Total seats
Conservative	318,279	16.6	3	296,929	15.7	15	18
Labour	663,585	34.6	46	561,879	29.8	4	50
Liberal Democrat	294,347	15.4	13	225,810	12.0	4	17
Scottish National Party	455,742	23.8	9	399,659	21.2	18	27
Scottish Green Party	0	0.0	0	132,138	7.0	7	7
Scottish Socialist Party	118,764	6.2	0	128,026	6.8	6	6
Others	65,877	3.4	2	143,908	7.6	2	4
Total	1,916,594	100.0	73	1,888,349	100.0	56	129

Elections to the National Assembly of Wales, 6 May 1999

Additional Member System (AMS)
Turnout: 46%

	Constituency votes	%	Constituency seats	Regional votes	%	Top-up seats	Total seats
Conservative	162,133	15.8	1	168,206	16.5	8	9
Labour	384,671	37.6	27	361,657	35.5	1	28
Liberal Democrat	137,857	13.5	3	128,008	12.5	3	6
Plaid Cymru	290,572	28.4	9	312,048	30.6	8	17
Green	1,002	0.1	0	25,858	2.5	0	0
Others	46,990	4.6	0	24,210	2.4	0	0
Total	1,023,225	100.0	40	1,019,987	100.0	20	60

Elections to the National Assembly of Wales, 1 May 2003

Additional Member System (AMS)
Turnout: 38%

	Constituency votes	%	Constituency seats	Regional votes	%	Top-up seats	Total seats
Conservative	169,832	19.9	1	162,725	19.2	10	11
Labour	340,515	40.0	30	310,658	36.6	0	30
Liberal Democrat	120,250	14.1	3	108,013	12.7	3	6
Plaid Cymru	180,185	21.2	5	167,653	19.7	7	12
Green	0	0.0	0	30,028	3.5	0	0
Others	40,575	4.8	1	70,475	8.3	0	1
Total	851,357	100.0	40	849,552	100.0	20	60

Elections to the Northern Ireland Assembly, 25 June 1998 and 26 November 2003

STV system of PR

Party	1998 Turnout 68.8%			2003 Turnout 64.0%		
	First preference votes	%	Seats	First preference votes	%	Seats
Democratic Unionist Party	146,989	18.1	20	177,944	25.7	30
Sinn Féin	143,647	17.7	18	162,758	23.5	24
Ulster Unionist Party	172,225	21.3	28	156,931	22.7	27
Social Democratic & Labour Party	177,963	22.0	24	117,547	17.0	18
Alliance Party	52,636	6.5	6	25,372	3.7	6
United Kingdom Unionist Party	36,541	4.5	5	5,700	0.8	1
Progressive Unionist Party	20,634	2.5	2	8,032	1.2	1
Northern Ireland Women's Coalition	13,019	1.6	2	5,785	0.8	0
Ulster Democratic Party	8,651	1.2	0	–	–	–
Others	38,012	4.7	3	31,959	4.6	1
Total	810,317	100.0	108	692,028	100.0	108

Election of Mayor of London, 4 May 2000

Supplementary Vote System
Turnout: 33.7%

Name	Party	First preference votes	%	Transfers	Final	%
Ken Livingstone	Independent	667,877	39.0	+108,550	776,427	57.9
Steven Norris	Conservative	464,434	27.1	+99,703	564,137	42.1
Frank Dobson	Labour	223,884	13.1			
Susan Kramer	Liberal Democrat	203,452	11.9			
Ram Gidoomal	Christian People's Alliance	42,060	2.5			
Darren Johnson	Green	38,121	2.2			
Michael Newland	British National Party	33,569	2.0			
Others		40,675	2.4			
Total		1,714,072				

Election of Mayor of London, 10 June 2004

Supplementary Vote System
Turnout: 35.9%*

Name	Party	First preference votes	%	Transfers	Final	%
Ken Livingstone	Labour	685,541	36.8	+142,839	828,380	55.4
Steve Norris	Conservative	542,423	29.1	+124,765	667,188	44.6
Simon Hughes	Liberal Democrat	284,645	15.3			
Frank Maloney	UK Independence Party	115,665	6.2			
Lindsey German	Respect	61,731	3.3			
Julian Leppert	British National Party	58,405	3.1			
Darren Johnson	Green	57,331	3.1			
Ram Gidoomal	Christian People's Alliance	41,696	2.2			
Others		16,234	0.9			
Total		1,863,671	100.0			

* Turnout 37.0% including spoilt and invalid papers

Election of London Assembly, 4 May 2000

Additional Member System (AMS)
Turnout: 31.2% (constituency) / 32.6% (list)

Party	Constituency votes	%	Constituency seats	List votes	%	Top-up seats	Total seats
Conservative	526,707	33.2	8	481,053	29.0	1	9
Labour	501,296	31.6	6	502,874	30.3	3	9
Liberal Democrat	299,998	18.9	0	245,555	14.8	4	4
Green	162,457	10.2	0	183,910	11.1	3	3
Christian People's Alliance	0	0.0	0	55,192	3.3	0	0
Other	95,612	6.0	0	191,046	11.5	0	0
Total	1,586,070	100.0	14	1,659,630	100.0	11	25

Election of London Assembly, 10 June 2004

Additional Member System (AMS)
Turnout: 34.7% (constituency) / 36.0% (list)*

Party	Constituency votes	%	Constituency seats	List votes	%	Top-up seats	Total seats
Conservative	562,047	31.2	9	533,696	27.8	0	9
Labour	444,808	24.7	5	468,247	24.4	2	7
Liberal Democrat	332,237	18.4	0	316,218	16.5	5	5
Green	138,242	7.7	0	160,445	8.4	2	2
UK Independence Party	181,146	10.0	0	156,780	8.2	2	2
British National Party	–	–	0	90,365	4.7	0	0
Respect	79,476	4.4	0	87,533	4.6	0	0
Other	65,211	3.6	0	59,882	3.1	0	0
Total	1,803,167	100.0	14	1,873,166	100.0	11	25

* Turnout 37.0% including blank, spoilt and invalid papers (not published separately for constituency and list)

Referendum on the status of Northern Ireland, 8 March 1973

Question: 'Do you want Northern Ireland to remain part of the United Kingdom, or do you want Northern Ireland to be joined with the Republic of Ireland, outside the United Kingdom?'

	Votes	%
Remain part of United Kingdom	591,820	98.9
Joined with the Republic of Ireland, outside the United Kingdom	6,463	1.1
Total	598,283	Turnout 58.7%

Referendum on the Common Market, 5 June 1975

Question: 'Do you think that the United Kingdom should stay in the European Community (the Common Market)?'

	Votes	%
Yes	17,378,581	67.2
No	8,470,073	32.8
Total	25,848,654	Turnout 64.5%

Referendum on Devolution for Scotland, 1 March 1979

Question: 'Do you want the provisions of the Scotland Act 1978 to be put into force?'

	Votes	%
Yes	1,230,937	51.6
No	1,153,502	48.4
Total	2,384,439	Turnout 63.6%

Referendum on Devolution for Wales, 1 March 1979

Question: 'Do you want the provisions of the Wales Act 1978 to be put into force?'

	Votes	%
Yes	243,048	20.3
No	956,330	79.7
Total	1,199,378	Turnout 58.8%

Referendums on a Scottish Parliament, 11 September 1997

Question: 'I agree that there should be a Scottish Parliament' or 'I do not agree that there should be a Scottish Parliament.'

	Votes	%
I agree that there should be a Scottish Parliament	1,775,045	74.3
I do not agree that there should be a Scottish Parliament	614,400	25.7
Total	2,389,445	Turnout 60.4%

Question: 'I agree that a Scottish Parliament should have tax-varying powers' or 'I do not agree that a Scottish Parliament should have tax-varying powers.'

	Votes	%
I agree that a Scottish Parliament should have tax-varying powers	1,512,889	63.5
I do not agree that a Scottish Parliament should have tax-varying powers	870,263	36.5
Total	2,383,152	

Referendum on a National Assembly for Wales, 18 September 1997

Question: 'Yr wyf yn cytuno y dylid cael Cynulliad Cymreig/I agree that there should be a Welsh Assembly' or 'Nid wyf yn cytuno y dylid cael Cynulliad Cymreig/ I do not agree that there should be a Welsh Assembly.'

	Votes	%
Yr wyf yn cytuno y dylid cael Cynulliad Cymreig /I agree that there should be a Welsh Assembly	559,419	50.3
Nid wyf yn cytuno y dylid cael Cynulliad Cymreig /I do not agree that there should be a Welsh Assembly	552,698	49.7
Total	1,112,117	Turnout 50.1%

Referendum on a Greater London Authority, 7 May 1998

Question: 'Are you in favour of the government's proposals for a Greater London Authority, made up of an elected mayor and separately elected authority?'

	Votes	%
Yes	1,230,715	72.0
No	478,413	28.0
Total	1,709,128	Turnout 34.1%

Referendum on the Good Friday Agreement (Northern Ireland), 22 May 1998

Question: 'Do you support the agreement reached in the multi-party talks on Northern Ireland and set out in Command Paper 3883?'

	Votes	%
Yes	676,966	71.1
No	274,879	28.9
Total	951,845	Turnout 81.0%

Appendix 3
Proxy and Postal Voters

Voters who wish to vote by post or proxy should obtain the appropriate form from their local council. (Most councils now have websites from which the forms can be downloaded directly.)

Postal votes were formerly subject to the same restrictions as proxy votes, set out below, but are now available to all electors registered in Great Britain; in Northern Ireland, however, the restrictions are still in force. Voters may apply either for a postal vote at a particular election, or to vote by post at all elections for a specified or indefinite period. Applications must be made at the latest by 5 p.m. on the sixth day before polling day (excluding Saturdays, Sundays and public holidays).

The former regulation that postal votes could only be sent out to addresses in the United Kingdom no longer applies. However, voters should bear in mind the potential delays involved in overseas postage, and that ballot papers will not be sent out until ten working days before the election at the earliest; they may be better advised to apply for a proxy vote if there is any risk they might not be able to receive and return their ballot paper in time.

Once a postal ballot paper has been issued, the voter will not be able to vote at a polling station; anyone who has previously applied for a postal vote and wishes to cancel it must notify the council in writing at least eleven working days before the election to ensure they are not sent a postal ballot paper.

There are two broad categories of **proxy voters**: those who wish to be registered as such for an indefinite period, and those who are seeking a proxy vote for a particular election. Proxy votes may be claimed *for an indefinite period* by those unable, or unlikely to be able, to go to vote in person, because of:

1. The general nature of their employment, service or occupation (for example, long-distance lorry drivers and merchant seamen), or attendance away from home on a course. Such applications need to be countersigned by an employer or representative of the educational establishment or, in the case of the self-employed, some other responsible person.
2. Blindness or other physical incapacity. Except in the case of registered blind persons and people in receipt of the higher rate of the mobility component of the disability living allowance, a counter-signature is required from a doctor or other qualified person – such as first level nurses trained in general nursing, Christian Science practitioners, those in charge of residential care homes and local authority residential accommodation and resident wardens. (GPs are required by law to deal with applications for absent voting attestation free of charge.[1])
3. Having to make a journey by sea or air in order to be able to vote in person. (This applies mostly to Scottish electors who live on islands away from a polling station.)

4. Service voters and overseas voters can also vote by post or proxy. Service voters can obtain forms from their commanding officers, Crown servants from their own government departments and overseas electors from British embassies and consulates abroad, or, in each case, from the local authority where they are registered to vote.

In addition, a proxy vote may be claimed *for a particular election only*, if the elector cannot reasonably be expected to vote in person at that election. The reason must be stated on the form and the application may be rejected if it is inadequate.

Applications for proxy votes must be made, on an appropriate form, by 5 p.m. on the sixth day before polling day (excluding Saturdays, Sundays and public holidays). Forms are obtainable from the electoral Registration Officer (that is, at the local council offices or, often, via its website). The applicant must name his or her proxy, who must be qualified to vote in the type of election(s) concerned. Nobody may act as proxy for more than two electors excluding family members.

A proxy records the vote at the same polling station at which the absent voter would otherwise be entitled to vote; a proxy voter may vote by post if he or she has made the appropriate application.

An elector, even having appointed a proxy, may vote at the polling station personally if a ballot paper has not already been issued to his or her proxy. However, an elector who has applied for a postal vote (or whose proxy has done so) may not vote in person at the polling station once a postal ballot paper has been issued.

Appendix 4
Election Timetable

The following chart lists the important days to remember during a general election campaign. It is important to remember to exclude Saturdays, Sundays and bank or public holidays in any part of the United Kingdom in the count of 17 days between the Proclamation and polling day.

Day

0	Dissolution
	Proclamation
1	Receipt of writ
3	Notice of election (by 4 p.m.)
4	First day for nomination
6	Last day for nomination (by 4 p.m.)
11	Last day for applications for postal or proxy votes
17	Polling day

Example (based on 2001)

Chart days   *Calendar dates*

0	M	14 May	Dissolution
			Proclamation
1	Tu	15	Receipt of writ
2	W	16	
3	Th	17	Notice of election (by 4 p.m.)
			Last day for registration of political parties
4	F	18	First day for nomination
–	Sa	19	
–	Su	20	
5	M	21	
6	Tu	22	Last day for nomination (by 4 p.m.)
7	W	23	
8	Th	24	
9	F	25	
–	Sa	26	
–	Su	27	
–	M	28	Bank holiday
10	Tu	29	
11	W	30	Last day for applications for postal or proxy votes
12	Th	31	
13	F	1 June	
–	Sa	2	

–	Su	3		
14	M	4		
15	Tu	5		
16	W	6		
17	Th	7 June	Polling day

In a **by-election**, some discretion is allowed in the choice of polling day, which may be on the 17th, 18th or 19th working day (counting from the receipt of the writ on day 1). Nominations will open on day 4, regardless, but will close on day 6, 7 or 8 depending on polling day.

In elections to the **European Parliament**, notice of election must be given not later than the 25th day before polling day. Nominations open the day after publication of the notice of election, and close on the 19th day before polling.

Death of a candidate. If the Returning Officer is notified of the death of a nominated candidate at any time before the result is declared, the poll is abandoned, and the timetable starts afresh as if the writ had been received 28 days after the Returning Officer was notified of the candidate's death. This last occurred in a Parliamentary election at the 1951 general election, when the Labour candidate for Barnsley died shortly before polling day.

Appendix 5
Summary of Election Offences

(This table is only a summary and should not be taken as being an authoritative or exhaustive statement of the law.)

Corrupt practices

Offences

Penalties

BRIBERY. No gift, loan, or promise of money or money's worth must be made to a voter to induce him or her either to vote or abstain from voting. The offer or promise of a situation or employment to a voter or anyone connected with him, if made with the same object, is also bribery.

The consequences are the same whether bribery is committed before, during, or after an election.

Giving or paying money for the purpose of bribery is equivalent to the offence itself.

A gift or promise to a third person to procure a vote is bribery. Payment for loss of time, wages, or travelling expenses may be judged to be bribery. Any person who receives a bribe, or bargains for employment or reward in consideration of his vote, is guilty of bribery.

TREATING. No meat, drinks, entertainment or provisions can be paid for or provided for any person at any time, in order to induce him, or any other person, to vote or abstain from voting. The gift of tickets to be exchanged for refreshment is regarded as treating.

Treating the wives or relatives of voters is also forbidden.

On indictment, twelve months' imprisonment or an unlimited fine, or both. On summary conviction, six months' imprisonment, a fine not exceeding £2000, or both.

Deprivation of the right of voting at any election in the United Kingdom for five years.

Removal from, and disqualification for, any public office.

Payment of costs of an election inquiry in certain cases.

If committed by the candidate he or she also loses the seat, if elected, and is disqualified for ten years from representing the constituency and is disqualified for five years from sitting for any other constituency. If committed by any agent the election is void, and the candidate is disqualified for seven years.

NOTE: Any recognised active worker may be held to be 'an agent'.

The receiver of any meat, drink, etc., is equally guilty, and liable to the same consequences* (see note on p. 233)

UNDUE INFLUENCE. No force, threat, restraint, or fraud may be used to compel an elector to vote or abstain. Using or threatening any spiritual or temporal injury is undue influence. The withdrawal of custom, or a threat to do so, comes under this prohibition. A threat to evict a tenant will also be undue influence.
Any fraudulent device or contrivance (e.g. publication of misleading election material resembling a rival's publications), or other interference with the proper course of the election (e.g. a scheme to prevent an elector receiving a candidate's election literature) may be undue influence if it can be shown to have impeded the free exercise of a voter's franchise.

UNAUTHORISED EXPENDITURE. Incurring expenditure on account of holding public meetings or issuing advertisements, circulars or publications, by any person, other than the election agent, for the purpose of promoting or procuring the election of any candidate at a Parliamentary election, unless authorised in writing by such election agent and returned as an expense by the person incurring it.

Making a false statement in nomination papers (including falsifying the signature of an elector in support of a nomination).
Fraudulently purporting to be authorised to issue a certificate on behalf of the registered nominating officer of a political party.

FALSE DECLARATION. Knowingly making a false declaration as to election expenses.

As for other corrupt practices, but in addition may be punishable under the Perjury Act (1911).

PERSONATION. Applying for a ballot paper in the name of another person, whether alive or dead, or a fictitious person.

Voting or attempting to vote at any election under the authority of a proxy paper when knowing or having reasonable grounds for supposing that the proxy paper has been cancelled, or that the elector on whose behalf it has been issued is dead or not entitled to vote at that election.

Aiding or abetting the commission of the offence of personation.

On indictment, two years' imprisonment, an unlimited fine, or both.

Five years' incapacity to vote, or hold any public office.

If committed by any agent, the candidate loses his or her seat.

Illegal practices

Offences

Penalties

CONVEYANCE. Paying or receiving money for conveyance of voters to or from the poll. (Private conveyances lent gratuitously can alone be employed; hackney carriages – taxis – are prohibited except when hired by voters for their own exclusive use.)

ADVERTISING. Paying money to an elector for exhibiting bills, etc. The receiver is also guilty.

VOTING OFFENCES. Voting when prohibited or inducing a prohibited elector to vote (whether in person, by post or by appointing a proxy).

Voting twice in the same constituency in the same election, or voting in more than one constituency in a general election.

Voting or attempting to vote in person knowing that one's proxy has already voted.

Voting or attempting to vote as proxy on behalf of more than two absent voters at an election in any constituency, unless voting as the husband or wife, or the parent, brother or sister of the absent voter.

A fine not exceeding £5000. Incapacity to vote at any election in the constituency for five years.

If committed by a candidate, or with his knowledge and consent, the election may be rendered void and the candidate disqualified from representing the constituency for seven years. If by an agent, the election may be declared void and the candidate disqualified from representing the constituency until the next general election.

Making a statement one knows to be false in any declaration or form concerned with an application for a postal or proxy vote, or attesting such an application when one knows one is not qualified to do so.

FALSE STATEMENT. Publishing a false statement of the withdrawal of any candidate or as to his or her personal character or conduct.

POLL CARDS. Issuing at a Parliamentary election any poll card or document resembling an official poll card.

BROADCASTING. Broadcasting election propaganda from outside the United Kingdom (except by the BBC, S4C or one of the ITV companies).

DISTURBING AN ELECTION MEETING. Acting or inciting others to act in a disorderly manner for the purpose of preventing the transaction of the business for which a (legal) election meeting was called.

ELECTION EXPENSES. Failure by a candidate or his election agent to comply with the provisions regarding returns and declarations of election expenses (including inadvertently making an inaccurate declaration or return).
Knowingly incurring an expense in excess of the statutory maximum.
Paying election expenses other than through the election agent.

EUROPEAN ELECTIONS. Standing for the European Parliament both in the United Kingdom and in another member state.
Standing in more than one region or for more than one party.

A fine not exceeding £2000. Incapacity to vote at any election in the constituency for five years.
If committed by a candidate, or with his knowledge and consent, the election may be rendered void and the candidate disqualified from representing the constituency for seven years. If by an agent, the election may be declared void and the candidate disqualified from representing the constituency until the next general election.

PUBLISHING BILLS, placards or posters, or any other printed document circulated for the purpose of promoting or procuring the election of a candidate, without the printer's and publisher's name and address. (The election agent alone, or sub-agents in counties, may issue any printed matter at the election.) Any process for multiplying copies of a document other than by copying it by hand is deemed to be printing.

If the offender be the candidate or his agent, the full penalty attaching to an illegal practice as above.
If any other person, a fine not exceeding £5000.

Illegal payment, employment and hiring

ILLEGAL CONVEYANCE. Lending or using, for the conveyance of voters to or from the poll, horses or vehicles usually kept for hire (such as taxis). This does not prevent electors at their own cost from hiring such a vehicle for their own use.

A fine not exceeding £2000. If committed by a candidate or election agent, he/she is also guilty of an illegal practice and subject to the disqualifications outlined above.

EMPLOYMENT of any person as a canvasser.

USING OR HIRING A COMMITTEE ROOM in any maintained school.

ILLEGAL PAYMENTS. Payment to induce corrupt withdrawal of a candidate.
Providing money for illegal purposes.

FORGERY or counterfeiting a ballot paper is not a corrupt or illegal practice as such, but under the Forgery and Counterfeiting Act of 1981 is subject to a maximum penalty of ten years' imprisonment or an unlimited fine, or both. On summary conviction, the maximum penalty is six months' imprisonment or a maximum fine of £2000, or both.

OTHER ELECTIONS. The provisions for European, local and devolved assembly elections are generally similar, and the penalties the same, as for Parliamentary elections. At local elections, in circumstances where a Parliamentary candidate would be disqualified from representing the constituency in which the election concerned took place, the disqualification would apply to holding any corporate office in the relevant local government area.

REFRESHMENT FOR WORKERS. Whilst it is much better, and more prudent, to leave all workers, whether paid or unpaid, to find their own refreshments, the view has been expressed by some judges that 'the giving of refreshments to persons employed at the election, if *bona fide* and honestly done, *is not treating*, even though the workers be voters, if care be taken to confine it to persons actually engaged on the election'.

Appendix 6
Occupations of Candidates and MPs 2001

Occupation	Labour elected	Labour defeated	Conservative elected	Conservative defeated	Liberal Democrat elected	Liberal Democrat defeated
Professions:						
Barrister	13	12	18	28	2	7
Solicitor	18	10	13	34	4	19
Doctor/dentist/optician	2	1	3	7	3	13
Architect/surveyor	1	2	4	9	1	3
Civil/chartered engineer	5	5	1	12	1	14
Accountant	2	3	3	22	1	30
Civil servant/local govt	30	21	2	13	3	23
Armed services	1	1	11	9	0	8
Teachers:						
University	18	6	1	1	2	15
Polytechnic/college	31	11	0	5	1	16
School	49	32	6	19	9	66
Other consultants	3	6	2	12	0	24
Scientific/research	6	4	0	1	0	5
Total	*179*	*114*	*64*	*172*	*27*	*243*
	(43%)	*(50%)*	*(39%)*	*(36%)*	*(52%)*	*(41%)*
Business:						
Company director	5	5	18	57	6	23
Company executive	10	9	31	66	7	42
Commerce/insurance	2	8	6	46	0	33
Management/clerical	12	2	2	12	1	21
General business	4	4	3	23	0	27
Total	*33*	*28*	*60*	*204*	*14*	*146*
	(8%)	*(12%)*	*(36%)*	*(43%)*	*(27%)*	*(25%)*
Miscellaneous:						
Miscellaneous white collar	73	35	2	29	1	90
Politician/pol. organiser	44	16	18	29	4	39
Publisher/journalist	32	19	14	18	4	20
Farmer	0	1	5	12	1	4
Housewife	0	0	2	2	0	4
Student	0	1	0	3	0	14
Total	*149*	*72*	*41*	*93*	*10*	*171*
	(36%)	*(32%)*	*(25%)*	*(20%)*	*(19%)*	*(29%)*

Occupation	Labour		Conservative		Liberal Democrat	
	elected	*defeated*	*elected*	*defeated*	*elected*	*defeated*
Manual workers:						
Miner	11	0	1	0	0	2
Skilled worker	37	13	0	4	1	16
Semi/unskilled worker	3	1	0	1	0	9
Total	*51*	*14*	*1*	*5*	*1*	*27*
	(12%)	*(6%)*	*(1%)*	*(1%)*	*(2%)*	*(5%)*
Grand total	*412*	*228*	*166*	*474*	*52*	*587*

Source: Reprinted by kind permission from Byron Criddle, 'MPs and Candidates', in David Butler and Dennis Kavanagh, *The British General Election of 2001* (London: Palgrave, 2002), p. 204.

Appendix 7
Opinion Poll Surveys Published during the 2001 Election

Campaign polls

Fieldwork dates	Agency	Client	Publ'n date	Sample size	Con (%)	Lab (%)	Lib Dem (%)	Others (%)	Lab Lead (%)
8 May	MORI	Times	10 May	1,046	30	54	13	3	24
10–11 May	NOP	S. Times*	13 May	1,003	32	49	13	6	17
10–11 May	ICM	Observer*	13 May	1,011	32	48	15	5	16
10–12 May	MORI	S. Telegraph*	13 May	1,021	31	51	13	5	20
11–13 May	ICM	Eve. Standard*	14 May	1,437	32	48	14	6	16
12–13 May	Rasmussen	Independent**	15 May	1,030	32	46	13	9	14
13–14 May	ICM	Guardian*	16 May	1,004	31	46	16	7	15
10–14 May	MORI	Economist	18 May	1,846	26	54	14	6	28
14–15 May	Gallup	D. Telegraph*	17 May	1,004	32	48	13	7	16
15 May	MORI	Times	17 May	1,019	28	54	12	6	26
17–18 May	NOP	S. Times*	20 May	1,107	30	49	14	7	19
19–21 May	ICM	Guardian*	23 May	1,000	32	45	17	7	13
19–22 May	Rasmussen	Independent**	25 May	3,162	32	44	16	8	12
21–23 May	Gallup	D. Telegraph*	24 May	1,439	32	48	15	5	16
22 May	MORI	Times	24 May	1,066	30	55	11	4	25
24–25 May	NOP	S. Times*	27 May	1,001	30	49	14	7	19
26–27 May	Rasmussen	Independent**	29 May	1,227	32	44	17	7	12
26–28 May	ICM	Guardian*	30 May	1,000	28	47	17	8	19
29 May	MORI	Times	31 May	1,013	30	48	16	6	18
28–29 May	Gallup	D. Telegraph*	31 May	1,462	31	47	16	6	16
30 May–1 Jun	ICM	Channel 4*	1 Jun	1,007	31	43	19	7	12
31 May–1 Jun	NOP	S. Times*	3 Jun	1,105	30	47	16	7	17
31 May–1 Jun	ICM	Observer*	3 Jun	1,005	34	46	15	5	12
31 May–2 Jun	MORI	S. Telegraph*	3 Jun	1,070	27	50	17	6	23
2–3 Jun	ICM	Eve. Standard*	4 Jun	1,332	30	47	18	5	17
2–3 Jun	Rasmussen	Independent**	5 Jun	1,266	33	44	16	7	11
2–4 Jun	ICM	Guardian*	6 Jun	1,009	32	43	19	6	11
4–5 Jun	MORI	Economist*	7 Jun	1,010	31	43	20	6	12
5–6 Jun	MORI	Times	7 Jun	1,967	30	45	18	7	15
6 Jun	Gallup	D. Telegraph*	7 Jun	2,399	30	47	18	5	17
7 Jun	Result (GB)				32.7	42.0	18.8	6.5	9.3

* Telephone poll.
** Telephone automated response poll.

Exit polls

Company	Client	Sample	Con seats	Lab seats	Lib Dem seats	Other seats	Lab majority seats
MORI	ITV	13,667	154	417	58	30	175
NOP	BBC	17,638	177	408	44	30	157
Result			*166*	*413*	*52*	*28*	*167*

Source: Adapted with permission from tables in *British Public Opinion* Newsletter, Vol. 24 (June 2001), p. 32 (London: MORI, 2001).

Appendix 8
Other Electoral Systems[1]

There are three broad categories of electoral systems: plurality, majoritarian and proportional representation (PR).

The Plurality System

This system awards seat(s) to the candidate(s) who get the most votes even if this is less than an absolute majority. This is often known, particularly in the United Kingdom, where it is used for Parliamentary and local elections, as the 'first past the post' system.

Most frequently it is used in single-member constituencies, but it may equally be applied to multi-member constituencies where the voter normally has as many votes as there are seats to be filled (for example, in some local government elections in the UK). A unique example of the use of multi-member constituencies, where the elector has only one vote, was the system formerly used in Japan, known as the *single non-transferable vote.*

Plurality systems are very widely used for Parliamentary elections, though they are nowadays mostly restricted to countries (including the USA) which were once under British rule. For presidential elections however, where by definition only one person is to be elected, the plurality system is more widely employed.

The Majoritarian System

This means that only candidates winning more than 50 per cent of the votes cast may be elected. The system has two main sub-categories: the *two-ballot* system and the *alternative vote*. A variant of the alternative vote called the *supplementary vote*, which is not strictly majoritarian, is also discussed here.

In the two-ballot system, which is normally restricted to single-member constituencies, a second round of voting is held if no candidate gains more than 50 per cent of the votes cast in the first ballot. The second ballot is often legally limited to the two leading candidates in the first round. Historically it has been the system used most frequently in France in Parliamentary elections, but it was temporarily replaced by a proportional system in 1986. It is widely used, however, in presidential elections.

The alternative vote is used for the election of the Australian House of Representatives. Voters number the candidates in the order of their choice, and if no candidate wins more than 50 per cent of the votes cast the bottom candidate is eliminated and his or her votes are redistributed to their second choices. Further candidates may be eliminated until one candidate achieves an absolute majority. The alternative vote is also used in the Republic of Ireland in the event of Parliamentary by-elections and for the election of the president.

The supplementary vote (SV) is similar to the alternative vote except that voters can only express their first and second choices; the two candidates with the highest number of first choice votes proceed to the second stage of the count, while all other candidates are eliminated, and the second choices of their voters redistributed if they are for one of the two candidates still remaining in the contest. Because a proportion of votes can be 'wasted' (voters whose first and second choice candidates are both eliminated at the first count get no chance to choose between the two candidates who remain), SV is not a fully majoritarian system. SV is used in the election of the Mayor of London.

Proportional Representation

This is the final broad category of election systems. As its name implies, it attempts to relate the allocation of seats as closely as possible to the distribution of votes. By definition, this requires more than one vacancy, so multi-member constituencies are necessary.

There are two distinct forms of proportional representation: party list systems, which explicitly recognise parties and assign them seats on the basis of the votes cast for them or their candidates, and the single transferable vote (STV), in which votes are cast only for individuals but the overall effect is to ensure that any group of candidates (including those belonging to any particular party) receive a total number of votes proportional to their collective support. Party list systems were mostly invented and adopted in continental Europe in the nineteenth and early twentieth century; STV was invented by British (and Irish) political philosophers around the same period, and has until recently been the preferred form of PR of most electoral reformers in the British Isles, though it is little used elsewhere.

The *party list* system is divided between two main sub-categories and a number of sub-sub-categories. The sub-categories are: *largest remainder* and *highest average (or divisor systems)*. These refer to the mathematical formulae by which the seats are allocated, as there is no way of ensuring 100 per cent proportionality. In any given election, even the best PR system will be fractionally less fair to some parties than to others because parties cannot be awarded a fraction of a seat, and the number of votes each party receives are unlikely to correspond to exact whole number shares.

The largest remainder method is the simplest means of allocation. It involves setting a quota of votes which party lists of candidates must achieve in order to be guaranteed a seat. The most common quota is the *Hare quota*, named after Thomas Hare, a Victorian lawyer and associate of John Stuart Mill. This is derived by dividing the number of votes cast by the number of seats to fill. For example, in a four-member constituency where 20,000 votes have been cast the quota will be 5000.

In the example shown in Table A8.1 only two of the four parties achieve an electoral quota. So only two of the four seats can be directly allocated: one each to parties A and B. But under the *largest remainder* system the third seat also goes to party A and the fourth seat to party C. The *largest remainder* system is sometimes regarded as being favourable to smaller parties, and it is noteworthy in the above example that party C gets as many seats as party B while getting less than half the number of votes; but in fact it treats parties of all sizes equally, and examples can also be constructed where the larger parties are over-represented.

Table A8.1 Largest remainder, four-member constituency (20,000 votes cast. Hare quota 5000)

Party	Votes	Quota	Seats	Remainder	Seats	Total seats
A	8,200	5,000	1	3,200	1	2
B	6,100	5,000	1	1,100	0	1
C	3,000	–	0	3,000	1	1
D	2,700	–	0	2,700	0	0
Total	20,000		2		2	4

Two different quotas, whose practical effect is to allocate more seats by quota, leaving fewer to the remainders, are the *Hagenbach-Bischoff quota* and the *Imperiali quota*. The Hagenbach-Bischoff quota involves dividing the total votes cast by the number of seats plus one, and the Imperiali quota by the number of seats plus two. The *Droop quota*, which is equivalent to the Hagenbach-Bischoff quota plus one or the next whole number above it, is not normally used in list PR systems but is used to assign seats in the single transferable vote system.

The *highest average* system was devised by another nineteenth-century lawyer, the Belgian Victor D'Hondt, after whom it is named; this is the system which has been adopted for PR elections in Britain since 1997 (although only in the European Parliament elections is the pure D'Hondt system used – for the Scottish Parliament, Welsh Assembly and London Assembly it is used only for calculating 'top-up seats' in the hybrid AMS system, explained below). Its central idea is to minimise the over-representation of the most over-represented party by successively awarding each seat to the party which given that extra seat would have the highest number of votes per seat. This is achieved by dividing each party's votes by successive divisors, and then allocating the seats to the parties in descending order of quotients. Table A8.2 shows the same results in votes as Table A8.1, but under the D'Hondt system the allocation of seats is different.

Table A8.2 Four-member constituency (20,000 votes cast. Division by D'Hondt divisors)

Party	Votes	Divisor 1		Divisor 2		Divisor 3	Seats
A	8,200	8,200	(1)	4,100	(3)	2,733	2
B	6,100	6,100	(2)	3,050	(4)	2,033	2
C	3,000	3,000		1,500		1,000	0
D	2,700	2,700		1,350		900	0
Total	20,000						4

In the example in Table A8.2 the first seat will go to party A, the second to party B, the third to party A and the fourth to party B whose second quotient is 50 more than the first quotient of party C. Party C is left without a seat, which suggests that the D'Hondt system is less favourable to smaller parties than the Hare quota.

It is possible to produce a hybrid system, first assigning seats by quota or 'first past the post' and then allocating the remaining seats by D'Hondt divisors.

Different quotas and divisors have also been devised, with the objective of giving greater or lesser advantages to large, small or medium-sized parties.

Alternative divisors to those used in the D'Hondt system are the *Sainte-Laguë* and the *Sainte-Laguë modified divisors*. The first of these involves dividing each party's votes by 1, 3, 5, 7, and so on, instead of by 1, 2, 3, 4, and so on. The second, which has been adopted in several Scandinavian countries, involves setting the first divisor at 1.4 instead of 1 (1.4, 3, 5, 7, and so on). This has the effect of strengthening medium-sized parties in a multi-party system. The pure Sainte-Laguë divisors, which have rarely been chosen for national elections but are used to calculate the PR element of New Zealand's mixed-member electoral system, can be shown mathematically to be the most equitable in the sense that they do not systematically advantage or disadvantage any particular size of party.[2] It can be argued that in practical terms this results too often in small parties gaining an electoral foothold, to the detriment of the democratic process. On the other hand, those arguing this – and those with the legislative power to determine details of electoral systems – tend to belong to the larger parties.

Several countries practise a double allocation of seats, in so far as remainders are transferred to a regional or national pool before the remaining seats are allocated. The effect is usually to make the overall result more proportional.

Many countries apply a threshold, in any event, before parties can qualify for seats, either at a constituency or at national level. The size of the threshold varies from country to country, but the most common figure is 5 per cent. Other things being equal, the larger the number of seats in each constituency the more proportional a system will be. The extreme examples are Israel and the Netherlands, in each of which the entire country forms one constituency.

Party list systems can also be classified as 'open' or 'closed', depending on the way in which they decide which of a party's candidates are assigned the seats which the party has won. The simplest system is the closed list system (used in Britain for the 1999 European Parliament elections), where voters simply vote for a party, and candidates win seats in the order in which they appear on the party's list. At the other extreme, fully open lists, voters vote for individual candidates – the votes for each party's candidates are totalled to determine the party's entitlement, and these seats assigned to those individuals from that party who won the most votes. Many countries use an intermediate, 'semi-open' system, where voters can choose either to vote for an individual candidate or to accept the party's recommended ranking. (The best-known variant of this type is often called the 'Belgian system', since it is used there.)

A different form of proportional representation is the *Single Transferable Vote* (STV), which is used for Parliamentary elections in the Republic of Ireland and Malta, and for elections in Northern Ireland except those to the Westminster Parliament. Under this system the voter may list all the candidates on a ballot paper in his or her order of preference. The total number of votes cast is divided by the number of seats plus one, and one is added to the quotient. This is known as the *Droop* quota. Candidates achieving the Droop quota are allocated seats, and any excess votes are transferred to their second preferences. The process is repeated until all the seats have been filled, if necessary eliminating the bottom candidates and transferring their votes in the same way. The counting of votes under STV is a complicated procedure, often requiring a long series of separate counts. An example from the Irish general election of February 1982 is shown in Appendix 9.

The STV system as used in the Republic of Ireland is less proportional than most party list systems, mainly because the constituencies are relatively small (three to five members), but it gives a much larger choice of individual candidates to the voter; with comparable constituency sizes it would operate almost as proportionately as a party list system (and where it did not, it would be because the voters themselves had declined to vote along party lines, not because of any capriciousness of the electoral system).

Table A8.3 Quotas and divisors: the formulae

1. Hare quota = $\dfrac{\text{Votes}}{\text{Seats}}$

2. Hagenbach-Bischoff quota = $\dfrac{\text{Votes}}{\text{Seats} + 1}$

3. Imperiali quota = $\dfrac{\text{Votes}}{\text{Seats} + 2}$

4. Droop quota = $\left(\dfrac{\text{Votes}}{\text{Seats} + 1} \right) + 1$

5. D'Hondt divisors: 1, 2, 3, 4, 5, etc.
6, Sainte-Laguë divisors: 1, 3, 5, 7, 9, etc.
7. Sainte-Laguë modified divisors: 1.4, 3, 5, 7, 9, etc.

One other device, which also produces this effect, is *panachage*, as practised in Switzerland and Luxembourg. These countries employ party list systems, but the voter has as many votes as there are seats to be filled and may, if he or she chooses, distribute choices between candidates on several different lists.

The *Additional Member System* (AMS), also known as the Mixed Member Proportional System (MMP), is a hybrid containing elements of 'first past the post' and party list PR, and has been adopted in Britain for the Scottish Parliament, Welsh Assembly and London Assembly. The system was originally devised by the occupying powers in West Germany after the Second World War, and imposed for the first Bundestag elections, with the intention of modifying the excesses of list PR which were seen as having contributed to the rise of Hitler. The system has been used in West Germany, and since reunification throughout Germany, ever since, and more recently was also adopted in New Zealand. The basic idea is that a certain number of seats are filled by 'first past the post', with members elected by and representing individual constituencies; but then 'additional members' are added on a regional basis to 'top up' each party's representation so that overall the number of seats is proportional to party support. Voters normally have two votes, one for a constituency member and one for a regional list, and candidates may nominate themselves both at constituency and regional level. (Those candidates who have already won constituencies are ignored when the extra seats are allocated to the leading names on the lists.)

The exact effect of AMS on party representation depends on the ratio of constituency members to top-up members – if there are too few additional members, a party may win so many seats in the constituency section that the top-up is unable to compensate fully. This is what happens in the Scottish Parliament and Welsh Assembly, where there are more constituency members than top-up members. (In both cases the D'Hondt divisors are used to allocate the top-up seats.) Table A8.4 shows how this worked in one region in Scotland, and Table A8.5 shows how the top-up seats are distributed in the same election.

Table A8.4 Scottish Parliament seats and votes in the West of Scotland region, 1999

Party	Constituency voting		Regional voting		Total seats
	% votes	Seats	% votes	Seats	
Conservative	16.4	0	15.7	2	2
Labour	43.5	9	38.5	0	9
Liberal Democrat	11.3	0	11.0	1	1
SNP	26.9	0	25.9	4	4
Other	0.0	0	8.9	0	0
Total	100.0	9	100.0	7	16

Table A8.5 Distribution of top-up seats, West of Scotland

	Con	Lab	Lib Dem	SNP
Votes	15.7	38.5	11	25.9
Seats at start	*0*	*9*	*0*	*0*
Votes/Seats + 1	15.7	3.85	11	25.9
Seats after distribution 1	*0*	*9*	*0*	*1*
Votes/Seats + 1	15.7	3.85	11	12.95
Seats after distribution 2	*1*	*9*	*0*	*1*
Votes/Seats + 1	7.85	3.85	11	12.95
Seats after distribution 3	*1*	*9*	*0*	*2*
Votes/Seats + 1	7.85	3.85	11	8.63
Seats after distribution 4	*1*	*9*	*1*	*2*
Votes/Seats + 1	7.85	3.85	5.5	8.63
Seats after distribution 5	*1*	*9*	*1*	*3*
Votes/Seats + 1	7.85	3.85	5.5	6.47
Seats after distribution 6	*2*	*9*	*1*	*3*
Votes/Seats + 1	5.23	3.85	5.5	6.47
Seats after distribution 7	*2*	*9*	*1*	*4*

The result in this case is that the largest party (Labour in both cases in 1999) gets more than its proportional share of seats, but much less of an advantage than would be the case under 'first past the post'. In Germany, by contrast, half the seats are reserved for additional members, and it is much rarer for a party to win too many constituency seats in a region – but when this does happen (termed an 'overhang') extra top-up seats are added to restore proportionality, so that the Bundestag occasionally has more members than normal.[3]

AV-plus, a system devised and recommended by the Jenkins Commission for use in future British general elections, is a refinement of AMS. In each constituency it uses alternative vote (see above) rather than 'first past the post' to determine the constituency member. It also uses a far smaller proportion of top-up members than is usual with AMS, only around one in six of all members elected. This means that without increasing the size of Parliament it could use constituencies little bigger than those currently in place – so that most would continue to comprise small, recognisable communities of single towns, sections of cities or country areas – and with top-up regions also small, consisting of no more than a single county. For example, they suggested that Oxfordshire, instead of returning six constituency MPs would return five constituency MPs and one top-up MP representing the whole county (and belonging to the party which would otherwise be most under-represented).

AV-plus would not operate as a system of PR, but rather as a blunted version of 'first past the post'. The biggest party, even with less than half the votes nationally, could still hope to win half the seats and thus command a majority in the Commons, but would need a more convincing lead in votes to achieve it than has hitherto been the case. Meanwhile, every voter would be represented by two or three MPs instead of one, and many more of them would find that at least one of their MPs belonged to the party they had voted for. Looking back at the history of British elections since 1945, hung Parliaments would have been more common, but around half of elections would still have produced a majority government, experts have estimated.

The party effect of different systems

The exact effect which different electoral systems would have on the party balance in Britain can only be estimated, because voters would naturally behave differently under different circumstances, and even the best survey evidence is limited in the depth of local detail it can collect. The following table is based on published estimates from two sources of what the result would have been under different systems in 1997, but should only be considered a rough guide. (In particular, the two estimates were based on very different survey evidence about voters' second and subsequent preferences, and how likely the voters would be to express them, which led to very diverse results on the effects of introducing STV; and neither source made estimates for all the different systems.)

Table A8.6 Estimated outcome of the 1997 election (GB only) under different electoral systems

	Con	*Lab*	*Lib Dem*	*Others*
First past the post – votes (actual) %	31.4	44.4	17.2	7.0
Seats				
First past the post (actual result)	*165*	*419*	*46*	*11*
Alternative vote	103–110	436	84–91	11
Supplementary vote	110	436	84	11
AV-plus	167	367	92	15
D'Hondt (5 MPs per region)	205	345	72	19
AMS with 75% constituency seats	196	326	104	15
STV (4–8 MPs per region)	144–195	317–342	89–131	17–24
AMS with 50% constituency seats	203–207	303	111–115	20
National party lists with 5% threshold	208	300	113	20
Largest remainder (5 MPs per region)	205	295	121	20
Pure proportionality	*202*	*285*	*110*	*34*

Sources: Data from the British Election Study, reported by John Curtice and Michael Steed in David Butler and Dennis Kavanagh, *The British General Election of 1997* (Basingstoke: Macmillan, 1997), p. 319; and Patrick Dunleavy, Helen Margetts, Brendan O'Duffy and Stuart Weir, 'Remodelling the 1997 Election: How Britain Would Have Looked Under Alternative Electoral Systems', in *British Elections and Parties Review*, Volume 8 (London: Frank Cass, 1998), and, for AV-plus, Margetts and Dunleavy, 'Reforming the Westminster Electoral System: Evaluating the Jenkins Commission Proposals', in *British Elections and Parties Review*, Volume 9 (London: Frank Cass, 1999).

Appendix 9
The Single Transferable Vote

The Single Transferable Vote is a very simple system of voting, the voters merely numbering the candidates 1, 2, 3 and so on in their order of preference. The counting of the votes is more complicated, as the following not untypical result from Galway West, in the Republic of Ireland's general election of February 1982, illustrates. It took seven counts before the five seats were filled, only one candidate securing enough first preference votes to secure election on the first count.

Table A9.1   Galway West result, general election February 1982

Galway West (5 seats)
Total valid poll, 48,572; Quota 8,096
Turnout 67.5%

Candidate and party	Count 1	Count 2	Count 3	Count 4	Count 5	Count 6	Count 7
*Molloy (FF)	9,545*	−1,449					
		8,096					
*Donnellan (FG)	6,105	+38	+51	+30	+2,181	−309	
		6,143	6,194	6,224	8,405*	8,096	
*Higgins (Lab)	5,718	+129	+715	+214	+554	+2,970	−2,204
		5,847	6,562	6,776	7,330	10,300*	8,096
Fahey (FF)	6,019	+352	+99	+294	+97	+379	+431
		6,371	6,470	6,764	6,861	7,240	7,671†
*Geoghegan-Quinn (FF)	4,139	+475	+47	+1,716	+87	+221	+196
		4,614	4,661	6,377	6,464	6,685	6,881†
*Killilea (FF)	5,624	+198	+35	+242	+29	+212	+145
		5,822	5,857	6,099	6,128	6,340	6,485
McCormack (FG)	3,952	+24	+38	+41	+1,014		
		3,976	4,014	4,055	5,069**		
Coogan (FG)	3,746	+47	+145	+105			
		3,793	3,938	4,043**			
O'Connor (FF)	2,513	+171	+33				
		2,684	2,717**				
Brick (SFWP)	1,211	+15					
		1,226**					
Spoilt/non-transferable	391	0	63	75	81	1,287	1,432

General notes:

(i)   The quota = $\dfrac{48,572}{5+1}$ +1 = 8,096 (ignoring any fractions).

(ii)   The party abbreviations following each candidate's name are:
      FF   Fianna Fáil. (Literally translated this party name is 'soldiers of destiny'.)

FG   Fine Gael. (Literally translated the party name is 'family group of the Gaels'.)

Lab   Labour.

SFWP   Sinn Féin the Workers' Party.

(iii) An asterisk preceding a candidate's name, for example, *Molloy, indicates a member of the previous Dáil, that is, a sitting member.

A single asterisk following a number of votes indicates that the votes of that candidate have exceeded the quota and hence the candidate has been elected on that count.

A dagger following a number of votes indicates that the candidate has been elected at the final count without having exceeded the quota.

A double asterisk following a number of votes indicates that the candidate has been eliminated as a result of that particular count and the votes are to be transferred in the following count.

(iv) The candidates are listed in descending order of the final vote obtained by the candidate. This vote will be obtained in the count which results in the candidate being elected or eliminated. An alternative presentation which could be used is to list the candidates in alphabetical order, as they are on the ballot paper.

Count 1:   First preference votes counted: Molloy (FF) elected.

Count 2:   Distribution of surplus votes of Molloy (FF): Brick (SFWP) eliminated.

Count 3:   Transfer of votes of Brick (SFWP): O'Connor (FF) eliminated.

Count 4:   Transfer of votes of O'Connor (FF): Coogan (FG) eliminated.

Count 5:   Transfer of votes of Coogan (FG): Donnellan (FG) elected, McCormack (FG) eliminated

Count 6:   Transfer of votes of McCormack (FG): Higgins (Lab) elected.

Count 7:   Distribution of surplus votes of Higgins (Lab): Fahey (FF) and Geoghegan-Quinn (FF) elected without reaching quota.

Source: Adapted with kind permission from Paul McKee, 'The Republic of Ireland', in Vernon Bogdanor and David Butler (eds), *Democracy and Elections: Electoral Systems and their Political Consequences* (Cambridge: Cambridge University Press, 1983), pp. 170–1.

Table A9.2   **First preference votes and seats won**

Party	N votes	% votes	Seats won
FF	27,840	57.3	3
FG	13,803	28.4	1
Lab	5,718	11.8	1
SFWP	1,211	2.5	0

Source: Adapted with kind permission from Paul McKee, 'The Republic of Ireland', in Vernon Bogdanor and David Butler (eds), *Democracy and Elections: Electoral Systems and their Political Consequences* (Cambridge: Cambridge University Press, 1983), pp. 170–1.

Appendix 10
Miscellaneous Statistics, 2001 General Election

Number of registered electors (as reported by Returning Officers to the Electoral Commission)	44,403,238
Number of constituencies	659
Number of candidates	3,319
Number of polling stations	c. 46,500
Total valid votes cast	26,367,383
Turnout	59.4%
Number of postal voters on list	1,758,055
Number of postal ballot papers included at start of count	1,370,884
Total number of ballot papers rejected in the count	100,005
Ballot papers rejected as unmarked or void for uncertainty	69,910
Ballot papers rejected for want of official mark	2,548
Ballot papers rejected for voting for more than one candidate	22,590
Ballot papers rejected for writing or other mark that might identify the voter	3,760

Sources: Electoral Commission, *Election 2001: The Official Results* (London: Politico's Publishing, 2001); Electoral Commission, *Absent Voting in Great Britain* (London: Electoral Commission, 2003); *UK Election Statistics: 1918–2004* (House of Commons Library Research Paper 04/61).

Notes and References

Chapter 1

1. See C. Seymour, *Electoral Reform in England and Wales* (New Haven, 1915); H. L. Morris, *Parliamentary Franchise Reform in England from 1885 to 1918* (New York, 1921); D. E. Butler, *The Electoral System in Britain since 1918* (Oxford: Oxford University Press, 1963).
2. See Bill Jones, Dennis Kavanagh, Michael Moran and Philip Norton, *Politics UK*, 5th edition (Harlow: Longman, 2004) or Gillian Peele, *Governing the UK*, 4th edition (Oxford: Blackwell's Publishing, 2004).
3. See Vernon Bogdanor and David Butler (eds), *Democracy and Elections: Electoral Systems and their Political Consequences* (Cambridge University Press, 1983); Dick Leonard and Richard Natkiel, *World Atlas of Elections* (London: Economist Publishing Company, 1986); Bernard Grofman and Arend Lijphart (eds), *Electoral Laws and their Political Consequences* (New York: Agathon Press, 1986).

Chapter 2

1. In 2001 the general election and local government elections were also held on the same day, but not the first Thursday in May: both were held on 6 June, having been postponed because of the Foot and Mouth Disease epidemic. Unlike the date of the general election, which (with the concurrence of the Queen) is in the Prime Minister's gift, the date of the local government elections is prescribed by law, and the postponement required legislation.
2. The last Parliamentary election not held on a Thursday was the Hamilton by-election in 1978, held on a Wednesday to avoid coinciding with the opening game in the football World Cup finals, which was the following day.

Chapter 3

1. The local government franchise also applies to elections for the Scottish Parliament, Welsh Assembly and Greater London Authority.
2. In the special case of the City of London the business vote is still retained.
3. The qualifying date was 10 October in England, Wales and Scotland, but 15 September in Northern Ireland.
4. Indeed, until 1980, no changes could be made to the register after 16 December, and anybody mistakenly omitted was excluded until the next year's register was drawn up. In 1980, it became possible for late claims for inclusion to be considered up to the final date for the nomination of candidates, although the Registration Officer could only include the names of people who were duly qualified to be registered at a particular address on the qualifying date.

5. For similar reasons of cost, the annual register was adopted in 1949, to replace the twice-yearly register originally decreed under the 1948 Representation of the People Act, at an annual saving of £650,000 (£13m at current prices).

6. The annually updated register is published on 1 December; there are no monthly updates in September, October or November.

7. The Electoral Commission has suggested that a future reform should be to switch to registration on an individual rather than household basis; this is already the case in Northern Ireland since the Electoral Fraud (Northern Ireland) Act 2002.

8. In the past this has been interpreted in practice to prevent the registration of the homeless (who cannot provide a permanent address), and voluntary mental patients have also been excluded – even if otherwise fit to vote – because registration officers have not been allowed to accept mental hospitals as valid addresses. Changes in the regulations have now been brought into effect that allow both groups to vote. Voluntary mental patients can register in the ordinary way giving the hospital as their address; similarly, unconvicted prisoners who have been remanded in custody can register at the address where they are being held. (Convicted prisoners serving their sentence are at present not allowed to vote, but the European Court of Human Rights has recently ruled this to be a violation of their human rights, and the law may now be changed to allow them, too, to register and vote.) Homeless people who wish to be registered should contact the local council for the area where they are for the time being staying, and will be asked to sign a 'declaration of local connection' stating that they commonly spend a substantial part of the time (whether day or night) in the constituency; having signed such a declaration they may register. People making a declaration of local connection have the choice of providing an address to which correspondence from the registration officer or returning officer can be delivered, or of agreeing to collect such mail periodically from the registration officer's office.

9. It used to be generally assumed that it was legal to vote in local government elections for two different local authorities if resident and registered in both areas, but a recent Parliamentary answer from the Lord Chancellor's Department has stated the opposite. The state of the law is consequently not entirely clear unless it is tested in court.

10. The registration form normally includes an extra box for those aged over 70 to tick, so they can be marked as exempt on the copy of the register used for selecting names for jury service.

11. This is the form of words prescribed by statutory instrument to be included on the registration form.

12. The period was initially five years, increased to 20 years in 1989 and reduced to 15 years by the Political Parties, Elections and Referendums Act 2000.

13. The studies are reported in: P. G. Gray, T. Corlett and Pamela Frankland, *The Register of Electors as a Sampling Frame* (London: Central Office of Information, 1950); J. Todd and P. Dodd, *The Electoral Registration Process in the UK* (London: OPCS, 1982); S. Smith, *Electoral Registration in 1991* (London: OPCS, 1993). See also J. Todd and B. Butcher, *Electoral Registration in 1981* (London: OPCS, 1982), M. and S. Pinto-Duschinsky, *Voter Registration: Problems and Solutions* (London: Constitutional Reform Centre, 1987).

14. The extent and electoral effect of poll-tax deregistration are discussed in Jeremy Smith and Iain McLean, 'The Poll Tax and the Electoral Register', in Anthony Heath, Roger Jowell and John Curtice with Bridget Taylor (eds), *Labour's Last Chance?* (Aldershot: Dartmouth Press, 1994).
15. A detailed breakdown of registration figures for all groups in 1991, calculated by testing the electoral register against the Census, is given in S. Smith, *Electoral Registration in 1991* (London: OPCS, 1993).
16. In Northern Ireland postal votes remain restricted to those who cannot be reasonably expected to vote in person at the polling station for the address where they are registered – see Appendix 3.

Chapter 4

1. Detailed and entertaining pen-portraits of every constituency, and their MPs, their histories and political and social characteristics, can be found in Robert Waller and Byron Criddle, *The Almanac of British Politics*, 7th edition (London: Routledge, 2002). Simon Henig and Lewis Baston, *The Political Map of Britain* (London: Politico's Publishing, 2002) has similar coverage with comprehensive historical statistics.
2. Before 1832, the biggest constituency was Yorkshire, with an estimated 16,000 voters, although from 1826 to 1832 it had four MPs rather than the two it had up to that point. At the other end of the scale, there were many 'rotten boroughs' where the electorate was in single figures, and on one occasion, at Bossiney in Cornwall in 1784, there was only one qualified elector, electing both the borough's two MPs. Among the most notorious of the rotten boroughs were Old Sarum, where there was not a single building left standing in the borough so that the Returning Officer had to operate from a tent, and Dunwich, which was mostly underwater having been swept away by the sea centuries before.
3. Borough constituencies are called burgh constituencies in Scotland.
4. The history of the Boundary Commissions is told, and the effects of each of their boundary reviews analysed, in D. J. Rossiter, R. J. Johnston and C. J. Pattie, *The Boundary Commissions* (Manchester: Manchester University Press, 1999). For a wider view of the principles involved see Iain McLean and David Butler (eds), *Fixing the Boundaries* (Aldershot: Dartmouth, 1996) and Ron Johnston, Charles Pattie, Danny Dorling and David Rossiter, *From Votes to Seats* (Manchester: Manchester University Press, 2001).
5. *House of Commons Debates* (Hansard), Fifth Series, volume 535, columns 1839–41. Partially quoted by D. E. Butler in an article 'The Redistribution of Seats', *Public Administration*, Summer 1955. See also *The Electoral System in Britain since 1918* (Oxford University Press, 1963) by the same author.
6. By the time of the 2001 general election, the electorate of the Isle of Wight had grown further, to 104,431, while that of the Western Isles was only 21,706.
7. John Curtice and Michael Steed, 'An Analysis of the Voting', in David Butler and Dennis Kavanagh, *The British General Election of 1983* (London: Macmillan, 1984), p. 361.
8. John Curtice and Michael Steed, 'The Results Analysed', in David Butler and Dennis Kavanagh, *The British General Election of 1992* (London: Macmillan, 1992), p. 351.

9. Rossiter *et al.*, *Boundary Commissions* (p. 359), disagreed. Using a different method from the other analysts to estimate the effect of the boundary changes, they concluded that the Conservatives gained a net 24 seats over other parties. For details of the 1994 boundary changes and calculations of their electoral effect in individual constituencies by the more generally accepted method, see Colin Rallings and Michael Thrasher, *Media Guide to the New Parliamentary Constituencies* (London: BBC Publications, 1994).

10. John Curtice and Michael Steed, 'The Results Analysed', in David Butler and Dennis Kavanagh, *The British General Election of 1997* (Basingstoke: Macmillan, 1997), p. 315.

11. John Curtice and Michael Steed, 'The Results Analysed', in David Butler and Dennis Kavanagh, *The British General Election of 2001* (Basingstoke: Palgrave, 2002), pp. 331–2.

12. John Curtice and Michael Steed, 'The Results Analysed', in Butler and Kavanagh, *The British General Election of 1992*, pp. 352–4.

13. See John Curtice and Michael Steed, 'Electoral Choice and the Production of Government: The Changing Operation of the Electoral System in the United Kingdom since 1955', *British Journal of Political Science*, July 1982, and their appendices to Butler and Kavanagh's books on each election. For the cube law to operate, there need to be about 180 seats that would be marginal in a close election; if the number falls to 65, the electoral system will be broadly proportional. Between 1955 and 1970, the number averaged 159, but fell to a low of just 80 in 1983. After that it rose at each election until 1997, when it reached 114.

14. These figures refer to the situation immediately after the 2001 general election and make no allowance for the effect of likely boundary changes in Scotland.

Chapter 5

1. The best up-to-date study of British political parties is probably *The Modern British Party System* by Paul Webb (London: Sage, 2000). See also *The British Party System* by Stephen Ingle, 3rd edition (London: Pinter, 2000).

2. The precise law on nominating under a misleading name or description was rather unclear, and was interpreted by different Returning Officers in different ways. The courts could intervene if they were convinced that voters might be misled – for example, in 1997 the Attorney General Sir Nicholas Lyell secured an injunction against an independent who had changed his name by deed poll to 'Sir Nicholas Lyell', and the Labour Party was able to prevent three independents running as 'New Labour'. But short of court action, most Returning Officers felt compelled not to interfere.

3. The task is not necessarily straightforward. At the 1999 Scottish Parliament elections (before the Electoral Commission had been set up, when registration was being administered by Companies House), the Scottish Socialist Party and Scottish Green Party were both initially told that they could not use those names because they were too similar to other party names already registered. In the case of the Greens this was a particular nonsense, since the name was registered to the Green Party in England and Wales, technically separate but allied to the Scottish Greens, and of course not likely to run candidates in

competition to it. After the unanimous intervention in their favour of the four major parties, however, both the SSP and Scottish Greens were eventually allowed to stand under their chosen labels and, indeed, both won a seat in the Parliament.
4. K. Maguire, 'Blair pleads to disaffected as membership plummets', *Guardian*, 12 April 2004.
5. UNISON, uniquely, is only partly affiliated to the party, because it was founded as an amalgamation of unions some of which were affiliated and some of which were not. The union maintains two political funds, one contributing to Labour and one not, and members may choose which to support.
6. Martin Bell at Tatton, standing against a Conservative incumbent, in 1997; Richard Taylor at Wyre Forest, standing against a Labour incumbent, in 2001. Both were successful.
7. For more information about the history of the minor parties see David Butler and Gareth Butler, *Twentieth Century British Political Facts 1900–2000* (Basingstoke: Macmillan, 2000), pp. 135–84, or the even more exhaustive catalogue in David Boothroyd, *The History of British Political Parties* (London: Politico's Publishing, 2001).
8. His constituency, North Down, has established something of a tradition of rejecting the established Unionist parties – his predecessor, Sir James Kilfedder, was elected for the Ulster Popular Unionist Party, which organised only in North Down and was in effect a personal organisation of his supporters, and unlike the other Unionists Sir James continued to take the Conservative Party whip. However, McCartney was beaten by the official Ulster Unionist candidate in 2001.
9. S. O. Davies at Merthyr in 1970, deselected because the CLP thought he was too old, and Dick Taverne (Lincoln) and Eddie Milne (Blyth), both deselected ahead of the February 1974 election for political reasons. Taverne, indeed, resigned immediately to call a by-election, and won both that (see Chapter 11) and the general election a few months later.

Chapter 6

1. The figures are cited in David Butler and Dennis Kavanagh, *The British General Election of 1997* (Basingstoke: Macmillan, 1997), p. 217.
2. In recent years the parties have begun to use the term 'Parliamentary spokesman/spokesperson' as an alternative to PPC.
3. *The Funding of Political Parties in the United Kingdom*, Fifth Report of the Committee on Standards in Public Life, Cm. 4057 (London: The Stationery Office, 1998), paragraphs 3.33–3.44.

Chapter 7

1. A comprehensive survey of the candidates in each recent election, and of how they came to be selected, can be found in Byron Criddle's chapter of the Butler and Kavanagh Nuffield studies. The recent overhaul in selection procedures awaits an updated and comprehensive treatment. Three earlier books which cover the process as it used to be are *Pathways to Parliament* by Austin Ranney

(Madison: University of Wisconsin Press, and London: Macmillan, 1965); *The Selectorate* by Peter Paterson (London: MacGibbon and Kee, 1967) and *The Selection of Parliamentary Candidates* by Michael Rush (London: Nelson, 1969). On Members of Parliament see *The Commons in Perspective* by Philip Norton (Oxford: Martin Robertson, 1981) and *The Backbenchers* by P. G. Richards (London: Faber, 1972).

2. *Age of Electoral Majority: Report and Recommendations* (London, Electoral Commission, 2004).

3. Indeed, one hereditary peer who no longer has a seat in the Lords, 3rd Viscount Thurso, has already been elected to the Commons, as a Liberal Democrat MP in 2001.

4. The passage of the bill solved the problem posed by the selection of David Cairns, a former Catholic priest, as Labour candidate in Greenock and Inverclyde; he was subsequently elected and, as a result of the new Act, was able to take his seat.

5. As a result of the Disqualifications Act 2000, which also removed the bar on members of the Dáil sitting in the Northern Ireland Assembly.

6. Although it should be noted that the Conservative candidate who was elected in this way immediately resigned the seat to allow a new by-election once the law had been changed so that Benn was once more qualified to sit.

7. Nigel Nicolson, *People and Parliament* (London: Weidenfeld and Nicolson, 1958), p. 40.

8. R. L. Leonard, *Guide to the General Election* (London: Pan Books, 1964), pp. 93–4.

9. In 2003, a Commission on Candidate Selection sponsored by the Electoral Reform Society and the Joseph Rowntree Charitable Trust reported on the efforts of the parties to select more women and more candidates from ethnic minorities, and suggested new guidelines to aid their success – see Peter Riddell, *Candidate Selection: The Report of the Commission on Candidate Selection* (London: Electoral Reform Society, 2003).

10. Trade unions may still financially assist their local Labour parties through Constituency Plan Agreements if the money is not linked to candidacies.

11. Margaret Thatcher, then still Margaret Roberts, was the defeated Conservative candidate for Dartford in 1950 and 1951; Tony Blair lost at Beaconsfield in a 1982 by-election.

12. Edmund Burke, Speech to the Electors of Bristol, 3 November 1774.

13. Byron Criddle, 'Candidates', in David Butler and Dennis Kavanagh, *The British General Election of 1983* (London: Macmillan, 1984), p. 241 (n. 5).

Chapter 8

1. For a more detailed survey of the campaign in the constituencies, see David Denver and Gordon Hands, *Modern Constituency Electioneering* (London: Frank Cass, 1997). For a readable and up-to-date account of the campaign from the candidate's point of view, see Paul Richards, *How To Win An Election*, 2nd edition (London: Politico's Books, 2004).

2. David Butler and Dennis Kavanagh, *The British General Election of 1997* (Basingstoke: Macmillan, 1997), p. 216.

3. But accidents do happen. In 2002, almost the entire Liberal Democrat slate for Harrow London Borough Council, including six sitting councillors, had their nominations deemed invalid and were therefore excluded as candidates, because of a clerical error by which the party description they gave on the nomination form did not match the description authorised by the party's national nominating officer.

4. An earlier edition of this book described the above programme as 'a cracking pace'. This provoked an astonished reaction from a leading political scientist, who wrote 'American visitors are always amazed by the soft lives that British politicians lead. This, by American standards, would be an easy day.' On the other hand, the author was light-heartedly rebuked by a well-known Labour MP, later a senior Cabinet minister. 'Before your book appeared,' he said, 'I had always succeeded in persuading my agent that candidates could not be expected to do any electioneering before lunchtime. Now he has me out canvassing after breakfast!'

5. In European elections, the Post Office is similarly obliged to make one delivery to each elector for each party list. At the election of the Mayor of London, a single manifesto booklet containing material from all the candidates is delivered.

6. However, the delivery was not achieved to everybody's satisfaction. The Electoral Commission reported that it had been made aware of 'a number of situations in which political parties were unhappy about the timeliness of the delivery, failures to deliver leaflets to properties with no other mail, the omission of some households owing to problems in matching postcodes to constituency boundaries, leaflets being delivered to the wrong constituency and, most seriously, instances where it is alleged that large numbers of election addresses from one particular party were not delivered at all'. It added that 'the Commission will pursue with the Royal Mail the various issues that emerged from the general election' (Electoral Commission, *Election 2001: The Official Results*. London: Politico's Publishing, 2001, pp. 54–5).

7. Although it is helpful if voters bring their poll cards to the polling station with them when they vote it is not necessary, and any elector who has lost or indeed for some reason not received a poll card may still vote at the polling station for the appropriate polling district (assuming his or her name is duly included in the electoral register).

8. It may be worth noting that in Northern Ireland, where personation was considered to be a problem in the past, the 1985 Representation of the People Act made specific provision to allow the Secretary of State to suspend postal voting (except for those on the permanent list of postal voters) if he was satisfied that it was necessary to do so to prevent serious abuse.

9. According to a Populus poll reported in *The Times* (8 June 2004), one in seven electors in the pilot areas had not received a ballot paper by the weekend before the election. In Bolton the council had to open polling stations after it was discovered that whole streets had had no ballot papers until it was too late to return them by post (*Financial Times*, 8 June 2004).

10. Nevertheless, it also agreed that the all-postal method should be retained for the referendum in the North-East on regional devolution, the arrangements being too far advanced to be easily changed.

Chapter 9

1. The government launched a consultation on the future of party political broadcasts in 2004 after receiving a report on the subject from the Electoral Commission, and it is possible that this will lead to a formalisation of the rules, and perhaps significant change to the practice, in the near future.
2. Martin Harrison's chapter on broadcasting, and Martin Harrop's and Margaret Scammell's on the press, in David Butler and Dennis Kavanagh *The British General Election of 1983* (London: Macmillan, 1984), *The British General Election of 1987* (Basingstoke: Macmillan, 1987), *The British General Election of 1992* (London: Macmillan, 1992), *The British General Election of 1997* (Basingstoke: Macmillan, 1997) and *The British General Election of 2001* (Basingstoke: Palgrave, 2002), have been important sources in compiling this chapter.
3. See, for example, Martin Harrop's comments in Butler and Kavanagh, *The British General Election 1983*, chapter 9, and especially pp. 214–15, and in Butler and Kavanagh, *The British General Election 2001*, pp. 181–2, and David Deacon and Dominic Wring, 'Partisan Dealignment and the British Press', in John Bartle, Simon Atkinson and Roger Mortimore (eds), *Political Communications: The General Election Campaign of 2001* (London: Frank Cass, 2002).
4. The evidence was examined by Martin Linton, then a *Guardian* journalist and now a Labour MP, in 'Maybe the *Sun* won it after all', *British Journalism Review*, November 1996.

Chapter 10

1. Acceptable forms of identification for this purpose are a passport issued by the United Kingdom or any other Member State of the European Community, a Northern Ireland or Great Britain driving licence (which must bear the photograph of the holder), a Senior SmartPass issued under the Northern Ireland Concessionary Fares Scheme, or an Electoral Identity Card (which can be obtained by application to the Chief Electoral Officer).
2. In recent elections, between 2000 and 3000 ballot papers have not been counted for this reason on each occasion. It is possible for such errors to affect an election result. At Winchester in 1997, the Conservative candidate lost by two votes and successfully petitioned to have the election result overturned by the courts because several votes in his favour had been ruled invalid – see p. 141.
3. Or for too many candidates in some local elections where voters are entitled to cast multiple votes.
4. David Butler and Richard Rose, *The British General Election of 1959* (London: Macmillan, 1960), p. 280, quote a senior party organiser on this point: 'If we lost a seat by one vote and I could clearly prove illegal practices by the other side I wouldn't try. It would cost perhaps £5000 and they might be able to show that our man had slipped up in some way. But worse than that, it might start tit-for-tat petitions and no party could afford a lot of them. On the whole, we are both law-abiding and it's as well to leave each other alone.'

5. Technically, neither the Glasgow Govan nor Newark cases were election petitions, since they proceeded by prosecution through the criminal courts. However, if the court had convicted, the MP would have forfeited his or her seat and a by-election would have been held.
6. The previous record, of 59 minutes, had stood since 1959, and had been particularly notable because it was set in the Essex constituency of Billericay, despite being at the time the constituency with the highest electorate in the country.

Chapter 11

1. See Pippa Norris, *British By Elections: The Volatile Electorate* (Oxford: Clarendon Press, 1990), and Chris Cook and John Ramsden (eds), *By-elections in British Politics* (London: University College London Press, 1997), which both include accounts of many of the most significant by-elections of the twentieth century.
2. Though in the latter case the public opinion poll trends, which fully confirmed the adverse by-election results, were probably equally responsible.
3. The standard work on local elections in Britain, by the accepted experts on the subject, Colin Rallings and Michael Thrasher, is *Local Elections in Britain* (London: Routledge, 1997). Results in detail for England and Wales are collected in the annual *Local Elections Handbook*, compiled by the same authors and published by Local Government Chronicle Communications; summary results are published in the annual *British Elections and Parties Review* (London: Frank Cass). For local elections in Scotland, results are collected by H. M. Bochel and D. T. Denver and published annually as *The Scottish Council Elections: Results and Statistics* (Newport on Tay: Election Studies). The House of Commons library now usually produces a research paper summarising each year's results which is available on the Internet. For a more general study of the structure and functions of local government, see J. A. Chandler, *Local Government Today*, 3rd edition (Manchester: Manchester University Press, 2001).
4. Exceptionally, in 2001 they were postponed to June because of the Foot and Mouth Disease outbreak, and in 2004 they were also moved to June so they would coincide with the European Parliament elections.
5. The government originally planned also to hold referendums at the same time in the North-West and Yorkshire and the Humber regions, but announced in July 2004 that these would be postponed.
6. Detailed accounts of the first two Euro-election campaigns in Britain are given in David Butler and David Marquand, *European Elections and British Politics* (London: Macmillan, 1981) and David Butler and Paul Jowett, *Party Strategies in Britain: A Study of the 1984 European Elections* (London: Macmillan, 1985). More recent Euro-elections are described and analysed in David Butler and Martin Westlake, *British Politics and European Elections 1994* (London: Macmillan, 1995) and David Butler and Martin Westlake, *British Politics and European Elections 1999* (Basingstoke: Palgrave, 2000). A volume on the 2004 elections by Butler and Westlake is forthcoming. Each election since 1984 has also been the subject of a special issue of the journal *Electoral Studies*.

7. The official figure given for turnout was 38.2 per cent, but this included spoilt, blank and invalid ballot papers, in defiance of previous practice.

8. On the history, principles and structure of devolved government in Britain, see Vernon Bogdanor, *Devolution in the United Kingdom* (Oxford: Oxford University Press, 1999).

9. Except that in the Scottish Parliament the Westminster constituency of Orkney and Shetland is split into two, so that there are 73 rather than 72 constituencies. When the number of Westminster constituencies in Scotland is reduced from 72 to 59 (probably at the next general election), the constituencies in the Scottish Parliament will remain unchanged and the link will be broken.

10. Until 1965, the outer areas which are now in London came under the county councils of Essex, Surrey, Kent and Hertfordshire, all of which lost territory to the GLC, and of Middlesex, abolished entirely.

11. On referendums in general, see Austin Ranney (ed.), *The Referendum Device* (Washington DC: American Enterprise Institute, 1981) and David Butler and Austin Ranney (eds), *Referendums around the World: The Growing Use of Direct Democracy* (Washington DC: American Enterprise Institute, 1994). For the constitutional context, see Vernon Bogdanor, *Politics and the Constitution* (Aldershot: Dartmouth Press, 1996), chapter 12. The *Report of the Committee on the Conduct of Referendums* (London: Constitution Unit, 1996) discusses the principles in a modern context. For studies of specific referendums: on the EEC referendum, see David Butler and Uwe Kitzinger, *The 1975 Referendum* (London: Macmillan, 1976), Anthony King, *Britain Says Yes* (Washington DC: American Enterprise Institute, 1977) and Philip Goodhart, *Full-Hearted Consent* (London: Davis-Poynter, 1976); on the 1979 Scottish referendum, see *The Referendum Experience, Scotland 1979*, edited by Jean Bochel, David Denver and Alan MacCartney (Aberdeen: Aberdeen University Press, 1981).

Chapter 12

1. The history of opinion polls in Britain is told in detail in Nick Moon, *Opinion Polls: History, Theory and Practice* (Manchester: Manchester University Press, 1999) and (up to 1987) in Robert M. Worcester, *British Public Opinion: A Guide to the History and Methodology of Political Opinion Polling* (Oxford: Basil Blackwell, 1991). Both discuss methodology and the issues that opinion polling raises. See also Robert M. Worcester and Roger Mortimore, *Explaining Labour's Landslide* (London: Politico's Books, 1999), and David Broughton, *Public Opinion Polls and Politics in Britain* (London: Prentice Hall, 1995). David Butler and Dennis Kavanagh in their *British General Election* series invariably include a chapter assessing the impact of the public and private polls on each individual general election.

2. The websites of the principal companies are: www.mori.com; www.icmresearch. co.uk; www.nopworld.com; www.populuslimited.com; www.yougov.com.

3. See *The Opinion Polls and the 1992 British General Election: A Report to the Market Research Society* (London: Market Research Society, 1994).

4. YouGov's methodology is explained, and its strengths and weaknesses debated, in the *International Journal of Market Research* Volume 46 (2004) by

Peter Kellner (chairman of YouGov) on one side and Nick Sparrow (head of ICM) and the psephologist John Curtice on the other.

5. Post-election analysis showed that the reason for the failure on that occasion was probably a combination of the constituency having an unusually high percentage of second-home absentee homeowners, and not allowing for the different voting patterns of farm owners and farm labourers.

6. See Philip Gould, *The Unfinished Revolution* (London: Little, Brown, 1998).

7. Figures from David Butler and Dennis Kavanagh, *The British General Election of 1987* (Basingstoke: Macmillan, 1987), pp. 140, 144.

8. See David Butler and Dennis Kavanagh, *The British General Election of 1992* (London: Macmillan, 1992), p. 151.

9. Conservative spending on opinion research in 1997 is reported in *The Funding of Political Parties in the United Kingdom*, Fifth Report of the Committee on Standards in Public Life, Cm. 4057 (London: The Stationery Office, 1998), but the figure was not broken out for either Labour or the Liberal Democrats.

10. See Robert Worcester (ed.), *Political Opinion Polling: An International Review* (London: Macmillan, 1983) pp. 109–10 for the full text of the 1974 Code of Practice. Details of the BPC's rules and membership can be found at its website, www.britishpollingcouncil.org.

11. A cross-national review of evidence on the impact of opinion polls was conducted in 2001 by Professor Wolfgang Donsbach of the University of Dresden, who concluded that 'any effects are difficult to prove and in any case are minimal' (Wolfgang Donsbach, *Who's Afraid of Opinion Polls?: Normative and Empirical Arguments for the Freedom of Pre-Election Surveys*. Amsterdam: Foundation for Information, 2001). For discussions by two leading pollsters on the influence that polls have on voters, see Worcester and Mortimore, *Explaining Labour's Landslide*, pp. 179–81 and Moon, *Opinion Polls: History, Theory and Practice*, pp. 207–12.

12. See Butler and Kavanagh, *The British General Election of 1992*, p. 146.

13. Dick Leonard, 'Belgian Leaders should read "Areopagitica"', *Wall Street Journal (Europe)*, 18 October 1985. See also Dick Leonard, 'Opinion Polls can't be Banned', *St. Louis Post-Dispatch*, 6 December 1985. Polling bans in France have been circumvented by publication of poll results in foreign media and, more recently, in Canada and Hungary by publication on the Internet. Donsbach (*Who's Afraid of Opinion Polls?*, see Note 11 above) also marshals the arguments in principle against banning polls in the light of recent experience.

14. Frits Spangenberg, *The Freedom to Publish Opinion Poll Results: Report on a Worldwide Update* (Amsterdam: Foundation for Information, 2003) reviews the state of the law on the publication of polls in 66 countries worldwide.

Chapter 13

1. David Butler and Donald Stokes, *Political Change in Britain*, 2nd edition (London: Macmillan, 1974); Bo Särlvik and Ivor Crewe, *Decade of Dealignment* (Cambridge: Cambridge University Press, 1983); Anthony Heath, Roger Jowell and John Curtice, *How Britain Votes* (Oxford: Pergamon Press, 1985); Anthony Heath, Roger Jowell, John Curtice, Geoffrey Evans, Julia Field and Sharon Witherspoon, *Understanding Political Change* (Oxford: Pergamon Press, 1991); Anthony Heath, Roger Jowell and John Curtice with Bridget Taylor (eds),

Labour's Last Chance? (Aldershot: Dartmouth Press, 1994); Harold D. Clarke, David Sanders, Marianne C. Stewart and Paul Whiteley, *Political Choice in Britain* (Oxford: Oxford University Press, 2004).

2. See the detailed bibliographies in the books listed above.

3. For a description of the methodology of these surveys see Clarke *et al.*, *Political Choice in Britain*, pp 329–39.

4. A 2003 MORI survey for Nestlé UK, which interviewed secondary school children rather than their parents, found that the same effect still seems to be present; but it also found a new development, that children of parents who do not vote have no intention of voting themselves. See Roger Mortimore and Claire Tyrrell, 'Children's Acquisition of Political Opinions', *Journal of Public Affairs* Volume 4 (2004), 279–98.

5. A strikingly similar 'generational effect' among US voters, which may largely have accounted for a long-term swing from Republican to Democrat, had earlier been detected by Angus Campbell, Philip Converse, Warren Miller and Donald Stokes, *The American Voter* (New York: Wiley, 1960), especially pp. 45–6.

6. Särlvik and Crewe, *Decade of Dealignment*. See also Ivor Crewe, Bo Särlvik and James Alt, 'Partisan Dealignment in Britain 1964–74', *British Journal of Political Science* Volume 7 (1977), 129–90.

7. Heath, Jowell and Curtice, *How Britain Votes*. See also Heath *et al.*, *Understanding Political Change*.

8. Heath, Jowell and Curtice, *How Britain Votes*, pp. 35–9.

9. Anthony Heath, 'Comment on Dennis Kavanagh's "How We Vote Now"', *Electoral Studies* Volume 5 (April 1986), 30.

10. See Crewe, Särlvik and Alt, 'Partisan Dealignment in Britain 1964–74'.

11. Heath, Jowell and Curtice, *How Britain Votes*, p. 62. See also 'How did Labour lose in 1992?' by the same authors, *Independent on Sunday*, 29 May 1994.

12. Clarke *et al.*, *Political Choice in Britain*, especially chapters 2 and 10.

13. Anthony Downs, *An Economic Theory of Democracy* (New York: Harper, 1957), and see, more recently, David Robertson, *Class and the British Electorate* (Oxford: Blackwell, 1984).

14. See, in particular, chapter 7 of Heath, Jowell and Curtice, *How Britain Votes*.

15. Notably J. Lees-Marshment, *Political Marketing and British Political Parties* (Manchester: Manchester University Press, 2000).

16. See Mark Abrams, 'Opinion Polls and Party Propaganda', *Public Opinion Quarterly* Volume 28 (Spring 1964), 13–19.

17. See David Denver, Gordon Hands and Iain MacAllister, 'The Electoral Impact of Constituency Campaigning, 1992–2001', *Political Studies* Volume 52 (June 2004), 289–306.

18. P. M. Williams, 'Two Notes on the British Electoral System', *Parliamentary Affairs*, Winter 1966–7, pp. 13–30.

19. See Heath, Jowell and Curtice, *How Britain Votes*, chapter 11, pp. 157–69.

20. See much of the research on the Electoral Commission's website, www.electoralcommission.org.uk. Most of the books on the 2001 election cited in the bibliography also address the question.

21. See in particular Robert Worcester and Roger Mortimore, 'The Most Boring Election Ever?' in John Bartle, Simon Atkinson and Roger Mortimore (eds),

Political Communications: The General Election Campaign of 2001 (London: Frank Cass, 2002), pp. 143–58.

Chapter 14

1. This chapter deals solely with the cost of general elections; statistics are not readily available of total expenses incurred in local elections, though the sums involved are undoubtedly lower. Expenditure on Parliamentary by-elections is substantially greater than that in individual constituencies at a general election, as the spending limits are now much higher.

2. *The Funding of Political Parties in the United Kingdom*, Fifth Report of the Committee on Standards in Public Life, Cm. 4057 (London: The Stationery Office, 1998). A comprehensive historical account is contained in *British Political Finance 1830–1980* by Michael Pinto-Duschinsky (Washington DC: American Enterprise Institute, 1981). On the case for public subsidies see the Houghton Report, *Report of the Committee on Financial Aid to Political Parties* (London: HMSO, Cmnd. 6601, 1976) and *Paying for Party Politics: The Case for Public Subsidies* by Dick Leonard (London: Political and Economic Planning, 1975). The Electoral Commission also launched an investigation into party funding in 2003, and its report when published (no likely date is known at the time of writing) will probably provide the most up-to-date discussion of all the relevant issues.

3. *Election 2001: Campaign Spending* (London: Electoral Commission, 2002), available at www.electoralcommission.gov.uk.

4. These were three trade unions (Unison, MSF and USDAW), four groups campaigning principally on the issue of relations with the European Union (the Democracy Movement, the Yes campaign, the Campaign for an Independent Britain and the South Molton Declaration), Charter88, the Society for the Protection of the Unborn Child and Tacticalvoter.net.

5. David Butler and Richard Rose, *The British General Election of 1959* (London: Macmillan, 1960), pp. 144–5.

6. *Observer*, 11 April 1999.

7. Dick Leonard, *Paying for Party Politics* (London: Political and Economic Planning, 1975). See also Dick Leonard, 'Contrasts in Selected Western Democracies: Germany, Sweden, Britain', in Herbert E. Alexander (ed.), *Political Finance* (Beverly Hills and London: Sage Publications, 1979), pp. 41–73.

8. See, for example, the MORI research published by the Electoral Commission in September 2003.

9. For a thorough discussion of the issue, by an opponent of public funding, see Pinto-Duschinsky, *British Political Finance 1830–1980*. A less ambitious proposal for public funding was put forward by a committee set up by the Hansard Society, under the chairmanship of Edmund Dell – see *Paying for Politics* (London: Hansard Society for Parliamentary Government, 1981). A later Hansard Society inquiry, chaired by Christopher Chataway, split three ways on the issue – see *Agenda for Change* (London: Hansard Society for Parliamentary Government, 1991).

10. Although there has never been direct public subsidy of general election campaigning in Britain, at one point money was made available by the European Parliament to help towards parties' election expenses in European

elections, though it was distributed on a capricious basis. This peaked in 1984. Some 69 per cent of the money was supposed to be paid out in advance, but this was only available to parties already represented in the Parliament. The remaining 31 per cent was paid out afterwards on the basis of percentage votes cast. The result was that, apart from three Northern Irish parties, only the Tories (£2.4 million), the Labour Party (£600,000) and the Scottish National Party (£100,000) received any money in advance, though the Liberals were given £150,000 by other European Liberal parties who were shocked by their exclusion. (The SDP also collected £8000 on account of a Labour MEP who had defected to them.) After the election, the Conservatives collected a further £390,000 and the Labour Party £350,000, while the Liberals got £98,000, the SDP £89,000 and the SNP a further £16,000. In the subsequent Euro-election, in 1989, the parties were again heavily subsidised by the European Parliament, though the grants were distributed on a rather different basis. From 1994, however, following a court action brought by the French Green Party, no money was provided by the European Parliament for election expenses, though the parties' activities between elections still receive funding, which is no longer entirely confined to parties represented in the Parliament.

11. The forfeiture of deposits is the one small if regular source of income to the Treasury which an election provides to offset the other costs. This peaked at almost £800,000 in 1997, and brought in £588,500 in 2001. (The number of deposits lost at each general election is recorded in Appendix 1.)

12. Pinto-Duschinsky, *British Political Finance 1830–1980*, p. 267.

13. Electoral Commission, *Funding Democracy* (Consultation Paper, September 2002).

Chapter 15

1. With recent changes in departmental responsibilities, the Constitutional Affairs Committee rather than the Home Affairs Committee would probably now be the relevant one.

2. Electoral Commission, *Voting for Change: An Electoral Law Modernisation Programme* (London, 2003), available at www.electoralcommission.gov.uk.

Appendix 3

1. Legal advice from the Home Office to this effect was quoted in the Fourth Report of the House of Commons Home Affairs Select Committee 1997–8, paragraph 71.

Appendix 8

1. This appendix is largely an updating, by kind permission of the Economist Publishing Company, of the introduction one of the authors wrote to Dick Leonard and Richard Natkiel, *World Atlas of Elections* (London: Economist Publishing Co., 1986).

2. Readers interested in exploring the arcane mathematics of the benefits of the various systems to different sizes of party should consult M. Balinski

and H. P. Young, *Fair Representation* (New Haven: Yale University Press, 1982) and Iain McLean and Roger Mortimore, 'Apportionment and the Boundary Commission for England', *Electoral Studies* Volume 11 (1992).

3. Although AMS systems normally use two votes, allowing voters to distinguish between their preferred local candidate and preferred regional party, it is possible to adapt the system so that it requires only a single vote (the vote for the constituency candidate being also counted as a vote for his or her party). A report by the Hansard Society, *Commission on Electoral Reform* (London: Hansard Society, 1976), recommended such a system for Britain, but found little sympathy.

Bibliography

For further reading on the topics covered in each chapter, see the notes to the chapter, especially the first note in each case. [The publisher Macmillan (Basingstoke) changed its name to Palgrave Macmillan in 2000.]

Election results

Summary statistics of all elections in Britain (Parliamentary, European, and local) have been published since 1993 in the annual *British Elections and Parties Review* (London: Frank Cass).

Full results of general elections, together with biographical details of members and of defeated candidates are published shortly after each election in *The Times Guide to the House of Commons* (London: Times Books). The series goes back to 1929, and also appeared after the elections of January 1910, December 1910 and 1918. Less detailed results are given also in *Dod's Parliamentary Companion* (London: Vacher-Dod Publishing), published annually, *Vacher's Parliamentary Guide* (London: Vacher-Dod Publishing), quarterly and *Whitaker's Almanack*, annually (London: The Stationery Office).

Tabulated results for all constituencies from 1832 to 1983 inclusive are included in five volumes compiled by the late F. W. S. Craig: *British Parliamentary Election Results 1832–85*, 2nd edition (Aldershot: Dartmouth Press, 1989); *British Parliamentary Election Results 1885–1918*, 2nd edition (Aldershot: Dartmouth Press, 1989); *British Parliamentary Election Results 1918–49*, 3rd edition (Chichester: Parliamentary Research Services, 1983); *British Parliamentary Election Results 1950–1973*, 2nd edition (Chichester: Parliamentary Research Services, 1983) and *British Parliamentary Election Results 1974–1983* (Chichester: Parliamentary Research Services, 1984). The series has now been taken up by Colin Rallings and Michael Thrasher, *British Parliamentary Election Results 1983–1997* (Aldershot: Ashgate, 1999). In 2001 for the first time official results were published by the Electoral Commission, again collated by Rallings and Thrasher and accompanied by the Commission's initial report on the election: *Election 2001: The Official Results* (London: Politico's Publishing, 2001). Summaries are included in *Twentieth Century British Political Facts 1900–2000* by David Butler and Gareth Butler (Basingstoke: Macmillan, 2000), and in Colin Rallings and Michael Thrasher, *British Electoral Facts 1832–1999*, 6th edition (Aldershot: Ashgate, 2000).

Results of elections to the European Parliament are given in *The Times Guide to the European Parliament* (Times Books, 1979, 1984, 1989 and 1994) and in *Europe Votes 2: European Parliamentary Election Results 1979–84*, Thomas T. Mackie and F. W. S. Craig (eds) (Chichester: Parliamentary Research Services, 1985) and *Europe Votes 3* by Thomas Mackie (Aldershot: Dartmouth Press, 1990). Local election results in detail are collected in the annual *Local Elections Handbook*, compiled by Colin Rallings and Michael Thrasher and published by the *Local Government Chronicle*.

Results of the elections to the Scottish and Welsh Parliaments are reported in *Whitaker's Almanack* (London: The Stationery Office) for the following year.

General elections

A general overview of all the elections from 1945 to 1987 is given in *British General Elections since 1945* by David Butler (Oxford: Basil Blackwell, 1989). More detailed accounts of individual elections are provided in a series of books sponsored by Nuffield College, Oxford: *The British General Election of 1945* by R. B. McCallum and Alison Readman (London: Macmillan, 1947); *The British General Election of 1950* by H. G. Nicholas (London: Macmillan, 1951); *The British General Election of 1951* by D. E. Butler (London: Macmillan, 1952); *The British General Election of 1955* by D. E. Butler (London: Macmillan, 1955); *The British General Election of 1959* by D. E. Butler and Richard Rose (London: Macmillan, 1960); *The British General Election of 1964* by D. E. Butler and Anthony King (London: Macmillan, 1965); *The British General Election of 1966* by D. E. Butler and Anthony King (London: Macmillan, 1966); *The British General Election of 1970* by David Butler and Michael Pinto-Duschinsky (London: Macmillan, 1971); *The British General Election of February 1974* by David Butler and Dennis Kavanagh (London: Macmillan, 1974); *The British General Election of October 1974* by David Butler and Dennis Kavanagh (London: Macmillan, 1975); *The British General Election of 1979* by David Butler and Dennis Kavanagh (London: Macmillan, 1980); *The British General Election of 1983* by David Butler and Dennis Kavanagh (London: Macmillan, 1984); *The British General Election of 1987* by David Butler and Dennis Kavanagh (London: Macmillan, 1988); *The British General Election of 1992* by David Butler and Dennis Kavanagh (London: Macmillan, 1992); *The British General Election of 1997* by David Butler and Dennis Kavanagh (Basingstoke: Macmillan, 1997) and *The British General Election of 2001* by David Butler and Dennis Kavanagh (Basingstoke: Palgrave, 2002).

A rival series, published by the American Enterprise Institute in Washington DC, first appeared in 1974. The titles were *Britain at the Polls: The Parliamentary Elections of 1974*, edited by Howard R. Penniman; *Britain at the Polls 1979*, edited by Howard R. Penniman; *Britain at the Polls 1983*, edited by Austin Ranney. A new series with the same title has covered the last three elections, all edited by Anthony King: *Britain at the Polls 1992* (Chatham, NJ: Chatham House, 1993), *New Labour Triumphs: Britain at the Polls* (Chatham, NJ: Chatham House, 1998), and *Britain at the Polls 2001* (Chatham, NJ: Chatham House, 2002).

A third series, focusing on the specific topic of political communications, has covered every election since 1979, usually including articles by the parties' own campaign chiefs. The titles are: *Political Communications: The British General Election of 1979*, edited by Robert Worcester and Martin Harrop (London: Macmillan, 1982); *Political Communications: The 1983 Election Campaign*, edited by Ivor Crewe and Martin Harrop (Cambridge: Cambridge University Press, 1986); *Political Communications: The General Election Campaign of 1987*, edited by Ivor Crewe and Martin Harrop (Cambridge: Cambridge University Press, 1989); *Political Communications: The General Election Campaign of 1992*, edited by Ivor Crewe and Brian Gosschalk (Cambridge: Cambridge University Press, 1995); *Political Communications: Why Labour Won the General Election of 1997*, edited by Ivor Crewe, Brian Gosschalk and John Bartle (London: Frank Cass, 1998) and *Political*

Communications: The General Election Campaign of 2001, edited by John Bartle, Simon Atkinson and Roger Mortimore (London: Frank Cass, 2002).

The last two elections are examined from the different dimension of public opinion of the issues and participants, as revealed by the opinion polls, by Robert Worcester and Roger Mortimore in *Explaining Labour's Landslide* (London: Politico's Publishing, 1999) and *Explaining Labour's Second Landslide* (London: Politico's Publishing, 2001).

Most recent elections have also produced a crop of more detailed studies of various aspects of the campaign and edited collections of articles. Books on the 1997 election include Andrew Geddes and Jonathan Tonge (eds), *Labour's Landslide: The British General Election of 1997* (Manchester: Manchester University Press, 1997); Pippa Norris and Neil Gavin (eds), *Britain Votes 1997* (Oxford: Oxford University Press, 1997) and *British Elections and Parties Review* Volume 8: The 1997 British General Election (London: Frank Cass, 1997). On 2001: Andrew Geddes and Jonathan Tonge (eds), *Labour's Second Landslide: The British General Election of 2001* (Manchester: Manchester University Press, 2002), Pippa Norris (ed.) *Britain Votes 2001* (Oxford: Oxford University Press, 2001) and *British Elections and Parties Review* Volume 12 (London: Frank Cass, 2002).

An interesting interpretation of recent election campaigns is provided by *Designer Politics: How Elections are Won*, by Margaret Scammell (London: Macmillan, 1995). Dennis Kavanagh assesses recent tactical and technological developments in *Election Campaigning* (Oxford: Basil Blackwell, 1995).

Voting studies

The major works are the successive volumes reporting the findings of the British Election Surveys, listed in the notes to Chapter 13. See also *The British Electorate, 1963–87: A Compendium of Data from the British Election Studies*, by Ivor Crewe, Neil Day and Anthony Fox (Cambridge University Press, 1991). A separate volume on Scotland is *The End of British Politics?* by W. L. Miller (Oxford: Clarendon Press, 1981). An offshoot of this series is *Class and the British Electorate* by David Robertson (Oxford: Basil Blackwell, 1984). For other analyses, see also *How Voters Decide* by Hilde T. Himmelweit, Patrick Humphreys and Marianne Jaeger (Milton Keynes: Open University Press, 1985, 2nd edition), *Electoral Change in Britain since 1945* by Pippa Norris (Oxford: Basil Blackwell, 1997), *Elections and Voting Behaviour in Britain* by David Denver (Basingstoke: Macmillan, 1998), *The Loyalties of Voters* by Richard Rose and Ian McAllister (London: Sage Publications, 1990), and Geoffrey Evans and Pippa Norris (eds), *Critical Elections* (London: Sage Publications, 1999).

The electoral system

The fullest and most up-to-date account is *The Electoral System in Britain* by Robert Blackburn (London: Macmillan, 1995). An authoritative historical survey is *The Electoral System in Britain since 1918* by D. E. Butler, 2nd edition (Oxford: Oxford University Press, 1963). Critical assessments are made in *Political Representation and Elections in Britain* by P. J. Pulzer (London: Allen and Unwin, 1968) and *British Elections* by Geoffrey Alderman (London: Batsford, 1978).

On the relationship between seats and votes in the electoral system, and reasons for the bias currently being shown towards Labour, see Ron Johnston, Charles Pattie, Danny Dorling and David Rossiter, *From Votes to Seats* (Manchester: Manchester University Press, 2001). An alternative electoral system for Britain is proposed in *The Report of the Independent Commission on the Voting System* (London: The Stationery Office, 1998), although this does not attempt to assess the case for replacing 'first past the post'.

The effects of different electoral systems on party systems and political culture are comprehensively examined in *Electoral Systems and Party Systems* by Arend Lijphart (Oxford: Oxford University Press, 1995); see also David Farrell, *Comparing Electoral Systems* (Basingstoke: Macmillan, 1998) and *Electoral Systems: A Comparative and Theoretical Introduction* by Andrew Reeve and Alan Ware (London: Routledge, 1992). Slightly older surveys containing information on other electoral systems and on elections in other democratic countries include Vernon Bogdanor and David Butler (eds), *Democracy and Elections: Electoral Systems and their Political Consequences* (Cambridge: Cambridge University Press, 1983), and *World Atlas of Elections: Voting Patterns in 39 Democracies* by Dick Leonard and Richard Natkiel (London: Economist Publishing Company, 1986).

Election law

The standard reference book is *Schofield's Election Law* (2nd edition) edited by Andrew Scallon and Rory Mates (Crayford: Shaw and Sons, 1996), loose-leaf with regular update supplements now accompanied by a CD-ROM of the entire text. See also *Erskine May's Treatise on the Law, Privileges, Proceedings and Usage of Parliament*, edited by William McKay, Frank Cranmer, *et al.*, 23rd edition (London: LexisNexis UK, 2004) and *Law and the Electoral Process* by H. F. Rawlings (London: Sweet and Maxwell, 1988). The Electoral Commission also issues regular detailed notes of guidance for candidates, agents, administrators and voters, which are available on its website (www.electoralcommission.gov.uk).

Internet sources

In recent years the Internet has emerged as a useful resource for statistics and reference, on politics as on other subjects, and can naturally be more up to date than the published texts, but often at the price of losing authoritative reliability. Among the relevant sites which can certainly be relied upon are the Research Papers in the House of Commons Library (www.parliament.uk/parliamentary_ publications_and_archives/research_papers.htm), and the Electoral Commission's website, mentioned above.

Index

1922 Committee, 48–9, 52, 53, 54, 58
abortion as election issue, 70, 125, 204
Abrams, Mark, 190–1, 260
absent voting *see* postal voting, proxy voting
abstention *see* turnout
Acting Returning Officer, 11, 15
Additional Member System (AMS) *see* electoral systems
adoption meetings, 107–8
advertising, political, 42, 69, 121–2
 cost of, 198–9
 in the press, 132
 on posters, 114, 193
age
 minimum for candidature, 83
 of candidates, 96
agents, 49, 77, 79, 108–17, 136, 202
 borrowed from other constituencies in by-elections, 147
 cost of employing, 77, 80, 100
 election agent, law regarding, 105–6, 201, 228–33
 liaison with party HQ, 44
 number falling in recent years, 77
Alderman, Geoffrey, 266
Alexander, Herbert E., 261
aliens, 12, 83
all-postal voting experiments, 8, 119–20, 157, 196, 255
Alliance Party (APNI) *see* Northern Ireland political parties
Alliance, Liberal-SDP, 62–3 *and passim*
Alt, James, 260
Alternative Vote (AV) *see* electoral systems
Ancram, Michael, 54
apathy and turnout, 195
Archer, Jeffrey (Lord Archer of Weston-super-Mare), 94
armed forces
 barred from candidature, 85–6

voting by servicemen *see* service voters
Ashdown, Paddy, 63
Asian candidates, 98
Asian voters, 19
Asquith, Herbert, 61, 62
Assheton, Sir Ralph, 24
Atkinson, Simon, 256, 260, 266
attainers, 13, 15, 17
Attlee, Clement, 5, 56

Balfour, Arthur, 45
Balinski, M., 263
Ballard, Jackie, 63
Ballot Act (1872), 209
ballot boxes, 118, 135, 136
 collection and transport to count, 138, 139
ballot paper, 135–6, 142
 counterfoils, 135, 138, 141
 interpretation of during count, 140
 mixing of papers from different ballot boxes, 139
 party names and symbols on, 43–4, 89, 107, 136, 210, 252
 retained after election, 141
 sent out to postal voters, 117–18, 120, 255
 spoilt and blank papers, 248, 258
 validation of, 135, 136, 140, 141, 248, 256
 See also counting of votes
ballot paper account, 138, 139, 141
bandwagon effect, 8, 175
bankruptcy as bar to candidature, 84, 145
Bartle, John, 256, 260, 265, 266
Baston, Lewis, 251
Beaufort Research, 166
Beckett, Margaret, 57
Beith, Alan, 63
Bell, Martin, 72, 253

Benn, Tony, 56, 86, 254
Bevin, Ernest, 1
bias in electoral system, 30–1
black candidates, 98
black voters, 19
Blackburn, Robert, 266
Blair, Tony, 5, 10, 34, 41, 46, 57, 60,
    67, 126, 129, 143, 174, 194, 254
Blakenham, Lord, 50
blind voters, 136, 224
block vote (of unions at Labour
    conference), 45, 57
Bochel, H. M., 257
Bochel, Jean, 258
Bogdanor, Vernon, 247, 249, 258, 267
Boothroyd, David, 253
borough and county constituencies,
    differences, 11, 22–3, 25, 200
borough councils *see* local
    government
Bossiney, 251
Boundary Commissions, 22–31, 201,
    251
Bowman, Phyllis, 204
British Broadcasting Corporation
    (BBC), 72, 125, 129
  election night exit poll, 143, 165
  election website, 125
  See also television, radio
British Election Panel Study (BEPS),
    191
British Election Studies (BES), 179–90
British Journalism Review, 256
British National Party, 67, 68, 125
British Polling Council, 175, 259
broadcasting *see* television, radio
broadcasts, party political, 42, 114,
    124–7, 199, 207
Broughton, David, 258
Bruce, Malcolm, 63
burgh *see* borough
Burke, Edmund, 101
business links with Conservative
    Party, 122, 204, 205
business vote, 13, 249
Butcher, B., 250
Butler swing, 37
Butler, David, ix–x, 36, 99, 107, 179,
    184, 202, 235, 245, 247, 249,

    251, 252, 253, 254, 256, 257,
    258, 259, 261, 264, 265, 266, 267
Butler, Gareth, 253, 264
by-elections, local, 6, 67, 155
by-elections, Parliamentary, 36, 86,
    87, 127, 134, 142, 144–53, 180,
    193, 253, 254
  and minor parties/independents,
    67, 69, 70, 71, 147
  and rise of the SDP, 62–3
  causes, 145
  effect of poor results on
    government, 7, 62, 148–51
  effect on election timing, 6, 7
  exit polls at, 143
  frequency of, 145
  imposition of candidates by Labour
    Party NEC, 93
  limit on expenses, 147, 200, 203
  nationalist gains at, 64, 65, 150,
    151
  opinion polls in, 164, 165, 171
  timetable for, 227
  timing of, 8, 145

Cairns, David, 254
Callaghan, James, 5, 7, 26, 62, 129,
    148, 174
campaign
  effect on voting behaviour, 191–4
  in the constituencies, 104–20
  length of, 10
  nationally, 121–33
Campbell, Angus, 260
Campbell-Bannerman, Sir Henry, 61
Canavan, Dennis, 72
candidate selection
  criteria, 95–101
  deselection and mandatory
    reselection of sitting MPs, 102–3
  influence of party headquarters, 90,
    92–3
  procedures, 87–95
  selection conferences, 90–2
  shortlists, 88–90, 93, 94–5
  shortlists, all-women, 93, 97
candidates, 83–103 *and passim*
  effect on voting behaviour, 78, 95,
    148, 193–4

eligibility, 83–7
  number of, 35
  occupations and professions of,
    98–100, 234–5
  training and vetting of, 43, 87
canvassing, 79–80, 81, 111–13, 114,
    116, 193, 199
'carpet baggers', 96
cars
  conveying voters to the poll, 115,
    117, 138, 230, 232
  for campaigning (by loudspeaker),
    137
casting vote in event of a tie, 140
Central Office *see* Conservative Party
Centre for Research into Elections and
    Social Trends (CREST), 179
Chandler, J. A., 257
Channel 4, 125, 236
Chiltern Hundreds, 145
city councils *see* local government
City of London, 249
civil servants, disqualified from sitting
    in Commons, 85
Clarke, Harold, 190, 260
Clarke, Kenneth, 53, 54
class and voting behaviour, 180–4
Clause Four of Labour Party
    constitution, 56, 60
clergy, eligibility as candidates, 84, 87
Commission on Candidate Selection,
    254
Committee on Standards in Public
    Life (Neill Committee), 81, 197,
    198, 206, 253, 259, 261
committee rooms, 80, 106, 137
Common Market *see* European
    Economic Community
Commonwealth citizens
  eligibility as candidates, 83
  voting rights, 12
Communicate Research, 166
Communist Party of Great Britain
    (CPGB), 65, 127
Community Charge ('poll tax'), 19,
    251
community councils *see* local
    government
compulsory voting, 196

computers, 43, 79, 112, 113, 142, 155,
    see also e-mail, Internet
conferences, party, 44–7, *see also under*
    party names
  local parties represented at, 76
Conservative Future, 49, 75, 77, 81
Conservative Party
  candidate selection and training,
    87–95
  Central Office, 41–2, 44, 48, 77, 87,
    93, 94, 98
  conference, 44–5
  election of leader, 49–54
  Ethics and Integrity Committee, 93
  history and organisation, 47–55
    and *passim*
constituencies, 22–31 and *passim*
  number of electors, 27–9
constituency campaigns, effect on
    votes, 193
constituency parties *see* local parties
Constituency Plan Agreements, 254
Constitutional Affairs Select
    Committee, 262
Converse, Philip, 260
Cook, Chris, 257
Co-operative Party, 59, 60, 61
Co-operative Societies, affiliated to
    Labour Party, 58, 76, 95, 106
Corlett, T., 250
corrupt and illegal practices, 115–16,
    119, 142, 228–33
  Corrupt Practices Act (1883), 209
  penalties for, 12, 84, 228–33
cost of elections, 197–207, *see also*
    finances of parties
councillors *see* local government
    elections
counting agents, 138
counting of votes, 117, 138–40, 207
county and borough constituencies,
    differences, 23, 25, 200
county councils *see* local government
Cowley Street *see* Liberal Democrats
Craig, F. W. S., 264
Crewe, Ivor, 180, 189, 259, 260, 265,
    266
Criddle, Byron, 235, 251, 253, 254
cube law, 32–3, 252

Curtice, John, 180, 245, 251, 252, 259, 260

D'Hondt divisors *see* electoral systems
D'Hondt, Victor, 240
Dáil *see* Ireland, Republic of
Daily Express, 131, 132
Daily Mail, 131
Daily Mirror, 130–1, 132
Daily Star, 130–1
Daily Telegraph, 131, 165, 166, 236
dates of general elections, 8
Davies, S. O., 253
Davis, David, 54
Day, Neil, 266
Deacon, David, 256
death of a candidate, 227
debates
  between constituency candidates, 111
  between party leaders, 129–30
declaration of election expenses *see* expenditure, limitations on
declaration of local connection, 250
deed poll to adopt misleading name for election, 252
Dell, Edmund, 261
Democratic Unionist Party *see* Northern Ireland political parties
Denver, David, 254, 257, 258, 260, 266
deposit, 86, 105, 108, 206, 262
  at non-Parliamentary elections, 105
  increased in 1980s, 35, 67, 147, 208
  number lost, table, 212–14
  recounts over lost deposits, 140
deselection of sitting MPs, 102–3
Dewey, Thomas E., 168
disabled voters, 117, 134, 211
disqualifications from membership of Commons, 83–7, 145
Disraeli, Benjamin (Earl of Beaconsfield), 6, 47, 130
dissolution of Parliament, 9, 10, 108, 122, 199, 226
district councils *see* local government
Dodd, P., 250
Donsbach, Wolfgang, 259
Dorling, Danny, 251, 267

Douglas-Home, Sir Alec (Lord Home of the Hirsel), 50, 127, 141, 149, 150
Downs, Anthony, 190, 260
Droop quota, 240, 241–2
Duncan Smith, Iain, 53, 54, 152
Dunleavy, Patrick, 245
Dunwich, 251
Durant, Henry, 165

Ecology Party *see* Green Party
Economic and Social Research Council, 179
economic confidence as factor in voting behaviour, 192
Economist, The, 236, 249, 262
Eden, Sir Anthony, 6
education and voting behaviour, 187
Edward I, 208
election address, 113–14, 123
election expenses *see* expenditure
election petitions *see* petitions
electoral college
  Conservative (Mayor of London), 94
  Labour Party, 56, 95, 102
Electoral Commission, 201, 208
  and all-postal voting, 119
  and party accounts, 174, 198–9, 201
  and party political broadcasts, 124, 125
  establishment of, 2, 201, 208, 211
  registration of parties, 44, 65, 252–3
  registration of 'third-party' campaigners, 199
  reports and recommendations, 83, 135, 163, 186, 198, 203, 207, 248, 250, 254, 255, 256, 261, 262, 264
  research commissioned by, 193, 260, 261
  to absorb Boundary Commissions, 25, 201
  website, 267
Electoral Fraud (Northern Ireland) Act (2002), 250
Electoral Reform Society, 34, 254

Electoral Registration Officer *see*
Registration Officer
electoral systems, 34–5, 238–45
Additional Member System (AMS),
34, 158, 161, 242–4
Alternative Vote, 34, 63, 238, 244
AV-plus, 34–5, 244
Belgian system, 241
D'Hondt divisors, 157, 240, 241,
243
'first past the post' (present system),
31–4, 156, 238
party effects of, 33–4, 68, 70, 244
party lists, 239–41
proposed referendum on, 162
Sainte-Laguë divisors, 241
Single Transferable Vote (STV), 34,
154, 157, 239, 241–2, 244,
246–7
Supplementary Vote, 160, 238, 239
eligibility to vote, 83–7, *see also*
Register of Electors
historic growth of franchise, 12–13
Elizabeth II, 10
e-mail, 78, 109, 114, 122
envelopes, addressing of, 113
Erskine May, 267
ethnic minority candidates, 90, 98
European Court of Human Rights,
204, 250
European Economic Community
(EEC), referendum on (1975),
162, 221
European Parliament elections, 134,
156–8
candidate stands as Literal
Democrat, 43–4
counting of votes, 138
deposit, 105
electoral system, 34, 157, 240, 241
eligibility of candidates, 83, 84
eligibility to vote, 12, 16, 17, 18
experimental voting method
(2004), 119
free delivery of election addresses,
255
Green Party in, 67, 68
offences at, 231, 232

public subsidies for campaigning,
261
results, 215–18
spending limits, 201
timetable for, 227
turnout, 195, 215–18
UK Independence Party in, 69
European Union
single currency, 48, 162
voting rights of EU citizens in
Britain, 12, 17
Evans, Geoffrey, 259, 260, 266
Evening Standard (London), 192, 236
Excalibur, 43
exit polls, 142–3, 165, 176, 237
expenditure, limitations on
by-elections, 147, 200, 203
in constituencies, 105, 127, 142,
200, 201–2, 229, 231
national, 198
non-Parliamentary elections, 200
third-party spending, 199, 204

Fabian Society, 55, 59, 60, 76
false names, standing for election
under, 252
Farrell, David, 267
Field, Julia, 259, 260
finances of parties
business contributions, 81, 205
foreign funding, 205
local, 81, 100–1, 106, 122
membership subscriptions, 55,
59–60, 74, 81, 204
national, 42, 204–6, 261
trade union contributions to
Labour, 44, 59–60, 74, 81, 100–1,
204, 254
Financial Times, 130–1, 165, 255
'first past the post' *see* electoral
systems
Fisher, Justin, 81
floating voters, 178, 188–94
focus groups, 173, 174
Foot and Mouth Disease (outbreak in
2001), 5, 10, 249, 257
Foot, Michael, 7, 10, 56, 129, 174, 206
football, 169, 249

foreign funding of political parties, 205
foreign residents, 12, 83
Fox, Anthony, 266
franchise *see* eligibility to vote
Frankland, Pamela, 250
Fraser, Hugh, 51
free delivery of election addresses, 113, 206, 207
free hire of meeting halls, 207
Freud, Clement, 176
fundraising *see* finances of parties

Gaitskell, Hugh, 40, 56
Galloway, George, 66
Gallup polls, 143, 170, 236
Gallup, George, 171
Gardiner, Sir George, 69, 71
Gavin, Neil, 266
Gavron, Nicky, 161
Geddes, Andrew, 266
gender and voting behaviour, 187
generational effect on voting behaviour, 180
gerrymandering, 25, 31
Gladstone, William, 61, 130
Goldsmith, Sir James, 69, 125
Goodhart, Philip, 258
Gordon Walker, Patrick, 150
Gosschalk, Brian, 265
Gould, Brian, 57
Gould, Philip (Lord), 174, 259
Government Social Survey, 19
Gow, Ian, 151
Granada TV, 127
Gray, P. G., 250
Greater London Authority (GLA), 160–1
    referendum to establish, 162
    result of referendum on, 223
Greater London Council (GLC), 95, 122, 160, 161, 258
Green Party, 65, 67, 68, 69, 161, 252
Grofman, Bernard, 249
Guardian, The, 130–1, 165, 236, 256

Hagenbach-Bischoff quota, 240
Hague, William, 47, 48, 53, 102
Halliwell, Geri, 127

Hamilton, Neil, 93
Hands, Gordon, 254, 260
Hansard Society, 13, 261, 263
Hardie, J. Keir, 55
Hare, Thomas, 239
Harris Research, 143, 166, 174
Harrison, Martin, 126, 256
Harrop, Martin, 256, 265
Hastings Agreement, 100
Hattersley, Roy, 56, 57
Healey, Denis, 56
Heath, Anthony, 180, 183, 187, 188, 189, 190, 251, 259, 260
Heath, Edward, 7, 45, 47, 50, 51
Heffer, Eric, 56, 57
Henig, Simon, 251
Heseltine, Michael, 51, 52
Himmelweit, Hilde, 266
Home Affairs Select Committee, 210–11
Home of the Hirsel, Lord (formerly 14th Earl of Home) *see* Douglas-Home, Sir Alec
homeless people, voting rights, 250
Houghton Report on party finance (1975), 206, 261
hours of polling, 134, 138, 210
House of Commons Disqualification Acts (1957 and 1975), 85, 145
House of Lords
    elevation to peerage as cause of by-elections, 145
    members' ineligibility to sit in Commons, 83, 86
    use of peers in election campaigns, 122
    voting rights of members, 12, 17, 162
housing and voting behaviour, 185
Howard, Michael, 49, 53, 54, 152
Howe, Sir Geoffrey, 51
Hudson, Hugh, 126
Hughes, Simon, 63
Hume, John, 70
Humphreys, Patrick, 266
Hurd, Douglas, 52

ICM Research, 165, 170, 172, 236, 259

identification, acceptable forms of, 256
ideology and voting behaviour, 188–90
illegal practices *see* corrupt and illegal practices
Imperiali quota, 240
incapacitated voters, 117, 134, 211
independent candidates, 44, 70, 86, 105, 106, 202
at local elections, 72, 95, 155, 161
in by-elections, 147
Independent Commission on the Voting System *see* Jenkins Commission
Independent Labour Party, 55
Independent Television (ITV), 125, 129, *see* also television
Independent, The, 130, 166
Ingle, Stephen, 252
Inglehart, Ronald, 189
Internet, 209
as reference source, 155, 267
BBC election website, 125
conducting opinion polls through, 171, 258–9
influence on voters, 193
provision of forms on, 20, 224, 225
publication of opinion polls on, 165, 259
use by MPs, 78
use by voters as information source, 114
IRA (Irish Republican Army), 71, 84, 151
Ireland, Republic of
electoral system (STV), 34, 242
eligibility of citizens as candidates, 83
members of Dáil and Seanad as candidates, 85
voting rights of citizens, 12, 15
ITN, 143, 165, *see* also television

Jaeger, Marianne, 266
James II, 47, 61
Jenkins Commission (Independent Commission on the Voting System), 35, 244

Jenkins, Roy (Lord Jenkins of Hillhead), 35, 62, 151
Jennifer's Ear, 126
Jewish voters, 136
Johnston, Ron, 251, 267
Jones, Bill, 249
Joseph Rowntree Charitable Trust, 254
Jowell, Roger, 180, 251, 259, 260
Jowett, Paul, 257
Junz, Alfred J., 13

Kaufman, Gerald, 123
Kavanagh, Dennis, 99, 107, 235, 245, 249, 251, 252, 253, 254, 256, 258, 259, 260, 265, 266
Kellner, Peter, 259
Kennedy, Charles, 63
Kennedy, John F., 129
Kidderminster Hospital and Health Concern Party, 72
Kilfedder, Sir James, 253
King, Anthony, 258, 265
Kinnock, Neil, 41, 56, 57, 60, 93, 102, 126, 129, 133, 194
Kitzinger, Uwe, 258
knocking up, 137, 138

Labour Party
candidate selection, 87–95
conference, 40, 41, 45, 46, 56, 59, 60, 93, 96
election of leader, 56–7
history and organisation, 55–60
National Executive Committee (NEC), 40, 42, 58, 93, 123
National Policy Forum, 46
party headquarters ('Old Queen Street'), 41–4, 59, 76, 88, 90, 159 *and passim*
Labour Party Young Socialists *see* Young Labour
Labour Representation Committee, 55
Labour Students, 59, 82
Labour Youth *see* Young Labour
leadership elections
Conservative, 49–54
Labour Party, 56–7
Liberal Democrats, 63
leaflets, 112, 114, 123, 125, 193, 204

Lees-Marshment, Jennifer, 260
length of campaign, 10
Leonard, Dick, ix, x, 249, 254, 259, 261, 262, 267
Liberal Democrats
  election of leader, 63
  federal headquarters ('Cowley Street'), 41
  federal party conference, 46, 64
  history and party structure, 60–4 *and passim*
Liberal Party (modern), 63, 68
Liberal Party (to 1988) *see* Liberal Democrats
Liberal Unionists, 47, 61
Lib-Lab pact, 62, 148
Lijphart, Arend, 249, 267
Lilley, Peter, 53
Linton, Martin, 256
Literal Democrat, 44
Literary Digest poll, 171
Livingstone, Ken, 72, 95, 161
Lloyd George, David, 5, 62
local government elections, 80, 105, 107, 153–6, 257, 264
  date of, 8, 10
  effect on general election timing, 7, 8
  electoral system, 155, 238
  eligibility of candidates, 83, 84, 85
  eligibility to vote, 12, 16, 17
  expenditure, 201
  experimental voting methods, 8, 119, 157, 196
  far-right parties in, 67
  hours of polling, 134
  independent candidates in, 71–2
  offences at, 232
  proportional representation, 34
  spending limits, 200–1
  turnout, 195
local government reorganisation, 26, 154, 156
local parties, 73–82, 88, 113, 123
  finances, 81, 100–1, 106, 122
  officers and committees of, 75, 76
  representation at national level, 45, 47–8, 56, 58, 64
  selection of candidates, 90–103
  See also campaign in the constituencies

London *see also* Greater London
London Assembly, 68, 160–1
  election results, 220–1
  electoral system, 34, 240, 242–3
  eligibility of candidates, 84
  franchise, 249
  selection of candidates, 94
London Mayor, 72, 160–1
  candidate selection, 94–5
  election results, 220
  eligibility of candidates, 84
  franchise, 249
lots drawn in event of a tie, 140
lunacy, 84, 145
Lyell, Sir Nicholas, 252

McAllister, Ian, 266
MacAllister, Iain, 260
McCallum, R. B., 265
MacCartney, Alan, 258
McCartney, Robert, 70
MacDonald, James Ramsay, 62
McKee, Paul, 247
Mackie, Thomas, 264
McLean, Iain, 251, 263
McLoughlin, Patrick, 98
MacManaway, Revd J. G., 87
Macmillan, Harold, 149, 150
Mail on Sunday, 130, 166
Major, John, 7, 10, 52, 53, 126, 129, 133, 174, 194
majoritarian systems *see* electoral systems
manifestos, 122–4, 157
  drafting of, 46, 123
  launch obscured by other events (2001), 129
Marek, John, 72
Margetts, Helen, 245
marginal seats, 34, 75, 82, 122, 143, 148, 202, 252
  by-elections in, 147
  campaign in, 112–13, 116, 118, 121
  candidates, 95–6
  definition, 36
  exit polls in, 143
  number, 33, 36
  spending higher, 77
  visits by party leaders, 129

Market Research Society, 168, 169, 258
Marplan, 165
Marquand, David, 257
Maslow, Abraham, 189
Maudling, Reginald, 50
Maxwell, Robert, 132
media *see* television, radio, newspapers
meetings, public, 77, 111, 114, 115, 128, 148, 231
membership of political parties, 54, 55, 59, 205
    affiliated members (Labour), 59, 74, 76, 87, 204
    subscription fees, 55, 59–60, 74, 81, 204
mental illness
    effect on voting rights, 12, 250
    lunacy a disqualification from membership of Commons, 84, 145
Meyer, Sir Anthony, 51
Militant Tendency, 93
Mill, John Stuart, 239
Miller, Warren, 260
Miller, William, 266
Milne, Eddie, 253
minor parties, 65–70, 93, 104, 201
    in by-elections, 147
    party political broadcasts by, 125
    treatment by electoral system, 34, 70
minority ethnic candidates, 90, 98
Molotov, Vyacheslav, 1
Montfort, Simon de, 208
Moon, Nick, 258, 259
Moran, Michael, 249
MORI (Market & Opinion Research International), 114, 143, 165, 170, 172, 174, 236, 237, 261
    poll findings on voting behaviour, 179, 183–8, 260
Morris, H. L., 249
Mortimore, Roger, x, 168, 237, 256, 258, 259, 260, 263, 266
Murdoch, Rupert, 132

National Assembly of Wales *see* Welsh Assembly

National Executive Committee (NEC) *see* Labour Party
National Front, 67, 68
Natkiel, Richard, 249, 262, 267
neighbourhood effect, 185
Neil, Andrew, 92
Neill, Patrick (Lord) *see* Committee on Standards in Public Life
Nestlé UK, 260
News Chronicle, 164, 165
news management, 42–3, 128–9
News of the World, 130, 132
newspapers
    advertisements in *see* advertising
    commissioning opinion polls, 165–6
    election coverage, 130–2
    influence on voting, 132–3, 193
    local newspapers, 79
    regional press, 132
    See also under titles of newspapers, news management
Nicholas, H. G., 265
Nicolson, Nigel, 91, 254
Nixon, Richard M., 129
Nolan, Lord, 197
nominating officer, 43, 44, 229, 255
nomination of candidates, 86, 108–9
    invalidation of (Harrow, 2002), 255
NOP (National Opinion Polls), 143, 236, 237
Norris, Pippa, 257, 266
Norris, Steven, 95, 161
Northern Ireland
    differences in procedure at general elections, 11, 15, 116, 135, 224, 249, 250, 251, 255
    political parties, 2, 33, 36, 47, 65, 70–1, 86
    referendum (1973), 162, 221
    referendum (1998), 162, 223
    representation in Commons, 27
    Single Transferable Vote, 34, 157, 241
Northern Ireland Assembly, 71, 160, 254
    election results, 219
    eligibility of candidates, 83, 84
Northstead, Manor of, 145

Norton, Philip (Lord Norton of Louth), 249, 254
notice of poll, 109
Nuffield College, Oxford, 265

O'Duffy, Brendan, 245
Observer, The, 130, 203, 236, 261
observers banned at polling stations, 135
occupation and voting behaviour, 180–4
occupations of candidates, 98–100, 234–5
Office of Population Censuses and Surveys (OPCS), 19
offices of profit under the Crown, 85, 145
official mark *see* ballot paper, validation of
Official Monster Raving Loony Party, 69
Official Unionist Party *see* Northern Ireland political parties
Old Queen Street *see* Labour Party
Old Sarum, 251
'one member, one vote' (OMOV), 57, 95, 102
Onslow, Cranley, 52
opinion polls, 164–77
  banning, 176, 259
  British Polling Council, 175
  constituency polls, 171–2
  during the 2001 election, 236
  effect in by-elections, 148
  exit polls, 142, 165, 176
  findings on voting behaviour, 178–96
  focus groups, 173, 174
  influence on election timing, 6–7, 150
  influence on voters, 176, 193
  Internet polls, 171
  phone-in polls ('voodoo polls'), 172
  private polls, 173–5, 199
  sampling methods, 170–3
Opinion Research Centre (ORC), 166, 169
Orkney and Shetland Movement, 64
overseas voters, 17, 21, 44, 208
Owen, Dr David, 62, 63

pagers, 109
Paisley, Ian, 70
Palmerston, 3rd Viscount, 61
panachage, 242
parental influence on voting behaviour, 179
parish councils *see* local government
Parkinson, Cecil, 9
Parliament Act (1911), 4
Parliamentary Constituencies Act (1986), 25
Parliaments, length of, 4
parties
  funding *see* finances of parties
  number registered, 65
  organisation at constituency and ward level, 73–82
  organisation at national level, 39–72
  staff levels and cost, 42, 204, 205
party lists *see* electoral systems
party names
  registration of, 44, 252–3
  use of misleading labels on ballot paper, 43–4, 252–3
party political broadcasts, 42, 124–7, 193, 207
  cost of, 199
Paterson, Peter, 254
Patten, Chris, 122
Pattie, Charles, 251, 267
Peart, Fred, 148
Peele, Gillian, 249
peers *see* House of Lords
Penniman, Howard R., 265
People, The *(Sunday),* 130
personal vote of popular candidates, 78, 95, 148, 194
personation, 116, 119, 230
petition against election result, 127, 141–2
Peyton, John, 51
Pinto-Duschinsky, Michael, 198, 207, 250, 261, 262, 265
Pinto-Duschinsky, S., 250
Pitt, William, 151
Plaid Cymru, 36, 65, 125, 159
  at by-elections, 65, 150

plurality system ('first past the post')
    see electoral systems
Political Parties, Elections and
    Referendums Act (2000), 25, 163,
    250
poll cards, 117, 207, 231, 255
poll tax *see* Community Charge
polling clerks, 117, 134–7, 207
polling districts, 16, 139
polling stations, 117, 134–7, 248
Poole, Lord, 6
Populus, 166, 255
Portillo, Michael, 52, 53, 54
positive discrimination in candidate
    selection, 96–7
Post Office, delivery of election
    addresses, 113, 206–7, 255
postal voting, 20–1, 79–80, 117–20,
    135
    and party campaigns, 79–80, 112,
        118–19
    ballot box for, 118, 139
    experimental all-postal voting, 8,
        119–20, 157, 196, 255
    extent at 2001 election, 117, 248
    how to apply, 20, 224
    timetable for applications, 20, 224,
        226
posters *see* advertising
Powell, J. Enoch, 50
Prescott, John, 56, 57, 129
Presiding Officer, 134–6, 138
press conferences, 122, 128, 133
Press, The *see* newspapers
priests, eligibility as candidates, 84,
    87
Prior, James, 51
prisoners
    eligibility as candidates, 84
    voting rights, 12, 250
private polls, 173–5, 199
Pro-Life Alliance, 70, 125
Prolongation of Parliament Acts, 4
proportional representation *see*
    electoral systems
proposers of candidates, 108
prospective Parliamentary candidate,
    49, 77, 107, 200, 253
protest votes, 68, 153

proxy voting, 21, 135, 226, 230
    election offences connected with,
        230
    eligibility and making applications,
        224–5
public funding of political parties,
    proposals for, 206
Pulzer, P. J., 266

qualifying date for inclusion on
    electoral register, 249
Queen, The, theoretical powers of, 4
quota, constituency (Conservative
    Party), 55
quota, electoral, 28, 29
quota sample *see* opinion polls

radio, 42, 73, 121, 122, 123, 127, 128,
    130, 133, 142, 172, 193, 207,
    209, 231
Rallings, Colin, 252, 257, 264
Ramsden, John, 257
Ranney, Austin, 253, 258, 265
Rawlings, H. F., 267
Readman, Alison, 265
recounts, 140, 142
Redgrave, Vanessa, 66
redistribution of seats *see* Boundary
    Commissions
Redwood, John, 52, 53
Reeve, Andrew, 267
Referendum Party, 69, 71, 125, 198
referendums, 161–3
    on Scottish devolution (1979), 64
    results of, 221–3
Reform Acts (1832, 1867), 22, 47, 208
region and voting behaviour, 185
regional devolution, 156
Register of Electors, 13–21, 108, 113,
    135
    accuracy, 19–20, 194, 210, 250, 251
    cost of compiling, 206–7, 250
    double registration, 15
    'ex-directory' registration, 16
    illustration, 18
    late claims for inclusion, 249
    marked, by Presiding Officer on
        issue of ballot paper, 136, 138,
        141

marked-up registers for
campaigning, 79–80, 111, 112,
137
objections to errors and omissions,
15
open to public inspection, 16
qualifying date, 19, 249
rolling register, 13, 19, 211
sale of, 16
use as a sampling frame for opinion
polls, 170
use for crime prevention and credit
checks, 16
used for selecting juries, 16, 250
Registration Officer (ERO), 13, 15, 16,
249
religion, 70
religious objections to voting, 8, 136
remand prisoners, voting rights of,
250
Rendel, David, 63
Representation of the People Acts, 12,
17, 22, 25, 107, 127, 139, 209,
210
reselection of candidates, 102–3
residency requirements for
candidates, 84
Respect, 66
Returning Officer, 11 *and passim*
Returning Officers' expenses, 207
Richards, P. G., 254
Richards, Paul, 254
Riddell, Peter, 254
Robertson, David, 266
Rodgers, William, 62
Roosevelt, President Franklin D., 171
Rose, Richard, 202, 256, 261, 265, 266
Rossiter, David, 251, 252, 267
rotten boroughs, 22, 251
Royal Mail *see* Post Office
Royal Proclamation of dissolution, 9,
11, 145
Rush, Michael, 254

safe seats, 24, 36–8, 110, 122, 133, 148
sampling methods of opinion polls,
170–3
Sanders, David, 190, 260
Sands, Bobby, 84

Särlvik, Bo, 180, 189, 259, 260
Scammell, Margaret, 256, 266
Scargill, Arthur, 67
Schofield's Election Law, 267
Scotland, over-representation in
Commons, 27, 29
Scottish National Party (SNP), 36,
64–5, 125, 158–9, 189
at by-elections, 64, 150, 151
Scottish Opinion Limited, 166
Scottish Parliament, 27, 64, 66, 68,
72, 158–60, 252–3, 258
candidate selection, 94, 98, 103
deposit, 105
election results, 218
electoral system, 34, 240, 242–4
eligibility of candidates, 83, 84
franchise, 249
result of referendums on, 222
spending limits, 200
Scottish Socialist Party, 66, 252
scrutineers, 138
Seanad *see* Ireland, Republic of
secrecy of the ballot, 119, 136, 139
service voters, 15
sex and voting behaviour, 187
sex of candidates, 96–8
Seymour, C., 249
Shandwick, 133
Sheridan, Tommy, 66
Shore, Peter, 57
'Short money', 204
single european currency, 48, 162
Single Transferable Vote *see* electoral
systems
Sinn Féin *see* Northern Ireland
political parties
Smith Square, 41
Smith, Jeremy, 251
Smith, John, 41, 56, 57, 60, 102, 194
Smith, S., 250, 251
Social and Liberal Democratic Party
(SLD) *see* Liberal Democrats
Social Democratic and Labour Party
see Northern Ireland political
parties
Social Democratic Federation, 55
Social Democratic Party (SDP), 2, 40,
41, 60, 150, *see also* Alliance

Social Science Research Council, 179
Socialist Alliance, 67
Socialist Labour Party, 67
Socialist Workers' Party (SWP), 66
Soskice, Sir Frank, 24
Spangenberg, Frits, 259
Sparrow, Nick, 259
Speaker of the House of Commons, 23, 55, 64, 72, 104, 141, 145, 209
Speaker's Conference, 209–10
  of 1944, 23, 25
  of 1965–8, 13, 176, 209
Spicer, Sir Michael, 54
'spin doctors', 42
sponsored candidates (Labour Party), 60, 100
Stansgate, 2nd Viscount *see* Benn, Tony
state funding of political parties, proposals for, 206–7
Steed swing, 37
Steed, Michael, 37, 245, 251, 252
Steel, David, 10, 62
Stewart, Marianne, 190, 260
Stokes, Donald, 179, 184, 259, 260
'stopwatch timing', 128
student political organisations, 81–2
subscription fees *see* membership of political parties
Sun, The, 130, 132, 133, 256
Sunday Express, 130
Sunday Mirror, 130
Sunday Telegraph, 130, 165, 236
Sunday Times, 130, 132, 166, 236
Supplementary Vote *see* electoral systems
surgeries, constituency, 78
Sutch, David ('Screaming Lord'), 69
swing, 36–8
  in by-elections, 149–53
System Three, 166

tactical voting, 172, 176
target seats, 116
Taverne, Dick, 150, 253
Taylor, Bridget, 251, 260
Taylor, Dr Richard, 72, 253
Taylor, Humphrey, 174
telephone canvassing, 112–13, 114, 116, 199

telephone polls *see* opinion polls
television
  effect of coverage on voting behaviour, 193
  effect of popular programmes on turnout, 138
  election night programmes, 142–3
  legal restrictions on coverage, 127–8, 231
  news coverage of campaigns, 127–30
  See also news management, party political broadcasts
tellers, 136, 137
Test Research, 133
Thatcher, Margaret, 7, 9, 10, 34, 51, 52, 63, 123, 129, 151, 206, 254
'third parties', regulation of spending by, 199, 204, 261
Thompson, Sir Kenneth, 24
Thompson, Malcolm, 86
Thrasher, Michael, 252, 257, 264
Thurso, John (3rd Viscount Thurso), 254
tie in number of votes, 140
  in Conservative leadership election, 53
time of day
  opening hours of polling stations, 134, 138
  when votes are cast, 138
Times, The, 9, 131, 132, 166, 176, 255
timetable of election campaign, 10, 226–7
timing of elections, 4–8
TNS System Three, 166
Todd, J., 250
Tonge, Jonathan, 266
Tories *see* Conservative Party
trade union links with Labour Party, 44, 45–6, 55, 56–60, 74, 76, 81, 87–8, 95, 100–1, 102, 204–5, 253
trade union membership and voting behaviour, 185
Trimble, David, 70
Truman, Harry S., 169
turnout, 20, 194–6
  calculation of statistics, 258
  effect of postal voting, 118

Tyrrell, Claire, 260

UK Independence Party, 69
Ulster Unionist Party *see* Northern
    Ireland political parties
uncontested seats, 35, 212–14
underdog effect, 175
unilateral nuclear disarmament, 40,
    56
unitary authorities *see* local
    government
unopposed elections, 109
urban/rural differences in voting
    behaviour, 186

voting age, reduction of (1969), 83
voting behaviour, 178–96
voting procedure on election day,
    134–7

Wales
    over-representation in Commons,
        27, 29
    referendums on devolution, 162,
        222–3
    See also Welsh Assembly
Wall, Pat, 93
Waller, Robert, 251
War of Jennifer's Ear, 126
ward party *see* local parties
wards (local government electoral
    districts), 16, 24, 73, 82
Ware, Alan, 267
Webb, Paul, 252
weekend voting, 8
Weir, Stuart, 245
Welland, Colin, 126
Welsh Assembly, 65, 72, 158–60
    candidate selection, 94, 98, 103

deposit, 105
election results, 219
electoral system, 34, 240, 242–4
eligibility of candidates, 83, 84
franchise, 249
spending limits, 200
Westlake, Martin, 257
Whitelaw, William, 51
Whiteley, Paul, 190, 260
Williams, P. M., 260
Williams, Shirley, 62, 151
Wilson, Harold, 6, 7, 150, 174
Winchester by-election (1997), 142,
    152
window bills, 105, 107, 112, 113
Winter of Discontent, 7
Witherspoon, Sharon, 259, 260
women as candidates, 96–8
    special provisions relating to, 90, 93
Worcester, Robert, 165, 168, 174, 237,
    258, 259, 260, 265, 266
Workers' Revolutionary Party, 66
Wring, Dominic, 256
writs to hold election, 141
    effect of, 11, 145, 200
    election timetable, 226, 227
    issue in by-elections, 145
    issue of, 11
    return to Clerk of Crown, 141

YouGov, 166, 171, 258
Young Conservatives *see* Conservative
    Future
Young Labour, 58, 75, 81, 82
Young Liberal Democrats, 75, 82
Young, H. P., 263
youth organisations, 81–2

zipping, 98